BUILDING A SMARTER UNIVERSITY

SUNY SERIES, CRITICAL ISSUES IN HIGHER EDUCATION
Jason E. Lane and D. Bruce Johnstone, editors

Building a Smarter University

Big Data, Innovation, and Analytics

Edited by
Jason E. Lane

Foreword by
Nancy L. Zimpher

For information, contact State University of New York Press, Albany, NY
www.sunypress.edu

Production, Ryan Morris
Marketing, Michael Campochiaro

Library of Congress Cataloging-in-Publication Data

Building a smarter university : big data, innovation, and analytics / edited by Jason E. Lane ; foreword by Nancy L. Zimpher.
    pages cm. — (SUNY series, critical issues in higher education)
Includes bibliographical references and index.
ISBN 978-1-4384-5453-5 (hardcover : alk. paper)
ISBN 978-1-4384-5452-8 (pbk. : alk. paper)
ISBN 978-1-4384-5454-2 (ebook) 1. Education, Higher—United States—Data processing—Congresses. I. Lane, Jason E., editor of compilation.
 LB2395.7.B85 2015
 378.00285—dc23

2014008138

10 9 8 7 6 5 4 3 2 1

To Kari and Emerson:
You have shown me the true meaning of life.

CONTENTS

ILLUSTRATIONS

FOREWORD

Building a Smarter University
Big Data, Innovation, and Ingenuity

NANCY L. ZIMPHER

This volume, the third in SUNY's Critical Issues in Higher Education series, is, like those that came before it, a companion piece to a conference—this one entitled, Building a Smarter University.

On October 29 and 30, 2013, in New York City, SUNY brought together hundreds of great minds from across several sectors—education, business, technology—to dive deep into one of the hottest topics of the day: Big Data. Specifically, for those of us at the conference and those who have contributed to this volume, the task was to plumb the possibilities of the 21st-century data explosion and come to a more intimate understanding of how data—Big Data—can be used to enhance education. Or, to put a finer point on it, we set about exploring the question: *How can we harness the untold power of the ever-swelling ocean of data and use it, purposefully, to build smarter, more innovative, resourceful, and effective universities that fully meet the needs of an increasingly complex society?*

With the help of our cosponsors, this year's conference gathered more than 400 participants from 25 states, Jamaica, and Mexico; 50 of our SUNY campuses; and 42 other colleges and universities. It included an impressive slate of 65 speakers and panels, which together sparked groundbreaking conversation on subjects like "How Will Big Data Transform Higher Education?," "Tapping Big Data to Strengthen the Education Pipeline," "The Cautionary Side of Big

Data," and "Data Scientist: The Sexiest Job of the 21st Century." We were also thrilled to introduce at the conference the inaugural class of SUNY Big Data Fellows, eight future leaders in data science from across multiple disciplines who are demonstrating the great potential of data usage in a range of fields, from psychology to finance to special education to nursing to applied mathematics.

But for all this "Big" talk, there was a rather unexpected moment at the conference when our keynote speaker, Harper Reed, cried foul at the term *Big Data*, the very subject he was there to discuss. The "Big," he asserted, is unnecessary, little more than a catchphrase meant to dress up a generic word. His deeper point, he went on to explain, was that "Big" doesn't describe a new kind of data or even a new phenomenon, that data are data are data, big or little. If anything, he argued, the adjective underscores new *potential* in collection, interpretation, and application of the volume of data that we are amassing daily and that the world is only beginning to understand.

To a point, I must beg to differ with Harper Reed on this one. The virtual tsunami of data created by technology as a by-product of the tools we now, rather suddenly, use in our everyday lives, is something *entirely* new, and learning what to do with it all—how to capture, share, store, manage, interpret, analyze, and, in effect, *use* it all—is our collective charge. The 2012 touchstone book *The Human Face of Big Data* reported that we now produce *every two days* the amount of data produced by all of human kind from the dawn of civilization until 2003—and the pace is accelerating.[1] If that's not big, I don't know what is.

But I fully agree with Harper's observation about potential. In terms of getting to know ourselves and how we tick, humanity is on the edge of something incalculably vast, something that will change us as a species, change how we move forward into the world and into the future. We owe it to ourselves to deeply and thoughtfully explore the possibilities of data and learn to wring from them as much life-enhancing information as possible.

The use of data to predict patterns and trends, to build better businesses, is, of course, nothing new. We each deepen our digital footprint with every credit card swipe, text, Tweet, and status update. All of this amounts to billions of data points we are putting out there for the world to use while hardly making an effort. Corporations are learning how to harness these data to transform the customer experience. If you shop at Amazon, you are prompted before checkout to look at a few other select items based on your pending purchase and similar buys by other customers. Netflix suggests movies or television series' you might enjoy based on past selections. Pandora uses complex algorithms to play songs you will like.

Beyond its commercial uses, we are seeing governments, cities, and hospitals adapt to the Big Data movement and use it to answer their own challenges. Polling data is one of the earliest versions of this trend. Transportation data are being used to decongest cities and get people to their destinations quicker and easier. Hospitals and healthcare systems are using electronic medical records so that patients can be consistently monitored, regardless of which hospital or clinic they check into.

Scholars within academia and working at colleges and universities have been among the leaders in harnessing data for all of these purposes. Yet, very little attention has been given to how we, as academic leaders, might ride the digital data wave to transform our institutions.

Higher education is in the business of building better lives and thriving societies. It's the business of helping people develop and reach their potential. As the largest comprehensive university system in the nation—with more than 463,000 students and 88,000 faculty and staff—SUNY is a powerful intellectual, research, service, and economic force for New York and, we think, a model for the nation. Our system of 64 diverse institutions maps like a central nervous system across the state, pulsing with knowledge-creation, economic promise, and cultural vibrancy.

At SUNY, we are moving forward propelled by the belief that if other major sectors can use data and information so precisely and innovatively, so can, and *must*, higher education. Data can help us run our physical plant more efficiently and at lower costs. Data can be used to strengthen and lengthen the education pipeline from one end to the other, from cradle to career. Data can allow us to provide real-time interventions to help at-risk students realize their full success.

So at SUNY, like so many other colleges and universities, we are doing all that—but we are also pushing the boundaries to consider what *more* we can do with data to make good on our mission, "To learn, to search, to serve." Let's really learn how to use data to reach more of today's youth and increase their access to college. Let's use data to play a greater role in their preparation for college so that we spend less time and money on remedial education. Let's use data to put students on a path to graduate on time, with less debt and more knowledge and experience that will benefit their lives—and our economy—when they set out into the workplace.

To do all this, don't we need to be certain—or at the very least, confident—that the services we are providing will have a positive impact on these outcomes? We absolutely do. And that is what data can tell us, if we use it effectively and consistently.

Look at the national spotlight cast on financial aid transparency in higher education in the last few years—it relies entirely on the smart collection of good data to help us inform and perform better for our target audience. If prospective students and their families have more uniform, easy-to-understand, comprehensive information about our universities, they can make smarter decisions about where to apply, where to enroll, and they can plan for their expenses end-to-end, borrowing with their head, not over it.

With more data about where students come from and what they have learned before they reach college campuses, we can be better equipped to help them select programs where they are most likely to thrive. At SUNY, we are working with the Community College Research Center at Columbia University to develop a data analytics method that will use data such as student test scores, course-taking patterns, and noncognitive assessments to help us offer guidance to prospective students about where within our system they should enroll to be the most successful.

Using data in partnership with state departments of labor and economic development, universities can take into account the types of degrees and programs that campuses offer alongside the jobs and training needed locally. SUNY has been doing this for years to target resources to train more nurses and engineers, and we recently reevaluated the program by gathering more data from our state partners. The process expanded our target careers, and we are actively investing in helping campuses start or expand programs that train students for fields that data show are high-need areas for New York, like information technology, human resources management, clinical laboratories technologies, and health resources administration.

It is the job of this volume to draw a line around data usage and education and look closely, from many angles, at how universities can use data to vastly improve their performance, their services, and their delivery of education to meet today's, and tomorrow's, complex needs. The State University of New York is honored and excited to be at the forefront of the charge to explore the deepest possibilities of what this data revolution holds for human kind, and, closer to home, how it can help us build smarter universities.

February 2014

NOTE

1. Smolan and Erwitt (2012, p. 1). The authors quote Eric Schmidt, executive chair of Google.

REFERENCE

Smolan, R., & Erwitt, J. (2012). *The human face of Big Data*. Sausalito, CA: Against All Odds Productions.

PREFACE

Like it or not, we have entered a new era in which nearly everything we do and everything our students do, particularly in the digital environment, generates data. For many readers, these data have remained untapped, unrefined, and unusable. However, there is also an increasing awareness among academic leaders that data are providing unparalleled opportunities to improve the academic experience, better understand the educational pipeline, and enhance the overall productivity of our colleges and universities. These opportunities are being sold as part of a data revolution being labeled Big Data; and many companies are taking advantage of this revolution to market new products and services to institutional leaders who know they should be harnessing this Big Data but are not entirely sure how to go about doing so.

The first step is not to be scared of Big Data. The term has come to represent a data revolution that takes advantage of both the massive amounts of new data being generated as well as more traditional data sets to improve how we play, work, and live. In fact, scientists and administrators are learning how to harness data to build smarter cities, smarter governments, and even a smarter planet. Strangely, there has been little concerted effort to understand how this data revolution might transform how we operate in higher education. The intent of this volume is to provide academic leaders with a basic understanding of what Big Data is, how it differentiates from traditional data, and how both can be used to build a smarter university.

In grappling with the big data tidal wave, one of the most important roles of colleges and universities will be to prepare the next generation of data scientists, which the *Harvard Business Review* has called "the sexy new job of the 21st century." Already faculties have led the development of advanced analytical methods needed to use Big Data, transforming the way some teach and research. As the need for data scientists grows, colleges and universities should be at the forefront of training the workforce for these next-generation careers. Infused throughout this volume are insights about the skill sets and knowledge that current and future administrators will need to serve as data scientists, and those same insights have relevance for those developing academic programs in these areas.

This volume focuses on three primary themes related to building a smarter university: (1) providing an overview of Big Data, including opportunities and challenges; (2) enhancing student access, completion, and success; and (3) improving policy making and institutional decision making. It is important to note that the chapters in this volume do not cover all of the areas where data, Big Data, and analytics may benefit the operation of the university—there is simply not enough room in a volume such as this to cover all of the functional areas of a university.

Overview of Big Data. The term *Big Data* is often widely used but not well understood. This lack of understanding can make it difficult for academic leaders looking to act in this area to do so in a meaningful way. In chapter 1, Jason Lane and Alex Finsel provide an overview of what Big Data is, how it differentiates from traditional data, and why both are important for creating a smarter university. They also discuss the potential pitfalls of the use of data in improving the student experience. Chapter 2, by Jeffrey Sun, explores the legal issues associated with Big Data, particularly related to privacy, data governance, and intellectual property. Then, in chapter 3, we move into a discussion of the difference between Big Data and Big-But-Buried Data, in which Elizabeth Bringsjord and Selmer Bringsjord highlight the important difference between using the outputs produced by new analytical models and actually understanding the math used to develop the models.

Student access, completion, and success. For decades, institutional research offices have been collecting student data to analyze things such as retention and graduation rates. As technology rapidly continues to evolve, the breadth and depth of data available to campuses is growing. Student ID cards allow institutions to track library usage, dining habits on and off campus, health center usage, medical treatments, attendance at cocurricular activities, and what residence halls or classrooms students access. Course management software can monitor student grades, which students access course material and for how long, and provide real-time learning assessments. Colleges and universities also generate the same infrastructure information that many cities are now using to improve their own effectiveness. This includes data created by parking enforcement, pedestrian patterns, traffic flows, energy usage, and recycling efforts. The amount of data is massive, and the possibilities for ingenuity are endless.

Chapter 4, by Jay Goff and Chris Shaffer, start part 2 with an examination of how Big Data can be used to improve the admission and recruitment processes at colleges and universities. In chapter 5, Fred Fonseca and Michael Marcinkowski utilize philosophical inquiry to examine who is the "Big Data Student." We then turn, in chapter 6, to college retention. Ben Wildavsky explores a number of new companies and products that are trying to use Big Data to improve student completion rates. Finally, in chapter 7, a case study of the State University of New York by Taya Owens and Dan Knox, highlights how data analysis can inform policies designed to improve student transfer, mobility, and ultimately their success in college.

Policy development and institutional decision making. Over the last several years, there has been a growing interest both inside and outside of the academy in better insulating the education pipeline, seeking to promote access, completion, and success of our students. There have been a number of efforts to capture and use data to better understand where students are coming from, how they experience college, and where they go after graduating. Moreover, new analytical methods being developed inside and outside of the academy are being used to transform the student experience and better insulate the pipeline.

Lisa Helmin Foss kicks off part 3 by distilling a nationwide survey of department chairs into strategies to encourage academic leaders to use data analytics in their decision making (chapter 8). John Cheslock, Rodney Hughes, and Mark Umbricht then explore how colleges and universities can better use their existing data to inform institutional strategy by integrating data sets and developing data integration standards. In chapter 10, Jason Lane and Rajika Bhandari move into the international higher education realm, discussing how international data are increasingly important as colleges and universities look to develop global engagements. Finally, in chapter 11 Brian Prescott provides an example of how merging state-level data sets from education and department of labor can help us better understand the career path of our students after they leave higher education.

This third volume in the SUNY Critical Issues in Higher Education series, *Building a Smarter University: Big Data, Innovation, and Analytics*, takes up this topic focusing on the opportunities and challenges of using Big Data to improve the academic enterprise. The book is intended to be thought provoking, analyzing some of the most pressing and complex issues about harnessing Big Data to build a smarter university, fostering innovation and ingenuity in the academy, and educating the next generation of data scientists. The authors, through their scholarly and practical insights, frame these issues for an international discussion.

ACKNOWLEDGMENTS

The SUNY Critical Issues in Higher Education series was developed to bring together thought leaders, through a national convening and an annual edited volume, to explore an issue of critical importance to the future of public higher education. In the first two years, we explored new roles for functions that have been part of the higher education landscape for several years. In 2011, we examined the role of colleges and universities as economic drivers. In 2012, we took a fresh look at the role of higher education systems in helping to fulfill the public agenda of states as well as provide additional support to constituent campuses. Both systems and the acknowledgment of higher education's role in economic development had been explored by previous conferences and academic writings. This body of existing work provided a solid foundation as we explored new paradigms for the future of each of these topics.

With SUNYCON 2013, we decided to tackle a topic that had recently attracted a great deal of popular attention in the media but had not been examined in the context of higher education: Big Data. At the time, there was beginning to unfold a broad awareness that massive amounts of data generated in the digital era were allowing for new insights into how we live, work, and play.

As we began to explore the topic, we uncovered pockets of interesting activities such as the work at Austin Peay State University to use students' past experiences to recommend future courses (in a fashion similar to Amazon's use of customer behaviors to suggest future purchases). Arizona State University, in partnership with Knewton, was using the digital footprint of their students to identify who might be at risk of dropping out and providing real-time interventions to improve student success. Higher education–focused media sources, such as *The Chronicle of Higher Education* and *Inside HigherEd*, had published a few articles on related topics, such as how the digital era was transforming research in the humanities. But, in all of our searching, we were unable to find any systematic exploration of how Big Data was being harnessed to improve the operations of colleges and universities.

And, so, we went to work researching how other sectors were using Big Data to improve their work. What we realized was that the Big Data revolution was really more about how to use data of all shapes and sizes to better understand human behavior, and, in turn, provide better services, make better decisions, and operate more effectively. And, thus, was born SUNYCON 2013: *Building a Smarter University: Big Data, Innovation, and Ingenuity*. At the conference, we gathered experts from a range of fields to discuss how higher education could benefit from this ever-increasing availability of data. Those same efforts led to the development of this volume, which was created in tandem with the conference and is intended to be an initial and more permanent scan of the ways in which higher education institutions can harness Big Data to improve student success. I hope that the volume can help raise awareness of the benefits of data to higher education and provide academic administrators with the tools to understand the opportunities and the challenges around their use.

I am indebted to many people for their hard work, thoughts, suggestions, and support in developing this volume. As with any attempt to give thanks to specific individuals, some will surely be omitted, and I apologize for these omissions in advance. B. Alex Finsel provided much-needed research support as we poured over hundreds of media and scholarly articles, seeking to identify key topics and speakers. He was also a valued coauthor in the development of the first chapter. Sarah Fuller Klyberg provided great support in the copyediting of the manuscript. Her knowledge of writing style and the study of higher education made this a much stronger contribution to the literature. Kaitlin Gambrill, Johanna Kendrick-Holmes, and Juliette Price were my compatriots in developing the conference and volume. We spent countless hours on the phone and in person developing the conference program and dealing with innumerable logistics. Lauren McCabe's outstanding organizational skills made it possible to pull together all the various pieces of such an activity and helped ensure we all crossed the finish line. As always, the team at SUNY Press has been great to work with—and special thanks go to Beth Boulou-kos, Donna Dixon, Fran Keneston, James Peltz, and Ryan Morris for shepherding the Critical Issues in Higher Education book series, bringing these volumes quickly to production, and promoting them broadly. The staff at the Rockefeller Institute of Government, particularly Tom Gais, Bob Bullock, Michael Cooper, Heather Trela, Michelle Charbonneau, Heather Stone, and Patty Cadrette have been incredibly helpful throughout the series by helping to pull the books together and raise awareness of them among key constituencies. Special thanks to all of the authors included in this volume. Their contributions shed light on this emerging field. Finally, great appreciation goes to SUNY chancellor Nancy Zimpher for her vision in creating this series and recognizing the importance of supporting research and writing on public higher education.

I've dedicated this volume to my wife Kari and our newborn daughter, Emerson, who entered this world while the book was being finalized. Her arrival added a new challenge to completing a manuscript, but I wouldn't trade it for the world (or all the data within it)!

Jason E. Lane
Albany, N.Y.

Part I

OVERVIEW

1

FOSTERING SMARTER COLLEGES AND UNIVERSITIES

Data, Big Data, and Analytics

JASON E. LANE AND B. ALEX FINSEL

ABSTRACT

Many sectors are looking for ways to harness data, particularly Big Data, to improve their operations to build smarter cities, smarter governments, smarter hospitals, and even a smarter planet. Yet, there has been little focus as to how this increasing interest in data actually can help build smarter colleges and universities. This chapter provides academic leaders with an introduction to Big Data and data analytics, exploring definition of terms, examining application to higher education operations, and raising related cautionary concerns.

We have reached a tipping point in the path of human evolution; billions of data points are being generated every minute of every day by humans, computers, and technological devices all around us, creating a real-time, digital footprint of our lives with every credit card swipe and smart phone use. With the availability of this ocean of information, the question becomes how to use the data to better engineer our world to serve our needs. This Big Data movement is transforming everything from healthcare delivery systems to the way cities provide services to citizens. Now is the time to examine how the Big Data movement could help build smarter universities—institutions that can use the huge amounts of data they generate to improve the student learning experience, enhance the research enterprise, support effective community outreach, and advance the campus's infrastructure. While much of the cutting-edge research being done with Big Data is happening at colleges and universities, higher education has yet to turn the digital mirror on itself to innovate the academic enterprise.

Let us put this data explosion in some perspective. From the dawn of civilization to 2003, humans created five exabytes worth of data. As of 2013, humans produced this same amount of information every two days (Miller & Chapin, 2013). The amount of information in the world today is so vast that it can be difficult to visualize, but one way to think about it is that "the world holds twice as many bytes of data as there are liters of water in all its oceans" ("The Big Bang," 2013). If harnessed, these data have the potential to create a feedback loop from human activity, which can be used to enhance institutional productivity and student success. This vast amount of information has become broadly labeled *Big Data*, a term that has come to symbolize the data revolution that we are now experiencing.

For all the hype about Big Data, no data—big or small—are useful unless they can be analyzed to develop meaning. It is similar to crude oil buried deep in the Bakken shale formation in western North Dakota. The formation is one of the largest repositories of oil in the world, but it remained nothing more than an interesting fact until the technological advances were discovered that allowed the oil to be extracted and refined. However, while the oil has become accessible and yielded great opportunities, the success of its extraction has been tarnished by the environmental dangers—many of which were unforeseen in the early years. The immense amount of data that is now being generated is only useful if it can be extracted and refined to be used to make decisions. And, in the same way that the new technologies used to extract the oil from the shale has a cautionary side, the extraction and use of Big Data also generate cautions of which we must be aware.

As the techniques to extract and refine Big Data improve, scientists at universities and corporations are learning how to use it to transform how we shop, work, and play. Analysis of these new data allows people to discover patterns that have been previously overlooked. One of the classic examples comes from when Target discovered that a teen girl was pregnant before her father did. By analyzing the shopping patterns of its customers, Target was able to predict fairly accurately which customers were pregnant and about when they were due. The company then sent coupons and flyers during key times of the pregnancy to encourage women to shop at Target for their pregnancy needs. One day, a father complained to a store manager that it was encouraging his teen daughter to get pregnant by sending her information on baby clothes and cribs. Two days later, the father apologized to the store manager, having just learned that his daughter was indeed pregnant (Hill, 2012).

Target is not alone in its close analysis of customer behavior. Walmart analyzed volumes of transaction data and discovered that consumers purchased a significant amount of Pop-Tarts in certain hurricane-prone areas during storm season. This information enabled the retail giant to increase its supply of Pop-Tarts, which led to increased sales and profits (Fourtané, 2013). Similarly, the Cincinnati Zoo chose to sell ice cream in the afternoon based on the rational expectation that warmer temperatures would lead to a higher demand for ice cream. However, zoo officials used Big Data analytics to determine that visitors significantly preferred ice cream earlier in the day, despite the conventional wisdom surrounding the impact of temperature. Accordingly, this meta-information helped the zoo to change when it offered ice cream to better satisfy customers and increase profits (Callaham, 2013; Vesset, 2013). Netflix analyzes the input of thousands of users to make personalized recommendations for what movie a customer might want to watch next. And, in early 2014, Amazon filed a patent for anticipatory package shipping, a process that would allow predictions of what some customers would buy next and then ship it to them before they actually purchased it (Matyszczky, 2014).

All these new data are being used in the development of smarter cities, smarter governments, and a smarter planet. So, why not smarter colleges and universities?

The intention of this volume is to unpack not just the phenomenon of Big Data but the corresponding renewed interest in how we analyze data of all sizes to build a smarter university. The remainder of this chapter is a primer on Big Data and data analytics and is intended to provide the reader with a basic understanding of related concepts, activities, and cautions. It is important to note from the outset that this volume does not focus on the more technical aspects of Big Data such as how to store and process large amounts of information; rather, it explores how colleges and universities might engage operationally with Big Data to improve student success and better understand the student pipeline.

UNPACKING BIG DATA

In the purest sense, the idea of Big Data is not new. It is actually a moving target. Big Data has always existed in that it is essentially data that exceed current standard abilities to manipulate them. Thus, much of the data that we easily and regularly analyze today was at one time considered Big Data. In fact, what Big Data is can even vary between different organizations as it is essentially data sets so large that they cannot be easily analyzed using available data management programs. What is different today, when the phenomenon is compared to previous eras, is that the amount of data being generated is growing at an unprecedented rate, and the utility of those data for understanding human behavior is unparalleled. Moreover, Big Data has generated a renewed awareness of the importance of using data to systematically improve the work of organizations. Therefore, not all of the data discussed in this volume may meet a purist's definition of Big Data, but it is part of the overall movement toward using data and analytics to improve how we work, play, and live.

Big Data has come to be described by five Vs: *volume, velocity, variety, veracity,* and *visualization.*[1] These terms are discussed in more depth in the following and provide a lens to understand the often ambiguous concept of Big Data, the technological equipment needed to process Big Data, and data themselves as both raw material and finished product. The first three Vs, volume, velocity, and variety, seek to describe the nature of Big Data. The other two Vs, veracity and visualization, are related to the outputs of Big Data.

Volume. There are a lot of data, and these data need to be stored. So how big is big? Although size is relative, the current data explosion creates a staggering amount of information on a scale that is difficult to comprehend. Again, humans create five exabytes of information every two days (Miller & Chapin, 2013). An exabyte is a billion gigabytes. (And a gigabyte is a billion bytes!) Thus, an exabyte is equivalent to a billion billion bytes, which is roughly equivalent to more than 4,000 times the information stored in the Library of Congress (McKinsey Global Institute, 2011). Accordingly, the unfamiliarly large petabyte, exabyte, and zettabyte are poised to become standard units of measure and more commonplace when discussing the size of today's Big Data volume. However, tomorrow's Big Data may extend well beyond the realm of yottabytes and force people to reconsider and redefine how we measure data's size (Foley, 2013). For many colleges and universities, administrative data sets this large may seem like fantasies (or nightmares) compared to the existing databases that track student enrollments and the like. Yet, many institutions now have software that can track how students engage with class materials available through course management software or which buildings they enter and when. These individual data points, when multiplied across an entire student population every day, can add up quickly.

Velocity. Even if one is able to store all of the data created and have room to spare, any storage space can be consistently constrained by the velocity, or the speed, at which data are created, processed, and/or transferred from one point to another. In other words, of importance is the velocity of the feedback loop—how quickly the new data can be harnessed and used to make decisions. At one time, the performance of a student in a given semester was not known until course grades were reported and a GPA calculated at the end of the semester. Now it is possible to track student activity on an almost daily basis and provide interventions in the middle of the semester—with the desire of supporting the success of the student.

Variety. Data can come from many different sources, and it rarely arrives in a form that is simple to process and through which leaders can easily make decisions. In the case of students, information can come from social networks, ID card usage, and the degree audit system. This information can then be married with more traditional data sets that are kept by the registrar or bursar, for example. This variety can make it difficult to realize the full potential of the data.

Identifying ways to get traditional and new data sets to talk with each other is a focus of chapter 4.

Veracity. A significant issue with the use of Big Data is determining its veracity in that the quality of the output depends on the quality of the input and the process used to refine it. Are the data being used meaningful to the analysis being performed? There is always the risk of collecting and analyzing flawed information, which could lead to flawed decision making. Such flaws may not be that significant when recommending a new movie, but they can have devastating effects if the wrong intervention is used to help an at-risk student.

Visualization. It can be difficult for individuals to "see" the patterns in the data. Thus, visualization is a critical part of the refining process that allows people to understand and use the knowledge created from Big Data. Visualization transforms abstract information into a physical image that has dimensions that humans can quickly see and understand, and from which they can extract meaning (Taylor, 2013). Although Big Data scientists have an intimate understanding of the Big Data process, visualization allows a greater number of lay people to access, understand, and use Big Data information to make decisions in day-to-day organizational operations. For example, eBay's online marketplace had almost 108 million users and sold $68 billion worth of merchandise in 2011. This activity generated 52 petabytes of user behavior, shipping, and online transaction data (Lampitt, 2012). Accordingly, visualization software transformed this large, diverse, and complicated data set into simple, insightful, and interactive graphics that employees can use to make decisions in real time.

DATA ANALYTICS, DATA MINING, AND MACHINE LEARNING

Indeed, the existence of data does not alone offer insights. Specific pieces of data need to be extracted and refined. How data are utilized has spurred a new industry of data mining, which is "the process of analyzing data from different perspectives and summarizing it into useful information—information that can be used to increase revenue, cut costs, or both. Technically, data mining is the process of finding correlations or patterns among dozens of fields in large relational databases" (Palace, 1996).

Another development is that of predictive analytics (or what is referred to as *machine learning* in the literature), where computer programs use algorithms to analyze volumes of data patterns to make automated and semi-automated decisions. The potential power of predictive analytics is summed up in the title of Siegel's (2013) book: *Predictive Analytics: The Power to Predict Who Will Click, Buy, Lie, or Die.* While readers may not be concerned about buying, lying, and dying, analytics can also predict who will apply, remain, struggle, and complete. Analytics also has the power to determine what interventions may be best to help students to succeed, including providing real-time interventions.

For example, Arizona State University's (ASU) eAdvisor program actively monitors student degree progress, Facebook information, student ID card swipes, and performance patterns to identify at-risk students for immediate intervention and then provides support to keep them on track toward graduation (Parry, 2012). Since ASU launched eAdvisor in 2008, the proportion of freshmen who did not return for their sophomore year decreased from 24% to 16%. Moreover, 42% of ASU's students graduated in four years, which was an increase from 26% in 1997 (Marcus, 2012).

The bulk of the use of data mining and predictive analytics has been within the corporate world, where there may be some inspiration for opportunities in higher education. Both data mining and predictive analytics can help organizations to identify consumer needs and wants to provide custom, tailored services to maximize satisfaction. For example, Netflix used data mining to create a software algorithm that recommends movies and television shows to its consumers based on their interests, often with surprising accuracy (Feinleib, 2012). Taking this concept to another level, Netflix used its data analysis to help create content for its successful series *House of Cards* by identifying and then combining a popular director, actor, and plot premise (Carr, 2013).

BIG DATA AND STUDENT SUCCESS

Today, human activity creates a tremendous amount of information, often in real time. Much of this digital explosion is borne from the technology that people use on a daily basis, such as cell phones, tablets, Internet search engines, online shopping sites, social networks, and GPS navigators. These gadgets and associated activities generate volumes of "sensor-like" information that can be mined for value. Much of this information is passive and reflects traces of human activity in the form of "digital exhaust" or "digital smoke" (Loukides, 2010). Moreover, all these sensory data create a virtual nervous system for our planet that can allow people to know more about themselves, respond in real time (like a reflex action), and predict how people and organizations might respond to a given stimuli.

For decades, researchers have been trying to unpack the black box of the college experience, working to understand how college affects students (Pascarella & Terenzini, 1991, 2005). Data would usually be gathered from surveys about student activities and characteristics and then attempted to be linked to outcomes. Conclusions were drawn about the aggregate, not the individual, and interventions were near impossible to personalize. Interventions are, in many cases, based on data gathered years before, and assumptions about students are often based on group behavior rather than individual activity. These observations are not meant to be critiques of how higher education has operated; they simply describe a reality based on the availability of past data. Information was gathered from surveys and interviews; the need for sampling made it important that data were as pristine as possible; and conclusions were based on groups of people, not individual activity. And, academic leaders should be applauded for their efforts to use the legions of research on this topic to improve the success of their students.

Big Data creates knowledge, but only if it is used with purpose and direction. While health, business, and government have increasingly turned to Big Data to improve their work, higher education has been slow to embrace it. For higher education, the benefits of Big Data extend well beyond Pop-Tarts, ice cream, and presidential elections. Today, we can track the activities of students in real time. Student identification cards can allow us to know when and where students shop, eat, and engage in student activities such as concerts and lectures. Their use of ID cards allows us to know when they access their residence hall, enter a classroom, or go to the recreational center. Course management software records what readings a student accesses and how long he or she engages with the material. We can even track when students sign up for classes, how well they are doing, and whether an intervention is needed—all in real time. The digital footprint of today's college student can be vast, and higher education institutions have not yet realized the full potential of this tidal wave of data. If harnessed correctly, however, all this information can be used to extrapolate models of student success.

The benefits of Big Data for higher education include the potential to provide customized learning experiences, real-time interventions, and a greater awareness of how students progress from cradle to career. For example, companies such as ETS are already capturing student learning data "to develop predetermined learning trees to track certain responses to questions that imply mastery of specific aspects" (Guthrie, 2013). This powerful information can improve student success by providing an individualized course of study, an enhanced student-instructor relationship, and a closer digital community through distance learning.

The digital revolution allows colleges and universities to collect fine-grain detail on a large scale that can enhance operational decisions. For example, in the private sector, businesses may desire to identify their most loyal and profitable customers and "microtarget" them with advertising instead of relying on more costly conventional advertising that appeals to everyone or broader groups. Microtargeting uses data mining and algorithms to predict a person's attitude, sentiment, or behavior concerning a given subject. Each individual is assigned a score, which represents his or her statistical likelihood of engaging in a certain behavior; these scores help the organization prioritize which individuals to focus their attention on (Gavett, 2012). Microtargeting has also transformed political campaign operations by helping political parties to aim "specific ads at potential supporters based on where they live, the Web sites they visit and their voting records" (Vega, 2012). And, such techniques are now coming to higher education. As the pool of high school graduates shrinks in many parts of the nation, college recruiters, many of whom are experienced with using data from groups such as the College Board and ACT to target their marketing, are increasingly augmenting those data sources with information from the web in order to identify the students who are most likely to enroll and those who are most likely to pay the full tuition rate (Rivard, 2013). Similar techniques can also be used to target likely donors.

Beyond recruitment, some higher education institutions have been successful in using data to improve the success of students in the midst of their studies. In 2011, Arizona State University contracted with Knewton to use its Adaptive Learning Platform to facilitate freshman remedial math courses. The platform records various student input data (e.g., mouse clicks, logon times, correct and incorrect answers, selected distracters, time spent logged in, etc.) and uses a computer algorithm to process this information against a larger data set. The program identifies individual input data and then recommends a custom learning path tailored to the student's learning style, strengths, and habits. In short, the Adaptive Learning Platform assesses how individual students learn. This information is shared with the student and the professor, who can make optimal instructional decisions to better suit the individual learning needs of student. This information is also a powerful tool for students to identify their own strengths and learning styles, which can be conscientiously employed in other courses to facilitate academic success. In the 2011–2012 school year, the pass rates for 5,000 freshmen enrolled in remedial math classes using Knewton's platform increased from 66% to 75% (Kolowich, 2013).

Drawing inspiration from Netflix's ability to recommend the next movie that a user may want to watch based on what they have already watched and liked, Austin Peay State University developed an online course advising system called Degree Compass (Young, 2013; see also chapter 6). This program, created by the institution's provost, Tristan Denley, a former professor of mathematics, uses the student's planned major, previous academic performance, and data about the success of similar students to suggest which courses a student should take next. The results so far suggest that the program has led to higher grades and fewer dropouts. By crunching huge amounts of data, something that human advisers are not capable of doing, Degree Compass creates personalized recommendations for students. Human interaction in advising remains important, and Austin Peay still provides advisers for students, but the recommendations from Degree Compass mean that less time is spent on course selection, which frees more time for discussing other issues.

We should note, though, that for higher education, the drive to embrace Big Data is really about more than Big Data. The phenomenon, and this book, raises awareness of the potential benefits (and cautions) of Big Data and encourages a more broad-based drive to better use the data that currently exist—such as linking disparate databases and thereby making all of the data more useful. For example, there are new efforts underway in several states to link higher education data to that from the K–12 sector and the department of labor, using unit record indicators so that one could track the performance of a student from cradle to career (see chapter 11). In many cases, these data sets have existed for decades, siloed from each other due to political or bureaucratic obstacles or a simple lack of awareness. Now, states and at least one group of states are merging these data, which allows the performance of a student to be tracked from first grade through retirement, permitting a more nuanced understanding of the experience at each level, and how that might influence later success.

The full range of possibilities for improving higher education through Big Data is still unknown. This volume provides insights into how some campuses are using Big Data to enhance their work in the areas of student access, completion, and success.

BIG DATA AND RESEARCH

Universities have been at the forefront of the data revolution, developing new analytical techniques to better understand a whole host of important societal issues. The Visualization Center at San Diego State University used thousands of pictures collected from a free app to develop a map of the impact of the BP oil spill on the Gulf of Mexico coastline. The Structural Analysis of Large Amounts of Music Information project, a collaboration between researchers at the University of Illinois, the University of Southampton, and McGill University, is collecting about 23,000 hours of digital music to allow researchers to study the structure of music. In 2005, researchers at the University of Memphis, in partnership with IBM and the City of Memphis, developed Blue CRUSH (Criminal Reduction Utilizing Statistical History) to track patterns of crime and predict when (and where) potential crime would occur to more efficiently direct police resources. The result was a 31% decrease in serious crime in the city of Memphis since 2006 (Henschen, 2010).

All these efforts would not be possible without the infrastructure investment and technological support from universities. While this book does not touch much upon the work of scholars to utilize Big Data in their research, it is important for academic administrators to be aware of their responsibility to support faculty work in this area. Moreover, the data and technology we are dealing with now are unlike much of what have been used by colleges and universities in the past. Inherent in the Big Data movement is the fact that it is difficult, if not impossible, for existing technology to store and analyze the amount of data that is now available. Institutions need to develop or obtain access to data warehouses to store the massive amounts of data that continue to grow rapidly. New techniques are needed to capture the data, whether it is downloading from social networks or uploading from an iPad used in health trials in Africa. New technology platforms are necessary to crunch the data and find meaningful patterns. And staff are needed who can work on infrastructure, analytical models, data sources, and application development.

The data and technology being used are also very different from previous generations, so existing staff members may not have the expertise to support these new initiatives. Academic leaders who are interested in providing a Big Data infrastructure for scholars (as well as building in-house analysis capacities) should be willing to invest in new staff and/or professional development for existing staff.

This new infrastructure can be quite expensive, so some institutions develop partnerships with business and industry to develop Big Data centers, such as the Cloud and Big Data Laboratory at the University of Texas at San Antonio. These centers tend to support cloud computing and provide the processing power necessary to work through a terabyte of data. Such centers can be advantageous as they provide universities with capacity to support the work of their faculty, while drawing on partners, who also have access to the facilities, to help cover the associated costs. Such arrangements are increasing since many organizations cannot fully use the capacity of such a center alone and recognize the value of partnerships. Moreover, colleges and universities tend to be viewed as neutral territory, allowing multiple companies to come together to support such a center without any one of them having the advantage of the investment being at their location.

BIG DATA AND EDUCATION: CREATING DATA SCIENTISTS

The data revolution has also created the need for colleges to prepare students for what the *Harvard Business Review* has called the sexiest new job of the 21st century: the data scientist (Davenport & Patil, 2012). Davenport and Patil (2012) describe this person as "a high-ranking professional with the training and curiosity to make discoveries in the world of big data." This generic description represents the persisting ambiguity in defining the exact nature of the role, but current job data suggest that there will be high demand for individuals with this general skill set. The McKinsey Global Institute (2011) reports that the demand for data scientists is expected to rise and exceed the available supply resulting in a 50–60% talent gap in the United States by 2018. This gap includes the unfulfilled need for "140,000 to 190,000 people with deep analytical skills as well as 1.5 million managers and analysts to analyze big data and make decisions based on their findings" (McKinsey Global Institute, 2011, pp.10–11).

The data scientists have a critical role in leveraging Big Data. First, they possess a broad range of technical skills, which includes computer science, programming, modeling, data management, advanced mathematics, and statistics. Additionally, data scientists possess strong business (or organizational) domain knowledge that enables them to become problem-solving artists. Data scientists know how to prioritize problems, what questions to ask, what to look for during data collection and analysis, and which Big Data tools to utilize. In this process they explore and examine data from a variety of sources and analyze Big Data challenges using multiple perspectives. IBM vice president of Big Data products Anjul Bhambhri remarked, "A data scientist is somebody who is inquisitive, who can stare at data and spot trends. It's almost like a Renaissance individual who really wants to learn and bring change to an organization" (Bhambhri, n.d.).

Data scientists are a combination of computer scientist, statistician, philosopher, and English major. Needless to say, many traditional academic programs do not provide the entirety of the skill set expected of such individuals. One way to overcome this shortcoming is to develop interdisciplinary programs such as the Institute for Advanced Analytics at North Carolina State University, where students can pursue a one-year master of science degree in analytics that includes courses dealing with data management and quality, mathematical and statistical methods for data modeling, and techniques for visualizing data in support of enterprise-wide decision making. More than a simple number cruncher, the data scientist needs to be able to bridge the communications gap between the detailed technical processes of Big Data and the individuals involved in decision-making processes. That is, they must have the ability to simplify, articulate, and present information derived from the data. Consequently, data scientists need to have some entrepreneurial insights as high-ranking professionals with the training and curiosity to make discoveries in the world of Big Data (Davenport & Patil, 2012).

Data scientists have to use creative problem-solving techniques to make enormous and complex problems smaller and simpler. One way to accomplish this is through "data jujitsu" or "the art of using multiple data elements in clever ways to solve iterative problems that, when combined, solve a data problem that might otherwise be intractable" (Patil, 2012). Integrating heterogeneous data from various sources to explore a Big Data problem is also known as "data mashup." This term reflects the data scientist's ability to overcome and embrace the "variety" constraint of Big Data.

After identifying various data sources and determining how to piece them together, data scientists must clean, condition, and prepare raw data for analysis. For example, privacy concerns over certain types of data, such as medical and financial data, require data scientists to "anonymize" or strip away sensitive personal information from collected data. Data conditioning may also require "tagging" certain data elements, which helps to organize and compare information during analysis. Data scientists must also confront the challenge of data veracity by effectively scrutinizing the quality and completeness of collected data.

HIGHER EDUCATION SYSTEMS: TAKING DATA ANALYTICS TO SCALE

Much of this volume focuses on the possibilities for Big Data at the campus level, yet systems and states are well poised to take advantage of the massive amounts of data now being produced in ways no single campus can. Systems and states provide an opportunity both to better understand the academic ecosystem and to provide more refined interventions based on the amount of data available across multiple campuses.

While this data movement will allow colleges and universities to better understand student behavior within their institutions, systems can amalgamate data from across multiple campuses. This practice allows systems to track the mobility (and success) of students as they move across campuses. Working with other agencies, the opportunity exists to follow students from when they begin school through their engagement in the workforce, enhancing understanding of how educational opportunities throughout the pipeline affect persistence in the educational system and performance in the workforce. Moreover, the scale of data available to a system provides for strategic decision making as well as development of more robust predictive models that can be used to improve student success.

As discussed in the foreword to this volume and in chapter 7, the State University of New York (SUNY) is harnessing data from its 64 campuses and 463,000 students to enhance understanding of student mobility. In fact, through some of its initial analysis, the system realized that a large percentage (26.2%) of students who transfer within the system transfer from a four-year institution to a two-year institution. This revelation resulted in retooling of SUNY's transfer policies to provide support for students who engage in this reverse transfer rather than seeing transfer as only an upward or horizontal practice. If all multi-campus systems of higher education in the United States were to pursue this level of multi-institutional analysis, we would have a much greater understanding of how a vast majority of students in public four-year institutions experience higher education.

Similar efforts are being developed through collaborations by higher education institutions, state education departments, and state labor departments to share unit-level data across agencies (see chapter 11). As opposed to looking at patterns of movement across institutions, these sorts of arrangements permit one to see how a student moves from cradle to career. Not only can one better understand how students progress through their educational paths, the data also allow for analyzing how different experiences along individuals' paths may affect their career choices, employment opportunities, and benefits accrued from their workplaces.

Not all the data used in such analyses may be Big Data in the strictest sense, but using data to look at trends across institutions and across lifetimes is an important aspect of the new way in which data are being aggregated to inform decision making.

THE CAUTIONARY SIDE

How does one safely harness the ability to predict who is likely to attend a college, complete a degree, and be successful in the workforce? What if that same ability allowed one to predict who would likely be a successful athlete, a frequent visitor of the campus judicial affairs office, or a defaulter on student loans? What if the information used also allowed one to discover private personal information about a student, such as their sexual orientation or online proclivities? Such questions are important to consider, as they frame important ethical considerations related to the increasing availability of data and their use to predict the future.

Fans of superhero comic books are likely have to have heard the phrase "With great power comes great responsibility." This saying is no less relevant to the power of data being discussed throughout this volume. The analysis of these massive data sets provides the opportunity to peer into individuals' likely futures and make decisions based upon those likelihoods. The analysis may also dictate certain organizational decisions that may have unintended consequences for individuals. For example, what if an institution is able to predict which students are likely to drop a class? Should such a student be dissuaded from enrolling as a way to save the student's money and the faculty member's time? If the faculty member is informed, will he or she ignore the student, thinking that interactions are wasted effort, or will the professor give special attention to the student in the hope of overcoming the predicted outcome? The ability to predict who is likely to drop a class can provide an opportunity to intervene and encourage student success, but such profiling may also create a self-fulfilling prophecy in that a student targeted as being at risk may end up acting that way even if he or she was not really at risk. As discussed in chapter 3, a myriad of concerns exist of which academic leaders need to be aware. We highlight four key areas here: data integrity, privacy, removing choice, and profiling.

Data integrity. There are many potential problems with the integrity of data. We address the primary issues here. In the digital realm, there are two types of data: generated and volunteered. Generated data come from the activities in which one engages, such as the type of course material one accesses via course management software. This type of data tends to be fairly accurate, although it is possible for someone to be acting as another student's digital persona. Volunteered data are actively created by a person (or a different person acting as that person). In this case, people choose which information to volunteer, and self-divulged information may not always be accurate—which may result in an inauthentic digital representation of themselves. Thus, programs that use data from Facebook and other social networks may not be capturing an accurate image of a student. Known as "the big lie," data made available on social media sites may reflect a gap between private reality and public social norms and opinions (DiResta, 2013). Accordingly, those engaging in data analysis need to be aware of this information fallacy since there is an important difference between generated and volunteered data.

Privacy. Most people realize that the digital era has diminished individual privacy. Many of us now make available pictures, opinions, and current locations on a regular basis to friends and strangers through such social networks as Facebook, Twitter, and Instagram. However, many people do not know that the data produced from their activities are being retained by organizations and refined for use in a variety of purposes. Student IDs can tell us what students eat (meal plans) and where they go (concerts, residence hall). Course management software allows us to know which course materials students access and how long they engage with it. It is also possible to discover other private information about students that they may not willingly disclose or want college administrators to know. These types of data give great power to those who possess them, and careful consideration should be given to who has access to such data and how the information is used.

Removing choice. Predictive analytics can help academic leaders make better-informed decisions about how to help students succeed. Many companies now track Internet searches, Facebook "likes," and GPS data to help measure and predict consumer preferences, which allows an organization to present preference-based options to its consumers. As discussed elsewhere in this chapter and in chapter 6, some campuses are doing similar analysis to advise students about which courses to take.

Predictive analytics may simplify the decision-making process and increase the likelihood of student success, but does the predictive process undermine a student's choice? For example, prediction relieves the individual from the full burden of the decision-making process, which includes gathering information, identifying and prioritizing alternatives, and carefully assessing the benefits against the costs. Thus, optimized selections provided by predictive analytics simultaneously simplifies (and optimizes) individual choices, but it also supplants individual critical thinking.

Profiling. Colleges and universities have already begun using predictive analytics to target students who may be at risk of failing a class or dropping out of school (see chapter 6). These predictions have allowed institutions to implement interventions, sometimes in real time, to help improve student success. While such predictions and interventions may seem to be a silver bullet for improving the rate of student completion, there are potential downsides that must be considered. For example, predicting a student's likelihood for success could dissuade institutions from marketing themselves to a student who may not have performed well in high school, thus reducing access. Similarly, in a technological version of what Burton Clark (1960) called the *cooling out* effect, if an institution predicts that a current student has a high likelihood of dropping out before completing his or her degree, the interventions provided may encourage the student to withdraw early rather than helping them persist through the end of their degree program. Moreover, these predictive models incorporate advanced statistical computer algorithms, which may not be accurate, or the outcomes could be used to implement interventions, for example, for which the algorithm was not originally designed. Analytics is a diagnostic tool that must be correctly matched to a given organizational problem.

Using Big Data and data analytics to create a smarter university is filled with ethical issues and measured risks. It is always important for academic leaders to remember that there is a huge difference between trusting Netflix to accurately recommend a movie and a university to accurately recommend a particular course and/or degree path.

THE WAY FORWARD

"You don't need these big platforms. You don't need all this big fancy
stuff. If anyone says 'Big' in front of it, you should look at them very
skeptically . . ."

—Harper Reed, CTO Obama for America 2012

Inclusion of this quote may seem strange for a book that incorporates
"Big" data in its name. This remark comes from a lecture given at
SUNY's 2013 conference on the role of Big Data in transforming
higher education.[2] The speaker's message was that issues around Big
Data had become distorted as companies and others invoked the term
to sell their services and products to those scared by the concept. The
reality, Harper Reed said, was that not everything about the current
data revolution was "big" and not everything labeled "big" really
deserved that description. And, before being scared into buying lots
of new equipment and software, institutions should pause and determine what data they want to use and how they want to use those
data.

In fact, one of the primary goals of this book is to decode a lot of
the mystery that currently surrounds the data revolution, including
the hyperfocus on Big Data. There is little doubt that there is something different about the world in which we now live. There is more
information today than one could fathom two decades ago; and new
information is being produced at an unprecedented rate. This situation makes it very difficult for current technologies to store and
process data, but for those who can harness the data, the insights are
unparalleled. As discussed throughout the remaining chapters of this
volume, colleges and universities can know more than ever before
about how their students study, play, and work. They can predict
who is likely to drop a course or drop out of school and provide interventions in the real time. Software can now advise students as to
which classes are most useful for their course of study and how well
they are likely to do, similar to how Amazon uses customers' information to suggest what else they might want to buy.

Such power raises many ethical questions around privacy, profiling, and individual choice. The data that are now available allow, for
those who control them, knowledge and insights about individuals
that can reveal a great deal of insights about them. How the data are

used can provide great benefits to student success, but if the data are inaccurate, or the algorithms used to process them are inappropriate, the interventions provided could do more harm than good. And, by limiting the choices available to students, it may remove personal choice and exploration from the college experience.

The bottom line, however, is that we are too early in this data revolution to fully understand its opportunities and challenges. There is no doubt that colleges and universities are using data to improve what they do, and such efforts will only increase in the future. Thus, academic leaders need to have a basic understanding of the issues surrounding Big Data and its implications for higher education.

NOTES

1. The first three Vs of Big Data (i.e., volume, velocity, and variety) were first reported by Laney (2001). Over the next several years, other V words have been added. We selected to include veracity and visualization as they seemed most applicable to the topic at hand. Some writers have included value as an additional descriptor.
2. SUNY hosts an annual Critical Issues in Higher Education conference. In 2013, the conference—entitled Building a Smarter University: Big Data, Ingenuity, and Innovation—focused on the role of Big Data in advancing student success, institutional infrastructure, and research.

REFERENCES

Bhambhri, A. (n.d.). *What is a data scientist*. Retrieved from IBM website: http://www-01.ibm.com/software/data/infosphere/data-scientist/

Callaham, J. (2013). *Microsoft's super-long infographic gives us the data on Big Data*. Retrieved from Neowin website: http://www.neowin.net/news/microsofts-super-long-infographic-gives-us-the-data-on-big-data

Carr, D. (2013, February 24). Giving viewers what they want. *New York Times*. Retrieved from http://www.nytimes.com/2013/02/25/

business/media/for-house-of-cards-using-big-data-to-guarantee-its-popularity.html

Clark, B. R. (1960). The "cooling-out" function in higher education. *American Journal of Sociology 65*(6), 569–576.

Davenport, T. H., & Patil, D. J. (2012, October). Data scientist: The sexiest job of the 21st century. *Harvard Business Review*. Retrieved from http://hbr.org/2012/10/data-scientist-the-sexiest-job-of-the-21st-century/

DiResta, R. (2013, September 25). Big Data and the "Big Lie": The challenges facing big brand marketers. *O'Reilly Radar*. Retrieved from http://radar.oreilly.com/2013/09/big-data-and-the-big-lie-the-challenges-facing-big-brand-marketers.html

Feinleib, D. (2012, July 20). How the Netflix Big Data approach is transforming education. *Forbes*. Retrieved from http://www.forbes.com/sites/davefeinleib/2012/07/20/how-the-netflix-big-data-approach-is-transforming-education/

Foley, J. (2013, October 9). Extreme Big Data: Beyond zettabytes and yottabytes. *Forbes*. Retrieved from http://www.forbes.com/sites/oracle/2013/10/09/extreme-big-data-beyond-zettabytes-and-yottabytes/

Fourtané, S. (2013, May 3). Big Data tales: Walmart's introduction. *Big Data Republic*. Retrieved from http://www.bigdatarepublic.com/author.asp?section_id=2747&doc_id=262692

Gavett, G. (2012, November 2). Electing a president in a microtargeted world. *Harvard Business Review*. Retrieved from http://blogs.hbr.org/2012/11/electing-a-president-in-a-micr/

Guthrie, D. (2013, August 15). The coming Big Data education revolution. *U.S. News & World Report*. Retrieved from http://www.usnews.com/opinion/articles/2013/08/15/why-big-data-not-moocs-will-revolutionize-education

Henschen, D. (2010, July 21). Memphis cuts crime with predictive analytics. *Information Week*. Retrieved from http://www.informationweek.com/healthcare/analytics/memphis-cuts-crime-with-predictive-analytics/d/d-id/1090960?

Hill, K. (2012, February 16). How Target figured out a teen girl was pregnant before her father did. *Forbes*. Retrieved from http://www.forbes.com/sites/kashmirhill/2012/02/16/how-target-figured-out-a-teen-girl-was-pregnant-before-her-father-did/

Kolowich, S. (2013, January 25). The new intelligence. *Inside Higher Ed.*

Retrieved from http://www.insidehighered.com/news/2013/01/25/
arizona-st-and-knewtons-grand-experiment-adaptive-learning

Lampitt, A. (2012, December 6). Big Data visualization: A big deal
for eBay. *InfoWorld*. Retrieved from http://www.infoworld.
com/d/big-data/big-data-visualization-big-deal-ebay-208589

Laney, D. (2001, February 6). 3D data management: Controlling data
volume, velocity and variety. Stamford, CT: META Group. Retrieved from http://blogs.gartner.com/doug-laney/files/2012/01/
ad949-3D-Data-Management-Controlling-Data-Volume-Veloci-
ty-and-Variety.pdf.

Loukides, M. (2010, June 2). What is data science? *O'Reilly Radar*.
Retrieved from http://radar.oreilly.com/2010/06/what-is-data-
science.html

Marcus, J. (2012, November 13). Student advising plays key role
in college success—just as it's being cut. *NBC News*. Retrieved
from http://usnews.nbcnews.com/_news/2012/11/13/15140302-
student-advising-plays-key-role-in-college-success-just-as-its-be-
ing-cut?lite

Matyszczky, C. (2014, January 19). Amazon to ship things before
you've even thought of buying them? *CNET*. Retrieved from
http://news.cnet.com/8301-17852_3-57617458-71/amazon-to-
ship-things-before-youve-even-thought-of-buying-them/

McKinsey Global Institute. (2011). Big Data: The next frontier for
innovation, competition, and productivity. Retrieved from McK-
insey & Company website: http://www.mckinsey.com/~/media/
McKinsey/dotcom/Insights%20and%20pubs/MGI/Research/
Technology%20and%20Innovation/Big%20Data/MGI_big_
data_full_report.ashx

Miller, K., & Chapin, K. (2013, February 15). How Big Data changes lives. Retrieved from WGBH website: http://www.wgbhnews.
org/post/how-big-data-changes-lives

Palace, B. (1996). What is data mining? Retrieved from UCLA Anderson Graduate School of Management website: http://www.an-
derson.ucla.edu/faculty/jason.frand/teacher/technologies/palace/
datamining.htm

Parry, M. (2012, July 18). Big Data on campus. *New York Times*.
Retrieved from http://www.nytimes.com/2012/07/22/education/
edlife/colleges-awakening-to-the-opportunities-of-data-mining.
html?pagewanted=all&_r=0

Pascarella, E. T., & Terenzini, P. T. (1991). *How college affects students: Findings and insights from twenty years of research.* San Francisco, CA: Jossey-Bass.

Pascarella, E. T., & Terenzini, P. T. (2005). *How college affects students: A third decade of research.* San Francisco, CA: Jossey-Bass.

Patil, D. J. (2012, July 17). Data jujitsu: The art of turning data into product. *O'Reilly Radar.* Retrieved from http://radar.oreilly.com/2012/07/data-jujitsu.html

Rivard, R. (2013, October 24). Micro-targeting students. *Inside Higher Ed.* Retrieved from http://www.insidehighered.com/news/2013/10/24/political-campaign-style-targeting-comes-student-search

Siegel, E. (2013). *Predictive analytics: The power to predict who will click, buy, lie, or die.* Hoboken, NJ: Wiley.

Taylor, C. (2013, August 26). Visualization: The simple way to simplify Big Data. *Wired.* Retrieved from http://www.wired.com/insights/2013/08/visualization-the-simple-way-to-simplify-big-data/

The big bang: How the Big Data explosion is changing the world. (2013, February 11). Retrieved from Microsoft News Center website: http://www.microsoft.com/en-us/news/features/2013/feb13/02-11BigData.aspx

Vega, T. (2012, February 20). Online data helping campaigns customize ads. *New York Times.* Retrieved from http://www.nytimes.com/2012/02/21/us/politics/campaigns-use-microtargeting-to-attract-supporters.html?pagewanted=all&_r=0

Vesset, D. (2013, February 11). Fun with Big Data: Cat ladies, soccer subs and sexy scientists. Retrieved from Microsoft News Center website: http://www.microsoft.com/en-us/news/features/2013/feb13/02-11bigdatafun.aspx

Young, J. R. (2013, April 10). The Netflix effect: When software suggests students' courses. *The Chronicle of Higher Education.* Retrieved from http://chronicle.com/article/The-Netflix-Effect-When/127059/

2

LEGAL ISSUES ASSOCIATED WITH BIG DATA IN HIGHER EDUCATION

Ethical Considerations and Cautionary Tales

JEFFREY C. SUN

ABSTRACT

This chapter examines key legal, ethical, and cautionary issues associated with Big Data. These topics include privacy, security, data retention, and intellectual property. The discussion of these topics illustrates that the legal environment offers guidance in practice areas for higher education administrators, yet it also draws attention to new and emerging legal challenges arising from Big Data. Given the latter, the chapter presents several legislative, regulatory, and practice recommendations, which are informed by the law yet move beyond a legal and regulatory framework and into data management strategies. This approach illuminates how the law serves as the connective intelligence to Big Data.

Data analytics has opened opportunities for postsecondary educational institutions to respond to student learning needs, identify student behaviors of concern, attract admissions prospects who are likely to attend, and examine levels of operational efficiency (Baer & Campbell, 2012; Bienkowski, Feng, & Means, 2012; Campbell, DeBlois, & Oblinger, 2007; Eduventures, 2013; Norris et al., 2011). According to an IBM case study, one university reports, "For the first time, we now have a statistical model than can show, based upon data, which students are most susceptible to attrition" (Campus Technology & IBM, 2012, p. 3). Further, the University of Kentucky attributes, in part, the use of data analytics to marginal gains of approximately 1.3% in freshman-to-sophomore retention, making the overall retention rate between freshman and sophomore years 81.5% (Straumsheim, 2013).

Given the characteristics of Big Data discussed in chapter 1, questions about legal and policy parameters around data collection, mining, storage, analytics, application, and destruction abound. Much of the referenced law applies to handling data generally, but Big Data pushes these issues forward through greater data exposure and heightened concerns. Accordingly, this chapter examines key legal issues of Big Data, specifically within the context of postsecondary education. These topics include privacy, security, data retention, and intellectual property. The discussion of these topics illustrates that the legal environment offers guidance in practice areas for higher education administrators, yet it also draws attention to new and emerging legal challenges arising from Big Data. Given the latter, the chapter presents several legislative, regulatory, and practice recommendations, which are informed by the law yet move beyond a legal and regulatory framework and into data management strategies. This approach illuminates how the law serves as the connective intelligence to Big Data.

PRIVACY AND EDUCATION RECORDS

Big Data is a major resource for postsecondary institutions to understand and perform in ways that improve student achievement, community engagement, and institutional accountability (Parry, 2012). Indeed, it is an asset for postsecondary institutions. At the same time, its benefits present several drawbacks, and one drawback is its challenge to privacy (Lohr, 2013; Rotenberg & Barnes, 2013). This concern, especially in terms of breaches to student records, is one of the principal fears (Dougherty, 2008; Rotenberg & Barnes, 2013). For instance, in August 2013, Ferris State University reported that its system may have been infected by malware that potentially compromised 39,000 student records ("Data security breach," 2013). This experience, as is the case for many other colleges and universities, is not the first. In November 2007, the media reported that Ferris State may have also compromised unencrypted applicant information such as names, addresses, telephone numbers, e-mail addresses, and academic records when a laptop was stolen from an admissions officer's car ("Ferris State University," 2007). As these data breach incidents illustrate, colleges and universities are highly susceptible to compromising information. While the scalability and access points are often different in Big Data breaches, the legal principles and policies follow the same general analysis. Thus, in light of these and other similar incidents, this section presents the legal parameters surrounding data privacy and education records with application to Big Data.[1]

The Family Educational Rights and Privacy Act of 1974 (FERPA) is a federal privacy law protecting student education records.[2] Its protections are particularly illustrative in four applications of Big Data: adaptive learning, statewide longitudinal data systems, education or treatment records that touch on health matters, and education records of minors.

Adaptive learning. Adaptive learning technology operates off information entered to determine the next lesson or module of educational content (Hartley & Bassett, 2013). As a form of artificial intelligence, the program mediates learning by assessing a student's knowledge level and presents a lesson or reinforcement activity before proceeding to the next module. Hence, the program adapts to the individual or mediates learning with a somewhat personalized set of education modules.

This technological approach to education has been in place since the 1990s. Educational testing and tutoring centers such as Sylvan and Kaplan have used adaptive learning technology to assist students in reading, language development, writing, and math. More recently, higher education's use of adaptive learning technology has demonstrated successes in writing, math, and foreign language classes—particularly developmental and remedial education courses (Baer & Campbell, 2012; Bienkowski, Feng, & Means, 2012).

Selingo, Carey, Pennington, Fishman, and Palmer (2013) highlight examples of how colleges have used adaptive learning technology in higher education. For instance, at Arizona State University, a student who enrolls in an adaptive learning class must master a set of concepts through which the student accumulates and earns badges.

An established number of badges qualifies the student to sit through the final exam to demonstrate course proficiency. As Selingo et al. (2013) report, Arizona State University has applied lessons from its experiences with adaptive learning technology to general education courses, into which they plan to integrate both an adaptive learning feature and an active learning classroom approach. That is, much of the traditional lecture portion can be offered through adaptive learning technology along with reinforcement activities. Further, the active learning classroom supports the integration with problem-solving activities. Accordingly, the "guiding principles for the course redesign are: 1) Mastery of each concept by every student, with mastery defined as proficiency at a predetermined level for all major concepts in a course; 2) Active learning using problem solving activities; and 3) Personalized, adaptive learning pathways" (Selingo et al., 2013, p. 11). However, Arizona State's work draws on the partnership of two for-profit companies, Pearson and Knewton. Pearson is an established company that provides educational solutions, which for many years has been through textbooks and learning aids. Founded in 2008, Knewton is a relatively new educational technology company that has gained significant traction in the field within the past few years. These companies, as third-party vendors of postsecondary institutions, hold confidential data of student records. Their access is permissible under the law.

FERPA permits use of student information without express consent when a university or state system office is using education records for predictive tests, student aid programs, or instructional improvements.[3] When Congress adopted this exception provision within FERPA, it conditioned the use of personally identifiable information with requirements that the data would not be released to outsiders and would be destroyed after the study is completed.[4] The U.S. Department of Education expanded those requirements by promulgating a rule that the study exception must be memorialized into a written agreement between the university and the organization authorized to conduct the study. The agreement must indicate the purpose, scope, and duration of the study along with the data to be disclosed; the restriction that personally identifiable information (PII) is used only for the purposes outlined in the agreement; the mandate that the organization may not release PII and use within the organization is restricted to representatives with legitimate interest (i.e., need-to-know basis); and the requirement of data destruction upon the study's completion.[5] So long as these provisions are fully executed, these parties have permissible access to these records as contractors.

Statewide longitudinal data systems (SLDS). Most states have moved forward on building a statewide longitudinal data system (SLDS), which contributes to the establishment of Big Data from a statewide source (see chapter 11). SLDS is a data warehouse of state educational information such as attendance patterns, test scores, and grades. While states such as Georgia, Maryland, and Oregon have been collecting student data in a systematic manner for many years, a national policy movement under the Educational Technical Assistance Act of 2002 incentivized states to move further on this initiative.[6] The Educational Technical Assistance Act authorized the U.S. secretary of education to award competitive federal grants to support states' creation and advancement of SLDS, including integration of an individual's data from early childhood through one's time in the workforce. Under this grant program and additional funds drawn from the American Recovery and Reinvestment Act of 2009, the U.S. Department of Education administered five rounds of grants between 2005 and 2012 to support statewide longitudinal data systems in 47 states plus the District of Columbia, Puerto Rico, and the Virgin Islands (National Center for Education Statistics, n.d.).

Although SLDS presents a useful data resource for education analytics, the growing prevalence of Big Data involving education records has raised concerns over data privacy. In particular, groups and individuals opposing SLDS development have argued that activities to create these systems violate FERPA.

As a federal law designed to protect student education records, FERPA prohibits educational institutions and state system offices from disclosing or using personally identifiable information absent consent or as statutorily permissible. Recent changes to the FERPA regulations in 2008 and 2011 make the law clearer about appropriate access and uses of student data, yet they have also raised the ire of privacy groups such as the Electronic Privacy Information Center (EPIC) (Rotenberg & Barnes, 2013).

Nonetheless, FERPA permits authorized state representatives and certain federal officials (e.g., U.S. secretary of education and the attorney general) to receive education records containing PII without the consent of students when they are needed for an audit or evaluation of a federal or state program and for the purposes of federal compliance.[7] Congress made clear in the law that data protections were critical by adopting steps to limit data access and put in place data destruction plans. In the regulations governing this provision, the U.S. Department of Education incorporated firm language that holds the official representative "responsible for using reasonable methods to ensure to the greatest extent practicable that any entity or individual designated as its authorized representative" complies with restrictions on the data use and handling.[8] Further, the regulations expressly indicate that a written agreement must be used when designating any authorized representative other than employees. The agreement must include who is the designated individual or entity; what PII from education records will be disclosed; what the purpose is, which must fall within one of the permissible bases (i.e., audit, evaluation, or a federal legal requirement); how the data will be used, giving "sufficient specificity to make clear that the work falls within the exception";[9] a statement that destruction will occur when the data are no longer needed; a time period for that destruction, and policies and procedures addressing protections and handling for unauthorized disclosure and use.[10]

Recently, questions arose on the application of FERPA and data reporting to states in which a university is not principally located but from which an institution draws students through online education. Specifically, in May 2013, the general counsel's office at the University of Massachusetts inquired about whether FERPA would permit the institution to comply with a Maryland law (King, 2013). The Maryland state law at issue requires postsecondary institutions operating in Maryland, even via online education, to register with the state and report PII from education records to the Maryland Longitudinal Data System (MLDS) Center. The University of Massachusetts has online programs that educate college students in Maryland, so it was unsure whether reporting its data would violate FERPA.

To resolve this legal matter, the governance structure of various state agencies is important to understand. On behalf of the state's executive branch, the Maryland Higher Education Commission (MHEC) serves as the coordinating board for higher education institutions. It is permissible under FERPA for the University of Massachusetts to disclose the data to MHEC. However, independent of

MHEC, the MLDS Center is a state agency responsible for data services, including information management and analyses. The MLDS
Center works with data from early childhood to higher education
to the workforce, which is referred to as the P20W continuum, as
the P20 refers to the full educational pipeline from early childhood
through higher education and the W refers to the workforce. Thus,
MLDS mines more than education records; it includes workforce records, and it is not a recognized higher education agency that may
simply receive education records without student consent. Given the
distinct nature of and separation between the two agencies, Dale
King, the director of the U.S. Department of Education's Family
Policy Compliance Office, informed the University of Massachusetts
that submission of education records to the MLDS Center would
be permissible only if the MLDS Center and MHEC had a written
agreement as outlined in the audit and evaluation exception requirements. The agreement requires MHEC to authorize MLDS as a third
party to act on MHEC's behalf. In other words, disclosure of education records to another state, pursuant to state authorization rules, is
not a violation of FERPA provided that the data are disclosed to an
authorized agency. In this case, the authorization must appear in the
form of a written agreement between MHEC and MLDS; otherwise,
the University of Massachusetts may not disclose the data to MLDS.

In short, the laws and regulations of FERPA have accounted for
the emergence of Big Data, particularly in terms of formation of an
SLDS. Specifically, FERPA permits disclosure of student data without
consent when the data are for an audit or evaluation of a federal or
state program. SLDS and other similar data mining efforts would
qualify. However, an audit or evaluation only permits data access to
governmental agencies explicitly charged with the responsibility of
postsecondary education. The privacy protections under FERPA do
not permit disclosure of education records to another governmental
agency unless an agreement is written addressing the uses, time period, and eventual data destruction.

Education or treatment records that touch on health matters.
Education or treatment records that touch on student health issues
may be helpful for postsecondary institutions to analyze when addressing student retention and behavioral matters (i.e., "students of
concern"). These records may be available, depending on how they
are treated and eventually classified.

For instance, colleges and universities are, at times, subject to a federal law, the Health Insurance Portability and Accountability Act of 1996 (HIPAA), which governs privacy policies of patient health information (PHI).[11] Colleges and universities that serve as a healthcare provider may be subject to HIPAA as a covered entity that participates in electronic transmissions of PHI for reasons such as claims, benefit eligibility inquiries, referral authorization requests, and other transactions specified by the U.S. Department of Health and Human Services. In 2009, the Health Information Technology for Economic and Clinical Health (HITECH) Act incorporated provisions of reports of data breaches.[12] These requirements include individual notification of persons affected by data breaches and public reports of data breaches when 500 or more individuals are affected.

While the law is detailed with many provisions, HIPAA represents the minimum required privacy protections for PHI. In many instances, state laws also govern handling of PHI, and these laws tend to be stricter. That is, state law often provides greater privacy protections to PHI.

However, student medical records from college health clinics are not necessarily an issue of HIPAA, but instead they fall within the purview of FERPA (U.S. Department of Education & U.S. Department of Health and Human Services, 2008). Depending on the record, it may fall under either an educational record or a treatment record. Health-related matters that enter the educational sphere, such as disability reports to establish reasonable accommodations, become education records under FERPA. As discussed earlier, education records are subject to the same access to third-party contractors or representatives of the postsecondary institutions. By contrast, medical records such as the campus psychologist or other student health matters are likely treatment records that are not governed by FERPA. Unlike education records, treatment records are not subject to a student's inspection of his or her records. Only an appropriate medical professional such as a medical doctor may inspect those records for the student. In addition, these records are typically covered by state PHI privacy laws.

Data on minors. For the most part, privacy in terms of education records at the postsecondary level is not an issue for minors. Under FERPA, when a student attends a postsecondary institution, the student, even if a minor, has rights over his or her education records.[13]

As Daniel, Gee, Sun, and Pauken (2012) indicate, the rights of parents, which are typically available when a student is under 18 years of age, do not apply to postsecondary education records, as those rights transfer to the student. Thus, in matters of students in dual enrollment or dual credit programs (i.e., simultaneously enrolled for high school and college credits), a student's education records at the college follow the statutory rule that the rights reside with the student, not the parents. However, the records at the high school follow typical standards for minors, which permit parental involvement.

Privacy versus openness. Legislation at the federal and state levels addresses many privacy and security protections, particularly over certain classifications of people (e.g., students and employees) and under certain transactions (e.g., transmissions of patient health information or processing credit cards). While the privacy laws and policies serve a role in protecting the rights of persons and groups as well as securing information from release to others, these privacy and security measures are, at times, asserted as justifications to counteract efforts of openness and transparency (Fairchild, 2013; Silverblatt, 2013). In light of these different interests, the debate continues about the line between maintaining privacy/security and providing openness/transparency. At times, this issue is settled by the legal source and strength. That is, federal law trumps state law, so whatever the federal law states prevails in the decision (McGee-Tubb, 2012).

When the federal-state distinction is not at issue, government documents such as a public university's student retention report and records of administrators' travel expenses are, in most states, subject to state open records laws. The public policy rationale is based on placing sunshine on government operations. For instance, in California, the open records law presents a foundational principal that "the Legislature, mindful of the right of individuals to privacy, finds and declares that access to information concerning the conduct of the people's business is a fundamental and necessary right of every person in this state."[14]

Colleges and universities often adopt strategies to overcome identifying personally identifiable information. For instance, colleges have relied on aggregated data or de-identified data. Pursuant to FERPA, data redaction presents a permissible approach to disclose education records without students' consent.[15] However, in other contexts, redaction may not be an option or sufficient to protect identities of individuals, identifiable groups, or organizations. For instance, the request may include the algorithm to predict employee performance and compare that figure to salary increases. These documents reflect sensitive information especially because the algorithm may be used for test calculations because the analysts are uncertain of the statistical validity.

Legal alternatives may exist to fend off these requests. As Fairchild (2013) points out, some states—including Arizona, Georgia, and Massachusetts—consider a balancing of interests between the parties' privacy and the public concern to examine government operations. Hutchens, Sun, and Miksch (2014) warn that individuals placing open records requests may not always have good intentions. They suggest that open records laws can present a tactic to intimidate and harass academic researchers and other members of the higher education community by placing an undue burden on them through the time, money, and mental energy dispensed to handle excessive record requests. One of their suggestions is that academic institutions receive an exempt status or classify certain mission-oriented work, such as research and educational activities, as unrelated to the government operations that open records laws were intended to address.

INTELLECTUAL PROPERTY

Access to and use of some data may be restricted through proprietary rights. Since Big Data involves data collection, mining, storage, analytics, and application, protections based on personal or organizational attribution, control, and ownership are often at issue. Those concerns reflect the law of intellectual property—a legal concept that is constantly evolving with technological advancements and competing interests from various actors involved in the property development.

Intellectual property refers to the intangible interest that often leads to the production or creation of products, processes, expressions, marks, or nonpublic information. Derived from the United States Constitution, "intellectual property law provides a personal property interest in work of the mind" (O'Connor, 1991, p. 598). Intellectual property has emerged as a significant issue with data as a general matter and has escalated with the emergence of Big Data.

Questions are posed in terms of: Who owns the data or the process in analyzing the data? How may one access the data or the analytic method? These questions present challenges for higher education through the constant tug between the academy's obligation to contribute to the academic commons or create a proprietary interest as mechanisms to reward creators or discoverers. Accordingly, Sun and Baez (2009) draw attention to the tension and describe the goal of achieving "an appropriate balance between incentives to innovate and diffusion of new knowledge, such that the economic costs of granting the right do not outweigh the benefits of increased innovation" (p. 1).

Intellectual property encompasses multiple types of protections, which are largely dependent on the protected interest. Given the need to protect different types of intellectual works with varying types of rights, the law of intellectual property appears in multiple forms—notably copyright, patents, trademarks, trade names, and trade secrets. Potentially all forms of intellectual property may be at issue when addressing legal aspects of Big Data, either as the Big Data center or the source to create the Big Data. For purposes of presenting a survey of legal issues, overviews of three typical concerns for Big Data, copyright, patents, trade secrets, and digital rights management follow.

Copyright. The federal copyright law applies to an original expression that is fixed onto some tangible format.[16] In other words, the copyrighted work must demonstrate some originality, which need only be a "minimal creative spark,"[17] and it must be contained in some real, material object. Practically speaking, Big Data applications of copyright law might be represented in protecting others from duplicating a manual addressing output findings, the specific data compilation, a survey instrument for data collection, and the code scripted to analyze the data.

Recent litigation on Big Data has addressed challenges to data collection processes involving web crawling and data scraping tools. In the case, *Associated Press v. Meltwater*,[18] the Associated Press (AP) sued Meltwater for copyright infringement when Meltwater reposted excerpts of selected AP articles. Meltwater is an internet media monitoring service for paid subscribers. It has an information-location tool that scrapes news articles, leading readers to brief article clips and hyperlinks to the full article. In its defense, Meltwater argued that its service presented transformative works, which would be a fair use of the articles. As the court's opinion explained, one may, under copyright law, use an originally copyrighted work as "raw material, transformed in the creation of new information, new aesthetics, new insights and understandings—this is the very type of activity that the fair use doctrine intends to protect for the enrichment of society."[19] By contrast, mere repackaging or republishing the same copyrighted work would not qualify as transformative and fail this qualification for fair use of the copyrighted works. Under the federal copyright law, courts actually undergo a four-prong analysis to determine if works would be considered transformative. They inquire about the purpose and character of the use, including whether such use is of a commercial nature or is for nonprofit educational purposes, the nature of the copyrighted work, the amount and substantiality of the portion used in relation to the copyrighted work as a whole, and the effect of the use upon the potential market for or value of the copyrighted work. In this case, the court ruled that Meltwater infringed on the AP's copyright, noting the commercial nature of the use, the republication of portions of the article with no commentaries, and its reliance on other organizations' works as the basis for its business model.

The *Associated Press v. Meltwater* case presents a significantly different outcome than *Authors Guild, Inc. v. HaithiTrust*.[20] HaithiTrust is a collective group of university libraries that entered into a contract with Google, an internet-related services and products company, to conduct a mass digitization project of books to create a shared digital repository. The Authors Guild, which represented numerous associational groups of writers, sued HaithiTrust for copyright infringement. HaithiTrust claimed that their work would transform the original works. The court relied heavily on the recognized purposes of the transformative works to preserve the original works as a way to advance knowledge and protect science, the capacity of the work to be located through a text search engine, and the accessibility of the works for persons with disabilities, particularly with visual impairments—as persuasive reasons to recognize a fair use application.

These two cases present several lessons for Big Data. First, one may use original copyrighted works as raw data if the works are transformed into a new state. As the *HaithiTrust* case illustrates, the massive digitization project enables new ways to analyze text or students' analysis of text, which may be connected to other behaviors in which data are available. Second, the commercial purposes versus advancement of knowledge and science construct a potentially different outcome. Viewed another way, a university's interest in examining educational interventions of its students as the rationale for use of copyrighted works may lead to a different outcome than a university's interest in engaging in educational services and products to other universities to raise revenue for its auxiliary operations. Third, digital tools such as mass scanning, web crawling, and data scraping present new ways in which to build Big Data.

Universities or internet sources may have contractual limitations on what may be accessed or used. While not necessarily a copyright infringement claim, websites and other posted sources may maintain "acceptable use" or "terms of use" policies that limit application to only personal and/or noncommercial uses. For instance, a website may assert browsewrap or a clickwrap agreement placing limitations on one's use of the site. As explained by two federal appellate courts,

> A **browsewrap agreement** discloses terms on a website that offers a product or service to the user, and the user assents by visiting the website to purchase the product or enroll in the service. **Browsewrap agreements** may be contrasted with "**clickwrap**" agreements, which require the user to manifest assent to the terms by clicking on an icon.[21]

With these statements, a user must review the agreement and consent to the terms by responding through an acknowledgment such as clicking a checkbox and entering personal information. These additional steps make enforcement of these provisions easier than other agreements, which require no additional steps, increasing the probability that the user bypassed the agreement and never fully consented. However, as covered in the data breaches discussion later, certain programs or steps may be taken to alert users of impermissible crawling and scraping of information. Software programming conventions such as a Robot Exclusion Standard send signals to potential users of unacceptable use of data collection beyond personal or noncommercial uses.

Patents. Another federal intellectual property protection recognized for Big Data activities is a patent. A patent protects others from using or selling inventions or discoveries that are novel, unobvious creations described and filed with the federal patent office.[22] With such levels of control over the invention as well as the corresponding rewards attached to the invention, such as royalties, actors who participate in the creation or discovery phases often desire some interest in it. In addition, as technology changes, the role and coverage of patents becomes refined, and policies and practices within the academic communities also change.

Under current U.S. patent law, the priority rule for patent filings relies on a principle of "first to invent." Accordingly, prior to a patent issuance, the patent officer determines whether an earlier filing or some other prior knowledge of the patent subject exists. In legal jargon, the patent officer inquires into the "prior art" or the "state of the art." Since knowledge about prior art may not be identical in description or contain precise details, the patent officer examines the components and description of the patentable subject either for comparison to other filings to determine if "prior art references" are mentioned because of close linkages or if the patent filing is not novel because prior art exists.

University patents have included technology transfer into drugs, machinery, food substitutes, and plants. The intent is to bring research to the marketplace. For Big Data, a patent might be used to establish rights in classroom response devices, high-speed cables, or a software program with artificial intelligence capabilities, such as one that predicts the likelihood of a college student's success and continuously improves its algorithm as the student body data changes. Thus, patents associated with Big Data may emerge in the form of programs, processes, and products.

Higher education has engaged in many patent cases involving life science and technology applications and software that resemble interactions seen in Big Data. In 2013, a complex patent litigation finally ended involving quick, high-level processes on the internet. The case started in 1999, in which the plaintiffs, the University of California and a start-up company, sued numerous companies, including Amazon, Yahoo, Google, YouTube, and JCPenney, for patent infringement.[23] The University of California and Eolas Technologies alleged that their patentable program served as a basis for certain web interactivity by supporting plugins making it easier to conduct search suggestions and play music. Microsoft was also one of the original defendants. It settled with the plaintiffs but the other defendants that remained on the suit for 14 years eventually won. As this case illustrates, the length of these disputes can be quite long when high financial stakes are at issue. Given the complex nature of building, maintaining, and mining data, Big Data cases are likely to be complex cases and involve well-recognized internet companies with a David versus Goliath experience.

In sum, as processing speeds continue to accelerate exponentially, postsecondary institutions will rely on programs and products that can process data-intensive information. The data processing may be derived from mined information such as the texts from hundreds of academic libraries, research findings from thousands of journals, student academic records and employee data for the past decade, and usage rates for all institutional operations. From that data, the mass analytic processes may include outputs of a campus master plan, research on a scientific phenomenon, and currently unknown academic interventions likely to increase student achievement. These analytic processes need protection through patents. Suffice it to say, the processes, programs, and products associated with Big Data in terms of analytic and other related artificial intelligence capacity represent a significant asset to the university, and a patent presents a practical option to protect the institution's intellectual property.

Trade secrets. Big Data may be protected under the law of trade secrets. Whereas copyrights and patents operate off a disclosure requirement to seek protection, institutions asserting trade secrets seek legal protections so as to not disclose information and to maintain competitive advantages over those who do not know the undisclosed information. Thus, trade secrets do not exist if the information is copyrighted, patented, or otherwise properly "known."

Unlike other intellectual property, which enjoys federal laws for protection, trade secret protection varies from state to state. Most states, however, have adopted the Uniform Trade Secrets Act, thus ensuring relative uniformity in defining trade secrets and misappropriations of those protected secrets among the adopting states. In California, a trade secret is defined as:

information, including a formula, pattern, compilation, program, device, method, technique, or process, that: (1) Derives independent economic value, actual or potential, from not being generally known to the public or to other persons who can obtain economic value from its disclosure or use; and (2) Is the subject of efforts that are reasonable under the circumstances to maintain its secrecy.[24]

Simply put, trade secrets protect information that attaches some economic value, whether definitively realized or not, and warrant justifiable reasons to block others from having the information (David, 1993).

Within the higher education context, trade secrets do not present as major a concern as patents and copyright. However, as institutions and faculty members look to private sources for funding of research, the private interests of those sources begin to shape what happens in universities, which includes the increasing focus on trade secret protections. Faculty members and students may be required to maintain secrecy over the results of research, for example, thus creating conflicts between their academic interests in making ideas freely accessible and the private entities' economic interests in keeping secrets to maintain their competitive advantages. University-industry collaborations present particularly difficult dilemmas in this regard (see, e.g., Blumenthal et al., 1986; Newberg & Dunn, 2002). For instance, a chemistry professor at Wayne State University misappropriated protected information that a chemist in New England classified as a trade secret (Blumenstyk, 1994, 1995). The protected information revealed a chemical composition that would glow in the presence of selected diseases in human bodies. Rather than complying with the nondisclosure of the trade secret, the professor used the information, patented it, and created a spinoff company. Later, he was sued, and Wayne State was required to surrender its interest in the company.

The reasons for trade secret protection may also serve the interests of the public. Trade secret protection potentially provides academics, particularly academic scientists, more time to study an issue such as a process, drug, or technique before placing it on the market. More in-depth studies may prevent unintended consequences or unknown variables related to the product or process that with time may be uncovered. However, a university's corporate partner may wish to roll out the product or process quickly to establish itself in the market. Further, Big Data projects may increase the classification of trade secrets as operations in higher education become more proprietary and less public.

Digital rights management. Ultimately, intellectual property serves to stake a claim in data or associated interests such as an algorithm or designed processes. The issue in intellectual property is how postsecondary institutions construct their digital rights management (DRM), while offering a proprietary interest presents one solution (Armstrong, 2006; Khan, 2009). Practically speaking, universities have DRM systems now that limit access to digital files such as e-publications or data video files. In the future, DRM may limit access to learning analytic codes to selected users such as other postsecondary institutions or may license analytic portals to generate revenue and build more data mining opportunities. Nonetheless, as Khan (2010) explains, "DRM encompasses technological measures built into physical devices that restrict content usage, such as access controls, copy restrictions, embedded identifications in content, and surveillance" (p. 604). Thus, the issue in intellectual property is how postsecondary institutions construct their DRM or certain controls to protect their interest.

SECURITY

Having a proprietary interest or the best data management policies in the world does not necessarily protect an institution against security breaches. In 2013, the Ponemon Institute conducted an international study on corporate data breaches. Based on a survey of 1,400 individuals from global organizations, Ponemon found that the average cost for U.S. firms to address data breaches is approximately $5.4 million per organization. In addition, based on experiences of the study's respondents, the source of the breaches occurred in three categories. Malicious attacks accounted for the largest share of breaches (41%), human factors such as accidental releases or mislaid laptops represented the next significant cause of breaches (33%), and system glitches reflected the remaining causes of breaches (26%).

These findings raise questions about legal recourse for universities and other effected parties (e.g., students and university staff) when the institution encounters data breaches.

Stored Communications Act (SCA). While the wiretap law covers an active movement of communication, within ECPA, a law known as the Stored Communications Act (SCA) prohibits unlawful access to stored communication such as data retention records on a server or in the Cloud.[25] The law has been asserted to protect organizations from hackers and other impermissible access to stored data. In addition, this law has application to protect individuals who may be subjects of the data collected or users of the data. Two cases discussed here illustrate the SCA's application.

Cases have ruled that a Facebook wall post is covered under SCA; the post can be subject to protections. In *Ehling v. Monmouth-Ocean Hospital Service Corporation*, the plaintiff, a nurse for a private hospital, filed several claims against her employer based on her termination.[26] Among the claims, she challenged the use of her Facebook post in a disciplinary action. The plaintiff posted the following statement on her Facebook wall.

> An 88 yr old sociopath white supremacist opened fire in the Wash D.C. Holocaust Museum this morning and killed an innocent guard (leaving children). Other guards opened fire. The 88 yr old was shot. He survived. I blame the DC paramedics. I want to say 2 things to the DC medics. 1. WHAT WERE YOU THINKING? and 2. This was your opportunity to really make a difference! WTF!!!! And to the other guards . . . go to target practice.

The employer suspended the plaintiff with pay indicating concerns about her deliberate disregard for patient safety. Other employment events eventually led to the plaintiff's termination.

The case outcome was largely based on other legal grounds, but its significance is the legal recognition that a Facebook wall post may qualify for protections. An important element of this case is that the plaintiff made efforts to keep her information and postings from individuals who were not designated as her "friends." However, in this case, one of the authorized users (i.e., a friend) disclosed the posting to the employer, making the posting's revelation an exception to the SCA coverage. However, if the employer had requested the authorized friend to disclose the information or taken other steps as a non-included user, the SCA would likely present a viable claim for individuals to assert. That assertion would have protected the Facebook posting from being used against the employee. Simply put, an employer may not actively seek out the information when the Facebook account is closed, but a Facebook friend may disclose the information permitting the employer access to the contents.

Similarly, a student's claim of rights under the SCA has also been presented in a legal opinion. In *Rodriguez v. Widener University*, a student sued the university on multiple counts based on his suspension from the institution.[27] The university suspended the student, asserting certain behaviors of concern such as the student's conflict with his adviser, a knife and marijuana in the student's backpack, and perceived interpretations of harm from e-mails and postings on Facebook. Among the student's arguments against the university were allegations that the university impermissibly accessed and used images that he posted on Facebook. According to the student, those actions constituted prohibited behaviors under the SCA. In response, the university expressed concerns about the student's display of guns on his Facebook wall as demonstration of harm. The university asserted that it obtained the Facebook information through public sources and individuals who brought the photos to the attention of university officials. Since the matter of access and use was a factual matter in dispute, the court determined that a trial should proceed to determine if the Widener officials accessed the photos in violation of the SCA.

Put simply, while the SCA protects universities from unlawful access to stored data from outside intruders, the SCA also presents a real concern for universities to be subject to suits as defendants subject to privacy guards in the data collection and mining processes. As the *Ehling* and *Rodriguez* cases illustrate, employees and students are viable litigants against a university when information access and use is restricted. Questions arise in terms of the actions the university took to gain data access and use.

Computer Fraud and Abuse Act (CFAA). A third law that presents a legal avenue to address data breaches is the Computer Fraud and Abuse Act (CFAA).[28] CFAA is a federal law designed to protect against individual or group access to a computer when the access is knowingly without authorization or exceeding authorized access.

There are two other conditions. Universities and others seeking application of this law must show that the data sought involve interstate commerce and lead to damages of at least $5,000.

The law allows two ways to seek redress for unauthorized entry into computers. As one federal court explained, CFAA is "primarily a criminal statute, intended to protect against traditional computer hacking."[29] The penalties include fines and imprisonment. Yet CFAA also maintains the possibility of civil damages, so losses incurred by the owner or holder of the computer may seek financial coverage. Thus, CFAA offers multiple enforcement options, especially since the damage may have been malicious, a prank, or simply serving a personal interest (e.g., deleting the hacker's discipline report of underage drinking).

One area in which the application of CFAA has not been resolved relates to recently departed employees and employees who are about to depart (whether by choice or not). The courts are split on whether CFAA or some other laws covering misappropriation of data are applicable claims against these individuals (Hargrove & Mischen, 2013). Recently, these cases have emerged from former or soon-to-be former employees' downloading data such as client lists or financial figures. These cases have also occurred where the individual at issue scrubs a computer clean, including works in progress such as data analytic reports or portions of a larger project. While the federal courts have been split on whether the CFAA applies, employers have other potential legal sources to draw upon including state laws that prohibit misappropriation of trade secrets, breach of employment contract, and unauthorized data/computer access.

Negligence and other state laws. State laws have played a significant role in responding to data security and privacy concerns (Fisher, 2013). For organizations that hold data and experience breaches, parties impacted by the breach may be able to assert a claim of negligence, which has a lower threshold than the federal crimes discussed earlier. Negligence claims refer to actions in which the holder of the data was obligated but failed to maintain reasonable care over the data (e.g., industry-accepted security mechanisms), and, as a consequence, the institution's failure to act reasonably caused foreseeable harm to particular persons or entities (e.g., students, faculty members, and alumni who were subjects of the data). Further, the harm unto the persons or entities resulted in damages such as loss of wages.

In many of the negligence cases for data breaches, plaintiffs have struggled to prevail. In particular, the calculation of damages to award plaintiffs has been a hurdle in these cases. That concept is illustrated in *Krottner v. Starbucks*.[30] In *Krottner*, an unknown person stole a laptop from a coffee company, Starbucks. The laptop held unencrypted data identifying the names, addresses, and social security numbers of approximately 97,000 of the company's employees. Two class-action suits by Starbucks employees were filed, with one of the principal claims alleging that Starbucks was negligent by failing to protect employee data. A federal appellate court recognized that an organization's loss of employee information may place the employees at risk of identity theft. Given the compromised employee data, the organization's negligence caused a legal injury requiring the employees to have credit monitoring. According to the court, the requirement of credit monitoring is analogous to situations in which an organization negligently exposes people to toxic substances who then need medical monitoring. Put simply, the first Starbucks case acknowledged that the employees had a legitimate lawsuit when Starbucks had compromised employee information in an unencrypted form.

However, the companion case was not as supportive of the employees when it addressed another part of the negligence claim. In another federal appellate court opinion for *Krottner v. Starbucks*, the court ruled that plaintiffs in a negligence suit, based on Washington law, must demonstrate an actual loss or damage such as costs associated with identity theft to plead the case properly.[31] Thus, the plaintiffs' case could not proceed because the employees did not have any calculated or articulated damage to request in its pleadings. Put simply, the lesson is that individuals or entities suing for negligence based on an organization's breach of security struggle to demonstrate economic loss arising for future harm to the plaintiffs—even though they are likely real issues, resembling cases in which persons are exposed to toxic substances.

In *Anderson v. Hannaford Brothers*, the data breach led to clear costs to the customers whose data were taken.[32] Hannaford is a national grocery chain that encountered a data breach involving approximately 4.2 million credit and debit card numbers, expiration dates, and security codes. In this case, the court recognized that the plaintiffs experienced real losses from the data breach such as loss of reward points and fees for card reissuances.

State laws vary in their handling data breaches. At least 40 states require a notification process to affected parties under certain conditions—typically when there is a reasonable likelihood or material risk of harm. The legal responsibilities of the organization experiencing the breach may differ if the data at issue are encrypted or redacted. Furthermore, some states involve reporting to the attorney general or another state agency to ensure oversight with addressing the current breach and take corrective actions to avoid future breaches.

RECOMMENDATIONS

While many scholars criticize the law as unable to respond to technological advances, the reality is that the law is not bereft of solutions. The preceding discussion outlined legal applications of privacy, access, intellectual property, security, and data breaches. This section offers recommendations that are informed by the law yet move beyond a legal and regulatory framework and into data management strategies.

Voluntary consensus standards. Postsecondary institutions must adopt practice standards that respond to legal and ethical concerns. Some industry and government standards already exist, and one of them may serve either as a guide or the adopted standards. For instance, federal agencies use the Fair Information Practice Principles (FIPPs). The FIPPs outline standards pertaining to data treatment in terms of notice/awareness, choice/consent, access/participation, integrity/security, and enforcement/redress. This approach would be consistent with the National Technology Transfer & Advancement Act,[33] which states, "all Federal agencies and departments shall use technical standards that are developed or adopted by voluntary consensus standards bodies," as well as the Higher Education Act's efforts to streamline the student aid delivery system, which encourages the adoption of voluntary consensus standards.[34]

Basic practices to maintain privacy. Postsecondary institutions should already have in effect basic practices to maintain privacy. While these standards may be elaborated once the voluntary consensus standards have been established, there are normative practices such as disclosure avoidance techniques that institutions may wish to consider now. These techniques include relying on aggregate information or using blind data; recoding data for de-identification, anonymization, or psuedonymization; using encryption, key-coding, and data sharding (Navetta, 2013; Tene & Polonetsky, 2013). Further, they include handling privacy and security concerns or data breaches such as data breach incident reporting protocols (Stiles, 2012).

Ethics review board. The standards and practices should be held with one institutional team. Postsecondary institutions may wish to establish a new ethics review board for Big Data concerns or incorporate oversight responsibilities to the existing institutional review board (IRB). The IRB should explore concepts such as a reasonable expectation of privacy for members of the campus community, dangers of behavioral targeting and predictive analytics, and options such as "do not track" or "surveillance free zones."

Data/record retention and destruction. Postsecondary institutions maintain some form of data or record retention and destruction schedule, adhering to legal requirements such as Equal Employment Opportunity Commission regulations,[35] state open records compliance, and state audit rules.[36] Further, data retention policies support historical knowledge and resources. These policies typically outline document management consideration addressing data production, extraction, archival repository, and record destruction or purging.

Data sanitation of equipment. Before returning or disposing of devices and equipment, organizations typically have protocols to sanitize and fully wipe information prior to releasing the equipment. Yet errors still occur. A matter involving a breach of electronic patient health information (ePHI), Affinity Health Plan (Affinity), a nonprofit managed health plan, illustrates these unintended breaches (U.S. Department of Health and Human Services, 2013). In that situation, Affinity returned photocopiers to its leasing agents. The photocopiers stored information on a hard drive, which had not been scrubbed. As part of an exposé on photocopier hard drives, *CBS News* purchased one of the Affinity photocopiers and uncovered ePHI for approximately 344,000 individuals. After an investigation, the U.S. Department of Health and Human Services fined Affinity over $1.2 million and placed the health plan organization under a corrective action plan to avoid future errors.

CONCLUSION

Big Data offers great opportunities to enhance learning and support services and campus operations. To appreciate these possibilities and better understand challenges that lie ahead, policy makers and campus leaders must evaluate the legal applications of privacy, access, intellectual property, security, and data breaches. In doing so, they should adopt a mindset that innovates the higher education enterprise by being informed by the law yet move beyond a legal and regulatory framework and into data management strategies. That is, the law should not be reified into an obligatory action based on restrictive parameters and organizational compliance. Instead, policy makers and campus leaders should reenvision the law as connective intelligence to Big Data.

NOTES

1. Admissions records are not necessarily covered by the Family Educational Rights and Privacy Act of 1974 (FERPA). FERPA only covers student records, so nonadmitted applicants and applicants who decline admissions are not included under this law. There are, however, other privacy protections for these individuals, such as state laws governing negligence, which are discussed later in this chapter.
2. 20 U.S.C. §§ 1232g, et seq. (2014).
3. 20 U.S.C. § 1232g(b)(1)(F) (2014); 34 C.F.R. § 99.31(a)(6)(i) (2014).
4. 20 U.S.C. § 1232g(b)(1)(F) (2014).
5. 34 C.F.R. § 99.31(a)(6)(i) (2014).
6. 20 U.S.C. § 9607 (2014).
7. 20 U.S.C. § 1232g(b)(1)(C), 20 U.S.C. § 1232g (b)(3) (2014); 34 C.F.R. § 99.31(a)(3), 34 C.F.R. § 99.35 (2014).
8. 34 C.F.R. § 99.35(a)(2) (2014).
9. 34 C.F.R. § 99.35(a)(3)(ii)(C) (2014).
10. 34 C.F.R. § 99.35(a)(3), (3)(i) through (v) (2014).
11. 42 U.S.C. § 201, et seq. (2014).
12. 42 U.S.C. § 17931, et seq. (2014).
13. 20 U.S.C. § 1232g(d) (2014).

14. Cal. Gov't. Code § 6250 (West 2013).
15. 34 C.F.R. § 99.31(b)(1) (2014).
16. 17 U.S.C. §101, et seq. (2014).
17. *Feist Publications, Inc. v. Rural Telephone Service Co.*, 499 U.S. 340, 362 (1991).
18. *Associated Press v. Meltwater U.S. Holdings, Inc.*, 931 F. Supp.2d 537 (S.D.N.Y. 2013).
19. 931 F. Supp.2d at 551 (citing a law review article by Leval, 1990).
20. *Authors Guild, Inc. v. HaithiTrust*, 902 F. Supp. 2d 445 (S.D.N.Y. 2012).
21. *Traton News, LLC, v. Traton Corp.*, 528 Fed. App'x. 525, 526, n. 1 (6th Cir. 2013); see also *Schnabel v. Trilegiant Corp.*, 697 F.3d 110, 129, n. 18 (2d Cir. 2012).
22. 35 U.S.C. §101, et seq. (2014).
23. *Eolas Technologies Inc. v. Amazon.com, Inc.*, 521 Fed. App'x 928 (Fed. Cir. 2013).
24. Cal. Civ. Code § 3426.1 (2014).
25. 18 U.S.C. § 2701 et seq. (2014).
26. *Ehling v. Monmouth-Ocean Hospital Service Corp.*, Civ. No. 2:11–cv–03305, 2013 WL 4436539 (D.N.J. 2013).
27. *Rodriguez v. Widener Univ.*, Civil Action No. 13–1336, 2013 WL 3009736(E.D. Pa. Jun. 17, 2013).
28. 18 U.S.C. § 1030 et seq. (2014).
29. *In re Google Inc. Cookie Placement Consumer Privacy Litigation*, MDL Civ. No. 12–2358–SLR, 2013 WL 5582866 *1, *8 (Oct. 9, 2013).
30. *Krottner v. Starbucks*, 628 F.3d 1139 (9th Cir. 2010).
31. *Krottner v. Starbucks*, 406 Fed. App'x 129 (9th Cir. 2010).
32. *Anderson v. Hannaford Bros. Co.*, 659 F.3d 151 (1st Cir. 2011).
33. National Technology Transfer & Advancement Act, 15 U.S.C. § 272 (2014).
34. Higher Education Act, 20 U.S.C. § 1018b(a) (2014).
35. 20 C.F.R. Part 1602 (2014).
36. See, e.g., Cornell University Retention/Archival Policy http://www.policy.cornell.edu/vol4_7.cfm; University of Iowa Records Management Policy http://www.uiowa.edu/~fusrmp/retention.html; University of Massachusetts Record Management, Retention, and Disposition Policy http://media.umassp.edu/massedu/policy/RecordsManagementRetention.pdf

REFERENCES

Armstrong, T. K. (2006). Digital rights management and the process of fair use. *Harvard Journal of Law & Technology 20*(1), 49–121.

Baer, L., & Campbell, J. (2012). From metrics to analytics, reporting to action: Analytics' role in changing the learning environment. In D. G. Oblinger (Ed.), *Game changers: Education and information technologies* (pp. 53–65). Louisville, CO: Educause. Retrieved from http://net.educause.edu/ir/library/pdf/PUB72034. pdf

Bienkowski, M., Feng, M., & Means, B. (2012). *Enhancing teaching and learning through educational data mining and learning analytics: An issue brief.* Retrieved from the U.S. Department of Education Office of Technology website: https://www.ed.gov/ edblogs/technology/research/

Blumenstyk, G. (1994, September 7). Trade-secret dispute. *The Chronicle of Higher Education 41*(2), A5.

Blumenstyk, G. (1995, April 14). Wayne State U. to surrender key patent rights to company. *The Chronicle of Higher Education 41*(31), A36.

Blumenthal, D., Gluck, M., Louis, K. S., Stoto, M. A., & Wise, D. (1986). University-industry research relationships in biotechnology: Implications for the university. *Science 232*(4756), 1361–1366. doi:10.1126/science.3715452

Campbell, J. P., DeBlois, P. B., & Oblinger, D. (2007). Academic analytics: A new tool for a new era. *EDUCAUSE Review 42*(4). Retrieved from http://www.educause.edu/ero/article/ academic-analytics-new-tool-new-era

Campus Technology & IBM. (2012). *Using data to boost student engagement and retention* (Document # YTL03117USEN). Retrieved from http://public.dhe.ibm.com/common/ssi/ecm/en/yt-l03117usen/YTL03117USEN.PDF

Daniel, P. T. K., Gee, E. G., Sun, J. C., & Pauken, P. D. (2012). *Law, policy, and higher education: Cases and materials.* New Providence, NJ: LexisNexis.

Data security breach at Ferris State University (2013, Aug. 16). *CBS Detroit.* Retrieved from http://detroit.cbslocal.com/2013/08/16/ data-security-breach-at-ferris-state-university/

David, P. A. (1993). Intellectual property institutions and the panda's thumb: Patents, copyrights, and trade secrets in economic theory and history. In M. B. Wallerstein, M. E. Mogee, & R. A. Schoen (Eds.), *Global dimensions of intellectual property rights in science and technology (pp.* 19–61). Washington, DC: National Academy Press.

Dougherty, C. (2008). Getting FERPA right: Encouraging data use while protecting student privacy. In M. Kanstoroom & E. C. Osberg (Eds.), *A byte at the apple: Rethinking education data for the post-NCLB era* (pp. 38–68). Washington, DC: Thomas B. Fordham Institute.

Eduventures. (2013). *Predictive analytics in higher education: Data-driven decision-making for the student life cycle.* Retrieved from http://www.eduventures.com/whitepapers/big-data-in-higher-education/

Fairchild, R. C. (2013). Giving away the playbook: How North Carolina's public records law can be used to harass, intimidate, and spy. *North Carolina Law Review 91*(6), 2117–2178.

Ferris State University applicants' info on stolen laptop. (2007, November 1). *SC Magazine.* Retrieved from http://www.scmagazine.com/ferris-state-university-applicants-info-on-stolen-laptop/article/155027/

Fisher, J. A. (2013). Secure my data or pay the price: Consumer remedy for the negligent enablement of data breach. *William & Mary Business Law Review 4*(1), 215–239.

Hargrove, S. H., & Mischen, C. (2013). *A potentially potent weapon for employers to combat misappropriation of trade secrets from former employees.* Raleigh, NC: Smith Anderson.

Hartley, Jr., J. F., & Bassett, E. (2013). *Market to watch: Adaptive learning in developmental education.* Retrieved from Eduventures website: http://www.eduventures.com/whitepapers/adaptive-learning-in-developmental-education/

Hutchens, N. H., Sun, J. C., & Miksch, K. (2014, January 10). Open records requests and academic freedom. *The Chronicle of Higher Education.* Retrieved from http://chronicle.com/blogs/conversation/2014/01/10/open-records-requests-and-academic-freedom

Khan, S. M. (2009). Copyright, data protection, and privacy with digital rights management and trusted systems: Negotiating compromise between proprietors and users. *I/S: A Journal of Law and Policy for the Information Society* 5(3), 603–628. Retrieved from http://moritzlaw.osu.edu/students/groups/is/archives/volume-53/

Leval, P. N. (1990). Toward a fair use standard. *Harvard Law Review* 103(5), 1105–1136.

Lohr, S. (2013, March 24). Big Data is opening doors, but maybe too many. *New York Times*. Retrieved from http://www.nytimes.com/2013/03/24/technology/big-data-and-a-renewed-debate-over-privacy.html

McGee-Tubb, M. (2012). Deciphering the supremacy of federal funding conditions: Why state open records laws must yield to FERPA. *Boston College Law Review* 53(3), 1045–1088.

National Center for Education Statistics. (n.d.). *Statewide Longitudinal Data Systems Grant Program*. Retrieved from http://nces.ed.gov/programs/slds/stateinfo.asp

Navetta, D. (2013). Legal implications of Big Data: A primer. *ISSA Journal* 11(3), 14–19.

Newberg, J. A., & Dunn, R. L. (2002). Keeping secrets in the campus lab: Law, values and rules of engagement for industry-university R&D partnerships. *American Business Law Journal* 39, 187–240. doi:10.1111/j.1744-1714.2002.tb00298.x

Norris, D., Baer, L., Leonard, J., Pugliese, L., & Lefrere, P. (2008). Action analytics: Measuring an improving performance that matters in higher education. *EDUCAUSE Review* 43(1). Retrieved from http://www.educause.edu/ero/article/action-analytics-measuring-and-improving-performance-matters-higher-education

O'Connor, K. W. (1991). Patenting animals and other living things. *Southern California Law Review* 65, 597–621.

Parry, M. (2012, July 22). Big Data on campus. *New York Times*. Retrieved from http://www.nytimes.com/2012/07/22/education/edlife/colleges-awakening-to-the-opportunities-of-data-mining.html

Ponemon Institute. (2013). *2013 cost of data breach study: Global analysis*. Retrieved from http://www.ponemon.org/library/2013-cost-of-data-breach-global-analysis

Rotenberg, M., & Barnes, K. (2013). Amassing student data and dissipating privacy rights. *EDUCAUSE Review* 48(1). Retrieved from http://www.educause.edu/ero/article/amassing-student-data-and-dissipating-privacy-rights

Selingo, J., Carey, K., Pennington, H., Fishman, R., & Palmer, I. (2013). *The next generation university.* Retrieved from New America Foundation website: http://higheredwatch.newamerica. net/blogposts/2013/the_next_generation_university-84378

Silverblatt, R. (2013). Hiding behind ivory towers: Penalizing schools that improperly invoke student privacy to suppress open records requests. *Georgetown Law Journal 101*(2), 493–517.

Stiles, R. J. (2012). *Understanding and managing the risks of analytics in higher education: A guide.* Retrieved from Educause website: http://www.educause.edu/library/resources/understanding-and-managing-risks-analytics-higher-education-guide

Straumsheim, C. (2013, October 18). Before the fact. *Inside Higher Ed.* Retrieved from http://www.insidehighered.com/news/2013/10/18/u-kentucky-hopes-boost-student-retention-prescriptive-analytics

Sun, J. C., & Baez, B. (2009). *Intellectual property in the information age: Knowledge as commodity & its legal implications for higher education.* San Francisco, CA: Jossey-Bass.

Tene, O., & Polonetsky, J. (2013). Big Data for all: Privacy and user control in the age of analytics. *Northwestern Journal of Technology & Intellectual Property 11*(5), 239–273.

U.S. Department of Education & U.S. Department of Health and Human Services (2008). *Joint guidance on the application of the Family Educational Rights and Privacy Act (FERPA) and the Health Insurance Portability and Accountability Act of 1996 (HIPAA) to Student Health Records.* Washington, DC: Authors.

U.S. Department of Health and Human Services, Office of Civil Rights. (2013). HHS settles with health plan in photocopier breach case [Press release]. Retrieved from http://www.hhs.gov/news/press/2013pres/08/20130814a.html

3

EDUCATION AND . . . BIG DATA VERSUS BIG-BUT-BURIED DATA

ELIZABETH L. BRINGSJORD AND SELMER BRINGSJORD

ABSTRACT

The technologized world is buzzing about Big Data and the apparent historic promise of harnessing such data for all sorts of purposes in business, science, security, and—our domain of interest herein—education. We distinguish between Big Data *simpliciter* (BD) on the one hand versus Big-But-Buried Data (B³D) on the other. The former type of data is the customary brand that will be familiar to nearly all readers and is, we agree, of great importance to educational administrators and policy makers; the latter type is of great importance to educators and their students but receives dangerously little direct attention these days. We maintain that a striking two-culture divide is silently emerging in connection with Big Data: one culture prudently

Selmer Bringsjord acknowledges, with deep gratitude, generous support provided by IBM to think about Big Data systematically, in connection with the seminal Watson system and is grateful as well for (a) data and predictive analysis (of the big *simpliciter* variety) regarding student performance in calculus at Rensselaer Polytechnic Institute (RPI), provided by institutional-research expert Jack Mahoney, and (b) enlightening conversations about Big-But-Buried Data and (differential and integral) calculus with Kayla Monahan and Thomas Carter.

driven by machine-assisted analysis of BD, and the other by both the quest for acquiring and bestowing mastery of B^3D and the search for the B^3D that confirms such mastery is in place within a given mind. Our goal is to introduce, clarify, and contextualize the BD-vs.-B^3D distinction to lay a foundation for the integration of the two types of data—and, thereby, the two cultures. We use examples, primarily that of calculus, to reach this goal. Along the way, we discuss the future of data analytics in light of the historic Watson system from IBM and the possibility of human-level machine tutoring systems, AI systems able to teach and confirm mastery of Big-But-Buried Data.

The technologized world is buzzing about Big Data, and the apparent promise of harnessing such data for all sorts of purposes in business, science, security, and—our domain of interest herein—education. We distinguish between Big Data *simpliciter* (BD) on the one hand versus Big-But-Buried (B^3D) data on the other. The former type of data is the customary brand that will be familiar to nearly all readers and is, we agree, of great importance to educational administrators and policy makers; the second type is of great importance to educators and their students but is dangerously overshadowed by attention paid these days to the first type. Part of this danger derives from the fact, explored later, that while Big-But-Buried Data is elusive and the technology to exploit it is expensive and still primitive, B^3D is absolutely central to first-rate teaching and learning.

One of the hallmarks of Big Data *simpliciter* is that the data in question, when measured against some standard yardstick (e.g., the *byte*, which is eight *bits* of data, where each bit is 0 or 1), are exceedingly large. For instance, internet traffic per month is known to be well over 20 exabytes (= 20×10^{18} bytes); hence an attempt to enlist software to ascertain, say, what percentage of internet traffic pertains directly to either student-student or student-teacher communication connected to some formal course would be a BD task. Or, more tractably, if one used R, by far the dominant software environment in the world used for all manner of statistical computing, and something that stands at the very heart of the Big-Data era, to ascertain what percentage of first-year U.S. college students in STEM disciplines graduate in those disciplines as correlated with their grades in their first calculus course, one would be firmly focused on BD.[1] We find it convenient to use a less pedantic yardstick to measure the size of some given collection of data. One nice option in that regard is simply the number of discrete symbols used in the collection in question. We are sure the reader will immediately agree that in both the examples of BD just provided, the number of symbols to be analyzed is staggeringly large.

Big-But-Buried Data is very, very different. What data does one need to master in order to thrive in the aforementioned calculus course and in those data-intensive fields (e.g., macroeconomics) that make use of calculus (and, more broadly, of real analysis) to model vast amounts of BD? And what data does a calculus tutor need in order to certify that his or her pupil truly has mastered elementary, single-variable calculus? In both cases, the answers exhibit not BD but rather B^{3}D. For example, one cannot master even the first chapter of elementary calculus unless one has mastered (in the first few pages of whatever standard textbook is employed) the concept of a *limit*, yet—as will be seen in due course—only 10 tiny symbols are needed to present data that express the schematic proposition that the limit of some given function f is L as the inputs to that function approach c.[2] Students who aspire to be highly paid data scientists seeking to answer BD problems (for Yahoo!; or for massive university systems like SUNY; or for those parts of the U.S. government that take profound action on the basis of BD, such as the U.S. Department of Education and the Federal Reserve; etc.) without truly understanding such little 10-symbol collections of data, put themselves, and their employers, in a perilous position. This assertion is confirmed by any respectable description of what skills and knowledge are essential for being a good data scientist (e.g., see the mainstream description in Minelli, Chambers, & Dhiraj, 2013). In fact, it may be impossible to know with certainty whether the results of analytics applied to BD can be trusted, and whether proposed, actionable inferences from these results are valid, without understanding the underlying B^{3}D-based definitions of such analytics and inferences. Of course, the results produced by BD analytics, and indeed often the nature of BD itself, are probabilistic. But to truly understand whether or not some proposition has a certain probability of being true, at least the relevant data scientists, and perhaps also the managers and administrators ready to act on this proposition, must certainly understand what probability *is*—yet as is well known, the nature of probability is expressed in none other than big-but-buried form.[3]

While we concede that there is some "crossover" (e.g., some ped-agogy, to be sure, profits from "analytics" applied to BD, and some educators, of course, are themselves administrators), nonetheless we maintain there is a striking two-culture divide silently emerging in connection with Big Data: one culture driven by machine-assisted analysis of BD and the fruit of that analysis, and the second by the quest for acquiring and bestowing mastery of B³D and by the search for the Big-But-Buried Data that confirms that such mastery is in place within a given mind. Our chief goal is to introduce, clarify, and contextualize the BD-vs.-B³D distinction to lay a foundation for the further integration of the two cultures via the integration of the two types of data around which each tends to revolve. The truly effective modern university will be one that embodies this integration.[4]

The plan for the sequel is straightforward: We first present and affirm a serviceable account of what data are, and specifically explain that, at least in education, *information* is key, and, even more specifi-cally, *knowledge* is of paramount importance (in the cases of *both* Big Data *simpliciter* and Big-But-Buried Data). Next, in the context of this account, we explain in more detail the difference between BD and B³D by presenting two competing sets of necessary conditions for the pair and some informal examples of these sets "in action." In the next section, we turn to the example of teaching calculus in the United States, to further elaborate the BD-vs.-B³D distinction and to illuminate the importance of uniting data-driven efforts from each side of the distinction.[5] Readers can rest assured that they will not need to know *any* calculus in order to understand what we say in this section, but we do explain that without appeal to calculus, human experience of even the simple motion of everyday objects, in light of Zeno's famous paradoxes, quite literally makes no sense (from which, as we point out, the untenability of recent calls to drop traditionally required precollege math courses follows). Next, we briefly discuss the future of BD analytics in light of the historic Watson system from IBM. We then confront the acute problem of scalability that plagues the teaching of Big-But-Buried Data and point to a "saving" future in which revolutionary artificial intelligence (AI) technology (advanced *intelligent tutoring systems*) solves the problem by teaching Big-But-Buried Data in "sci-fi" fashion. A short pointer to future research concludes the chapter.

DATA, INFORMATION, AND KNOWLEDGE

It turns out that devising a rigorous, universally acceptable definition of *data*[6] is surprisingly difficult, as Floridi (2008), probably the
world's leading authority on the viability of proposed definitions for
these concepts (and related ones), explains. For example, while some
are tempted to define data as collections of *facts*, such an approach is
rendered acutely problematic by the brute truth, routinely exploited
in our "data age," that data can be *compressed* (via techniques explained, for example, by Sayood [2006]): How could a fact be compressed?[7] Others may be inclined to understand data as knowledge,
but such a view, too, is untenable, since, for example, data can be
entirely meaningless (to wit, "The data you sent me, I'm afraid, is
garbled and totally meaningless."), and surely one cannot know that
which is meaningless. Moreover, plenty of what must be preanalyti-
cally classified as data seems to carry no meaning whatsoever; Floridi
(2005) gives the example of data in a digital music file. Were you
to examine any portion of this digital data under the expectation
that you must declare what it means, you would draw a blank, and
blamelessly so. Of course, when the data are processed, they *cause*
sound to arise, and that sound may well be eminently meaningful.
But the data itself, as sequences of bits, mean nothing.

In the interest of efficiently getting to the core issues we have
targeted for the present chapter, we affirm without debate a third
view of what data are, one nicely in line with the overall thrust of
the present volume: We adopt the *computational* view of data, according to which data are collections of strings, digits, characters,
pixels, discrete symbols, etc., all of which can be processed by algorithms unpacked as computer programs, which are in turn executed
on modern high-speed digital computers.[8] Affirmation of this view
would seem to be sensible, since after all the Big-Data rage is bound
up inextricably with computational analytics. When the institutional
research (IR) office staff at university *U* is called upon by its provost
to deliver a report comparing transfer and native-student graduation
rates, invariably its work in acceding to this request will require (not
necessarily on the part of the IR professionals themselves) the use of
algorithms, programs regimenting those algorithms, and the physical
computers (e.g., servers) on which the programs are implemented.

And, of course, the same tenor of toil would be found outside academia: If Amazon seeks to improve the automated recommendations that its browser-based systems make to you for what you are advised to consider purchasing in the future given your purchases in the past, the company's efforts revolve around coming up with algorithmically smarter ways to process data—and to enticingly display the results to you.

But we need a crisper context from which to move forward. Specifically, it is important to establish at the outset that universities and university systems, and indeed the academy as a whole, are most interested in a specific *kind* of computational data: data that are both well formed and meaningful. In other words, administrators, policy makers, analysts, educators, and students, all are ultimately interested in *information*. An elegant, succinct roadmap for coming to understand what information, as a special kind of data, is, and to understand the various kinds of information that are of central importance to the academy and the technologized world in general, is

Figure 3.1. Floridi's ontology of information

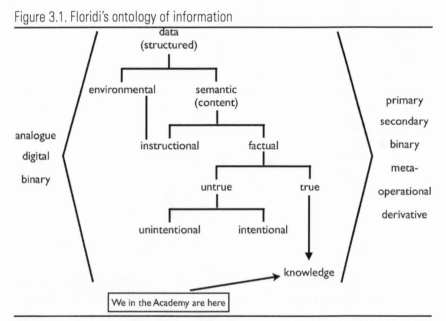

Source: Figure used by permission of Luciano Floridi, holder of the copyright. (Annotation by Selmer Bringsjord permitted by Floridi.)

provided by Floridi (2010).[9] This roadmap is summed up in figure 3.1. The reader should take care to observe that in this figure we pass to a kind of data that is even more specific than information: We pass to the subspecies of data that is a specific form of factual and true semantic information—that is, to *knowledge*. (Hence, while, as noted previously, data are not knowledge, *some* data do indeed constitute knowledge.) We make this move because, as indicated by the "We in the academy are here" comment that we have taken the liberty of inserting into figure 3.1, the cardinal mission of universities is the pursuit and impartation of knowledge. From this point on, when, following common usage (which frames the present volume), we refer to data, and specifically to the fundamental BD-vs.-B³D dichotomy, the reader should understand that we are referring, ultimately, to *knowledge*. In the overarching world of data, data analysis, and data science, it is knowledge that research is designed to produce; knowledge that courses are designed to impart; and knowledge that administrators, managers, and others in leadership positions seek out and exploit to enhance the knowledge that research yields and classrooms impart.

BIG DATA SIMPLICITER (BD) VERSUS BIG-BUT-BURIED DATA (B³D)

We provided a provisional account of the difference between BD and B³D. Let us now be more precise, but not *too* precise, as formal definitions are outside the scope and nature of the present chapter. In the present context, it suffices (a) to note some necessary conditions that must be satisfied by any data to qualify specifically as *Big* in today's technology landscape (i.e., as BD), or instead as *Big-But-Buried* (i.e., as B³D); and (b) to flesh out these conditions by reference to some examples, including examples that connect to elementary calculus as currently taught in the U.S. educational system. The "calculus part" of the second of these steps is, as planned, mostly reserved for the next section.

For (a), please begin by consulting figure 3.2, which sums up in one simple graphic the dichotomy between BD and B³D. Obviously, BD is addressed on the left side of this graphic, while B³D is addressed on the right. Immediately under the heading for each of the two sides

Figure 3.2. BD vs. B³D

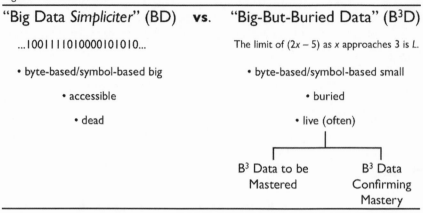

Source: Figure by Elizabeth Bringsjord and Selmer Bringsjord.

we provide a suggestive string to encapsulate the intuitive difference between the two types of data. On the left, we show a string of 0s and 1s extending indefinitely in both directions; the idea is that you are to imagine that the number of symbols here is staggeringly large. For instance, maybe there are as many symbols as there are human beings alive on Earth, and a 1 indicates a male, whereas a 0 denotes a female. On the right, we show a simple 12-symbol-long statement about a certain limit. The exact meaning of this statement is not important at this juncture (although some readers will perceive this meaning); it is enough to see by inspection that there are indeed only 12 symbols in the statement and to know that the amount of data "buried" in the statement far exceeds the data carried by the string of 0s and 1s to its left. This statement is true because the 12-symbol-long statement is making an assertion (given in prose form in endnote 3) about every single real number, and while there are indeed a lot of human beings on our planet, our race is after all finite, while there are an infinite number of real numbers in even just one "tiny" interval, say the real numbers between zero and .5. Now let us look at the remainder of figure 3.2.

Notice three attributes are listed under the BD heading, and a different, opposing trio is listed under the B³D heading. Each member of each trio is a necessary condition that must apply to each instance of any data in order for that instance to qualify, respectively, as BD or B^3D. For example, the first hallmark of BD is that (and here we recapitulate what has been said previously), whether measured in terms of number of bytes or in terms of number of symbols, the data in question is large. The second necessary condition for some data to count as Big Data *simpliciter*, observe, is that it must be "accessible." What does this mean? The idea is simple. BD must be susceptible to straightforward processing by finite algorithms. To see this notion in action, we pull in here the suggestive string for BD given on the left side of figure 3.2:

$$. . . 1001111010000101010 . . .$$
$$\uparrow$$

Suppose we wanted to ascertain if the data here contain anywhere a sub-string of seven consecutive 0s. How would we go about answering this question? The answer is simple: We would just engage a computation based on a dirt-simple algorithm. One such "mining" algorithm is: Moving simultaneously left and right, starting from the digit pointed to by the arrow (see the preceding string), start a fresh count (beginning with one) for every switch to a different digit, and if the count ever reaches seven, output "Yes" and halt; otherwise output "No" and halt when the digits are exhausted.

It should be clear that this algorithm is infallible because of the presupposition that the data in question are accessible. Sooner or later, the computation that implements the algorithm is going to return an answer, and the correct one at that, for the reason that the data are indeed accessible. This accessibility is one of the hallmarks of BD, and it is principally what makes possible the corresponding phenomenon of "big analytics." The techniques of statistical computing are fundamentally enabled by the accessibility of the data over which these techniques can operate.[10] Things are very different, though, on the other side of the dichotomy: Big-But-Buried Data is, as its name implies, buried.

Here's a simple example of some B^3D:[11] Suppose we are given the propositional datum that (a) everyone likes anyone who likes someone. And suppose as well that we have a second datum: (b) Alvin likes Bill. The data composed of (a) and (b) are how big? Counting spaces as separate characters, there are only 58 symbols in play; hence we certainly are not in the BD realm: We are dealing with

symbol-based small data, which is to say that the second hallmark of
B³D shown in figure 3.2 is satisfied. Or at least the reader will agree
that it is satisfied once the hidden data are revealed.

Toward that end, then, a question: (Q) Does everyone like Bill?
The answer is yes, but that answer is buried. Most people see that
data composed of (a) and (b) imply that (c) everyone likes Alvin; few
people see that (a) and (b) imply that (d) everyone likes Bill. Datum
(d), you see, is buried. And notice that (d) is not just buried in the
customary sense of being extractable by statistical processing (so-
called data mining): No amount of BD analytics is going to disclose
(c), accompanied by the justification for (d) on the strength of (a) and
(b).[12] If you type to the world's greatest machine for answering data
queries over BD, IBM's historic *Jeopardy!*-winning Watson system
(Ferrucci et al., 2010), both (a) and (b), and issue (Q) to Watson, it
will not succeed. Likewise, if you have R running before you (as the
second author does now), and (a) and (b) are represented in tabular
form and are imported into R, there is no way to issue an established
query to express (Q) and receive back in response datum (d)—let
alone a way to receive back (d) plus a justification such as is provided
via the proof in endnote 12. To be sure, there is a lot of machine intelligence in both Watson and R, but it is not the kind of intelligence
well suited for productively processing Big-But-Buried Data.[13]

It is crucial to understand that the example involving Alvin and
Bill has been offered simply to ease exposition and understanding
and is not representative of the countless instances of Big-But-Buried Data that make possible the very data science and engineering
heralded by the present book. It is student mastery of B³D that is
cultivated by excellent STEM education, in general.[14] And we are
talking not just about students at the university level; B³D is the key
part of the M in STEM education much earlier on. For instance,
just a few hundred symbols are needed to set out the full quintet of
Euclid's Postulates, in which the entire limitless paradise of a large
part of classical geometry resides. The data composing this paradise
are not just very large; they are flat-out infinite. Exabytes of data
do make for a large set to analyze, but Euclid, about 2.5 millennia
back, was analyzing data sets much bigger than those to which we
apply modern "analytics." And the oft-forgotten wonder of it all is
that the infinite paradise Euclid (and Aristotle, and a string of minds
thereafter; see, e.g., Glymour [1992]) explored and mapped can be

crystallized down to just a few symbols that do the magical "hiding." These symbols are written out in about one-quarter of a page in every geometry textbook used in just about every high school in the United States. And geometry is just a tiny exhibit to make the point.[15] The grandest and most astonishing example of Big-But-Buried Data in the realm of mathematics is without question the case of axiomatic set theory: It is now agreed that nearly all of classical mathematics can be extracted from a few hundred B³D symbols that express a few basic laws about the structure of sets and set operations. (Interested readers can see for themselves by consulting the remarkably readable and lucid text by Potter [2004].) A shortcut for the mathematically mature is to consult the set theory chapter in Ebbinghaus, Flum, and Thomas's 1994 work.[16]

Finally, with reference again to figure 3.2, we come to the third hallmark of BD ("dead"), versus the corresponding opposing hallmark of B³D ("live"). What are we here referring to? A more humdrum synonym in the present context for "dead" might be "prerecorded." In the case of BD, the data are prerecorded. The data do not unfold live before one's eyes. The *analysis* of BD is, of course, carried out by running processes; these processes are (by definition) dynamic and can sometimes be watched as they proceed in real time. For example, when Watson is searching BD in order to decide on whether to respond to a *Jeopardy!* question (or for that matter any question), human onlookers can be shown the dynamic, changing confidence levels for candidate answers that Watson is considering—but the data being searched are quite dead. Indeed, Big Data *simpliciter*, in and of itself, is *invariably* dead. Amazon's systems may have insights into what you are likely to buy in the future, but those insights are without question based on analysis of "frozen" facts about what you have done in the past. Watson did vanquish the best human *Jeopardy!* players on the planet, but again, it did so by searching through dead, prerecorded data. And IR professionals at university *U* seeking, for instance, to analyze BD to devise a way to predict whether or not a given first-year student is going to return for his or her second year will analyze BD that is fixed and prerecorded. But by contrast, B³D is often "live" data.

Notice we say *some* B³D is live. Not all of it is. This bifurcation is explicitly pictured in the bottom right of figure 3.2. What gives rise to the split? From the standpoint of education, the split arises from two different cases: on the one hand, situations where some Big-But-Buried Data is the target of learning and, on the other, situations like the first, *plus* the live production of Big-But-Buried Data by the learner to demonstrate that he or she has in fact learned. Accordingly, note that in our figure, the bifurcation is labeled to indicate on the left that which is to be mastered by the student and, on the right, the additional Big-But-Buried Data that, when generated, confirms mastery.

For a simple example of the bifurcation, we have only to turn back to this trio

(a) Everyone likes anyone who likes someone.
(b) Alvin likes Bill.
(c) (Q) Does everyone like Bill?

and imagine a student, Bertrand, say, who in a discrete mathematics class, during coverage of basic Boolean logic (upon which, by the way, modern search engine queries over BD on the web are based) is given this trio and asked to answer (Q). But what sort of answer is Bertrand specifically asked to provide? Suppose that he is asked only for a "yes" or a "no." Then, *ceteris paribus*, he has a 50% chance of getting the right answer. If Bertrand remembers that his professor in discrete math has a tendency to ask tricky questions, then even if Bertrand is utterly unsure, fundamentally, as to what the right answer is but perceives (as the majority of college-educated people do) that certainly from (a) and (b) it can be safely deduced that everyone likes Alvin, he may well blurt out "yes." And he would be right. But is mastery in place? No. Only the live unearthing of certain additional data buried in our trio can confirm that mastery is in place: That is, a proof (such as that provided in note 12) must be either written out or spoken by Bertrand.

TWO ANTICIPATED QUESTIONS, TWO ANSWERS

The first questions we anticipate are: "But why do you say the 'frozenness' or 'deadness' of Big Data *simpliciter* is a necessary condition of such data? Could the very systems you cite, for example Watson and Amazon's recommender systems, not operate over vast amounts of Big Data *simpliciter*, while those very data are being generated? It may be a bit creepy to ponder, but why could it not be that when you are browsing Amazon's products with a web browser, your activity (and for that matter your appearance and that of your local environment) is being digitized and analyzed continuously in real time? And in terms of education, why could not the selections and facial expressions of 500,000 students logged on to a MOOC session be collected and analyzed in real time? These scenarios seem to be at odds with the necessary condition you advocate."

These questions are excellent, and warrant a serious answer. Eventually, perhaps very soon, a lot of BD will indeed by absorbed and analyzed by machines in real time. Today, however, the vast majority of BD analytics is performed over "dead" data; figure 3.2 reflects the current situation. Clearly, BD analytics is not *intrinsically* bound up with live data. On the other hand, confirmation of the kind of mastery with which we are concerned *is* intrinsically live. Of course, we do concede that a sequence in which a student produces conclusive evidence of mastery of some B^3D could be recorded. And that recording is itself by definition—in our nomenclature—dead and can be part of some vast collection of BD. A MOOC provider, for instance, could use a machine vision system to score 500,000 video recordings of student behavior in a class with 100,000 students. But the educational problem is this: The instant this BD repository of recordings is relied upon, rather than the live generation of confirming data, the possibility of cheating rears up.[17] *If* one assumes that the recording of live responses is fully genuine and fully accurate, then, of course, the recording, though dead, conveys what *was* live. But that would be a big if. And given that it is, our dead-versus-live distinction remains intact.

Moreover, the distinction is further cemented because of what can be called the "follow-up" problem, which plagues all recordings. This problem consists in the fact that you cannot query a recording on the spot to further confirm that mastery is indeed in place. But a professor can, of course, easily enough ask a follow-up question of a student with whom he is interacting in the present.

In sum, then, there is simply no substitute for the unquestionably authentic live confirmation of deep understanding. And, accordingly, there is no substitute for the confirmatory power of oral examination, over and above the examination of dead data, even when those dead data are a record of live activity.

We also anticipate some readers asking: "But why do you say that the kind of data produced by Bertrand when he gives the right rationale is big-but-buried? I can see that (a) and (b) together compose a simple instance of B^3D. But I don't see why what is generated in confirmation of a deep understanding of (a) plus (b) is *itself* a simple case of Big-But-Buried Data."

The answer is that (1) as a rule, when a learner, on the spot before one's eyes, generates data that confirm mastery of Big-But-Buried Data, he or she has extracted those data from the vast and often infinite amount of Big-But-Buried Data that is targeted by the teacher for mastery; *and* (2) because the data that are unearthed are *themselves* Big-But-Buried Data, it is symbol-wise small yet hides a fantastically large (indeed probably infinite) amount of data. In the immediate case at hand involving Bertrand, if the correct rationale is provided (again, see note 12), what is really provided is a reasoning *method* sufficient for establishing an infinite number of results in the formal sciences.[18] In short, and to expand the vocabulary we have introduced, Bertrand can be said to have big-but-buried *knowledge*.

THE EXAMPLE OF CALCULUS

We now, as promised, further flesh out the BD-vs.-B^3D distinction by turning to the case of elementary calculus.

On Big Data simpliciter *and calculus.* We begin by reviewing some simple but telling BD-based points about the advanced placement (AP) calculus exam, in connection with subsequent student performance, in the United States. These and other points along this line are eloquently and rigorously made by Mattern, Shaw, and Xiong (2009), and especially since we only scratch the surface to serve our specific needs in the present chapter, readers wanting details are encouraged to read the primary source. We are generally interested in predictive BD analytics and specifically with the questions: Does performance on the AP calculus exam, when taken before college, predict the likelihood of success in college? And if so, to what degree?[19]

The results indicate that AP calculus performance is highly predictive of future academic performance in college. For example, using a sample size of about 90,000 students, Mattern et al. (2009) found that those students who scored either a 3, 4, or 5 on the AP

Calculus (AB) exam were much more likely to graduate from college within five years, when compared to those who either scored a 1 or a 2 or who did not take the test. With academic achievement identified with high school GPA (HSGPA) and SAT scores, the analysis included asking whether this result held true when controlling for such achievement. In what would seem to indicate the true predictive power of student command of calculus, even when controlling for academic aptitude and achievement (as measured by HSGPA and SAT, run as covariates), the result remained that those earning a 3, 4, or 5 were much more likely to graduate from college.

But *why* is the cognition cultivated in calculus apparently so powerful and valuable? This is something that BD will not reveal, for the simple and widely known reason that correlation does not explain causality. A professor, administrator, or policy maker could thus see in the analysis of BD evidence that such cognition highly *correlates* with desirable outcomes (timely graduation, for example) but would not see what underlying, buried data define calculus and would not see what mastery of the subject consists of. This brute fact is, of course, perfectly consistent with the real possibility that the administrator is a calculus whiz: The limitation is in the nature of BD, not in the mind of those analyzing BD. Likewise, even if an administrator had further correlation data (e.g., showing that achievement in economics and physics correlates stunningly well with high performance in calculus courses, which happens also to be true), no deep understanding of why the correlations hold is on the table. Indeed, one could, for all that the BD analytics tells us, view calculus as simply some kind of magical black box—but a black box to be advocated. We thus now look at calculus from a B³D perspective.

On Big-But-Buried Data and calculus. Calculus[20] is a tremendously important subject in the modern, digital economy—for many reasons. One reason is that, as the sort of BD analysis visited earlier indicates, apparently the cognition that goes hand in hand with learning calculus in turn goes hand in hand with academic success in STEM.[21] A second reason why calculus is crucial is that real analysis (of which the calculus is a part, and to which, in our K–16 educational system, calculus is the gateway) stands at the heart of many important approaches to the analysis of BD. Contemporary macroeconomics is based on real analysis; it is, for instance, impossible to understand the most powerful macroeconomic arguments in favor of generous Keynesian spending by the U.S. government, despite budget deficits and debt, without an understanding of calculus.[22]

To illustrate the prudence of a focus on B^3D at the present juncture in our discussion, consider the case of Johnny, who, upon arriving as a first-year student intending to major in math at university U, boldly announces to Professor Smith at orientation before the start of classes that he (Johnny) should leapfrog over the three math-major calculus courses (I, II, III) in the department, straight into advanced analysis.

Professor Smith: "You know, Johnny, our Calc III requires not just what some of our students call 'plug and chug' but proofs." One must be able to prove the formulas that are used *for* plugging and chugging.

Johnny: "Not a problem, sir."

Professor Smith, looking down at his desk, observes that Johnny received an A in precollege (single-variable) calculus and scored a 5 on the Calculus AB advanced placement test. Smith knows that this record is good enough, by a decision tree generated from analysis of relevant BD, to skip Calc I for math majors, but many students with super-high SAT scores do not even do that.

We make two claims:

Claim 1: Even if Professor Smith has at his beck and call all the BD in the world, and even if by some miracle he had the time right here on the spot to issue a hundred queries against these data while Johnny waits in silence, he can instead find out whether Johnny is all bluster, or the real deal, by asking one or two single-sentence questions and by then sitting back to see whether the young man writes out the one or two key proofs requested, or not.[23] In short, it will be live Big-But-Buried Data that settles the question, on the spot.

Claim 2: The best classroom teaching arguably proceeds by way of the teacher ascertaining directly, in decidedly low-tech, oral-exam fashion, whether a "golden," buried datum of true mastery or understanding is there or not. If not, the teacher then strives to get such understanding to take root, testing in like manner again so that the cycle continues until learning is confirmed.

This pair of claims can be put into action for teaching even very young students. For instance, by using visual forms of Big-But-Buried Data one can quickly make serious headway in explaining the

Figure 3.3. B³D-based representation of a limit in seventh-grade math

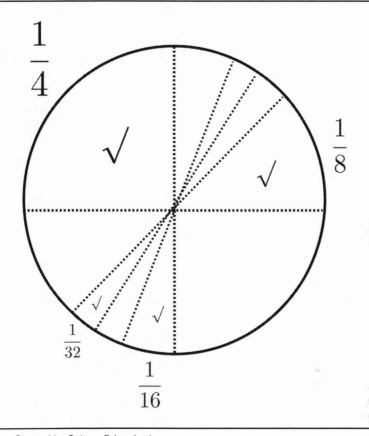

Source: Created by Selmer Bringsjord.

concept of a limit even to middle school students, thereby building a substantial part of a path to full-blown calculus for them. For example, see figure 3.3, which is conceptually similar to the kinds of suggestive geometric progressions seen in middle school textbooks [e.g., see Eicholz et al., 1995, p. 268]. Imagine that Alexandra, in the seventh grade, is asked to determine the "percent pattern" of the outer circle consumed by the ever-decreasing checked "pie peices." The pattern, obviously, starts at $\frac{1}{4}$ and then continues as $\frac{1}{8}$, $\frac{1}{16}$, $\frac{1}{32}$, and so on. When asked what percentage the shaded square would "get down to" if someone could forever work faster and faster, and smaller and smaller, at drawing the up-down and left-right lines that make each quartet of smaller pie pieces, Alexandra announces: "Zero." That is indeed none other than the limit in the present case: The percent "in the limit" the checked pie peice consumes of the original circle is indeed zero. The figure in question is tiny but hides in gemlike fashion an infinite progression.

Of course, asking for and assessing the kind of live Big-But-Buried Data that Johnny and Alexandra are here asked to produce, if in fact such techniques can scale to millions of students (an issue we take up later), is an expensive proposition, to put it mildly. Skeptics will pointedly ask why something as recherché as calculus would ever warrant the expenditure of all the time and money it would take to ensure mastery in this manner. Unfortunately, the mistaken view shared by many is that a deep understanding of calculus is a needless luxury.

In fact, even among many members of the academy in our day, the view that calculus has narrow value is firmly afoot. Many university professors are under the impression that calculus has value in fields such as engineering, math itself, and the like but does not reach across the human experience. Unfortunately, this view is inconsistent with intellectual history and specifically with the fact that without calculus, everyday concepts such as motion are incomprehensible. One way to reveal this fact, and thereby to reveal the ignorance behind sarcastic, short-on-ratiocination calls (such as the recent one from Baker [2013]) to block federal educational standards requiring higher-level mathematics in high school, is to turn to some of Zeno's paradoxes of motion, such as the Paradox of the Arrow. If such a paradox cannot be resolved, our everyday conception of motion leads us directly to contradiction.

THE PARADOX OF THE ARROW

Here then is, in our words, a summary of Zeno's reasoning:[24] Time is composed of moments, and hence a moving arrow must occupy a space filled by itself at each moment during its supposed travel. Our arrow is thus at a particular place at each moment during its supposed travel. Assuming for the sake of argument that an arrow (supposedly) travels only a short distance, the picture given in table

Table 3.1. Zeno's Framework for the Paradox of the Arrow

Moments	Places Where the Arrow Is Located			
m_1	→ @ place 1			
m_2		→ @ place 2		
m_3			→ @ place 3	
m_4				→ @ place 4

Source: Figure by Selmer Bringjord.

3.1 should be helpful. But there is no motion here whatsoever. After all, places certainly do not move. Hence, if, as shown, the arrow is at each moment at a particular place, occupying a space equal to its volume, the arrow cannot possibly ever really move: It is not moving at any of the moments m_i, since at each such moment it is simply at the place where it is, and there are no other moments at which it can move! The reasoning here can be effortlessly generalized to show that the movement of anything is an illusion.

The quickest way to reveal to an intelligent person in the modern information age the centrality and indispensability of calculus for understanding the world in more than a mere childlike, hand-wavy manner is to ask whether motion is real. Upon receiving an affirmative response, then ask how that can be in the light of the Zenoian reasoning given here. (It is not a cogent response to simply shoot an arrow or throw a baseball and say "See?"—since Zeno's claim is precisely that while things certainly *seem* to move, they actually don't. After all, we cannot confirm that day by day the moon changes shape and size on the strength of pointing up to the night sky and saying "See?") All cogent responses must include an appeal to calculus and all the Big-But-Buried Data that calculus, at bottom, is.[25] We might mention that in light of this, it is quite astonishing that, in response to Common Core math standards urged by the U.S. Department of Education and most states (the main rationale for which is, of course, based on analysis of BD showing that U.S. students, relative to those in other countries with whom they will be competing in the global, data-driven economy, are deficient), some maintain that mathematics should be simply an elective in high school. For instance, Baker (2013) stridently advances the claim that even a dedicated high school algebra course is, for most, downright silly, and downright painful; accordingly, no such course should be required.[26] Needless to say, if the ordinary motion of everyday objects makes no intellectual sense without at least a fundamental conception of calculus, without mastery of even algebra one quickly advances toward lowering a definition of the human from—to use Aristotle's phrase—*rational animal* to just *animal*. And, of course, it is impossible for our universities to produce the data scientists that our economy needs without taking in students who know algebra and who can then build upon that knowledge to gain knowledge of valuable analytics, including techniques requiring calculus.

THE FUTURE

As promised, we now briefly touch upon the future, in connection, respectively, with IBM's Watson system, and following naturally on that, with so-called intelligent tutoring systems (ITSs), AI systems able to tutor individual students in various disciplines.[27]

Watson, BD, B³D, and the future. Most people, at least those in the United States, are aware of the fact that Watson, an AI system engineered by IBM, triumphed to much fanfare in 2011 over the best (at the time) human *Jeopardy!* players. Most people are also aware of the fact that this victory for a machine over human experts in a particular game follows an entrancing pattern that IBM established and pulled off previously, when, in a 1997 rematch, its Deep Blue, a chess-playing computer program, with the world watching move by move, beat Gary Kasparov, at that time the greatest human chess player on the planet. Yet the pattern is not quite the same, for there is a big difference between the two AI systems in question: Whereas Deep Blue had narrow expertise and no capacity to process data expressed in so-called natural languages such as English and Norwegian, Watson does have such a capacity (with respect to English, currently). To put it bluntly, despite the fact that a chess-playing machine of the power of Deep Blue realized one of the long-standing and strategically targeted dreams of AI (e.g., see Newell, 1973), chess, compared to challenges that involve human language, is easy (Bringsjord, 1998). And yet Watson, too, has some noteworthy limitations.

For example, while Watson is able to return correct answers to many natural-language questions, it does so on the strength, specifically, of its having on hand not simply vast amounts of frozen BD but specifically vast amounts of frozen *structured* BD. The reader will recall that we defined data for purposes of the present inquiry, but we left aside the distinction between structured and unstructured data. Structured data are data nicely poised for profitable processing by computation. Paradigmatic structured data would for example be data in a relational database or a spreadsheet; the College Board data discussed briefly earlier, for instance, was all structured and housed in databases. Unstructured data include what we humans for the most part use for human-to-human communication: e-mails, narratives, movies, research papers, lectures, diagrams, sketches, and so on—all things that computers cannot currently automatically understand (to any real degree, anyway), not even Watson. Fortunately for fans of BD and BD analytics, and for IBM, this limitation on Watson can be manually surmounted via ingenious human engineering, carried out within a seminal framework that was invented long before Watson.[28] This engineering takes in unstructured data from a given domain as input and "curates" it to produce corresponding structured data that can be penetratingly analyzed by Watson and its wondrous algorithms.[29]

Can the manual "translation" from unstructured to structured data be automated? IBM recently announced a $1 billion expansion in the planned reach and power of Watson (Ante, 2014), but that expansion appears to sustain the need for engineers to "translate" unstructured information in some domain (e.g., medicine) into structured data. A profound and open question about the future is whether or not the process of passing from unstructured to structured data can be automated.[30] Without that automation in place, the cost of providing deep question-answering technology for the university community (and, indeed, *any* community) will continue to carry the large labor cost of data scientists and engineers having to configure Watson for deployment. That cost may or may not be surmountable.

But more to the points at hand in the present essay, we remark upon a second limitation that currently constrains Watson: It can only handle questions about BD, not B³D. Watson, as suitably pre-engineered for *Jeopardy!* competition, would presumably be able to answer, say, "Watson, what 'Little Flower' famously ran the Big Apple?"—and this capacity is without question a stunning achievement for AI. But Watson cannot currently handle this (now-familiar-to-our-readers!) question: "Watson, what is the limit of the function two times x, minus five, as x approaches three?"[31]

If in the future Watson developed an ability to answer such questions, the consequences for the academy would be momentous. For then "under one roof," Watson's analysis of BD would be powerful, and deep education centered around B³D could, in theory, be provided as well. In other words, Watson would be in position to function as a revolutionary component of an intelligent tutoring system (ITS), a category of intelligent machinery to which we now briefly turn our attention.

Intelligent tutoring systems and the future. It has doubtless not escaped the reader's attention that the kind of education on which we have tended to focus herein is certainly more akin to one-on-one tutoring than to, for instance, the kind of instruction offered by a professor teaching a MOOC to myriad students spread across the globe. Yet our focus is purely a function of the intimate relationship that undeniably exists between tutoring-style education and Big-But-Buried Data; the focus, for the record, is not reflective of any animus on our part toward other pedagogical structures. For example and for the record, we both regard peer-to-peer learning to be extraordinarily powerful. Regardless, in the future, why can ITSs not be imbedded within MOOCs? Why cannot each of the tens (or hundreds . . .) of thousands of students signed up to take calculus in a MOOC, or signed up to watch educational videos from Khan Academy (which offers many excellent ones on calculus), whether they are students at the high school or college level, *also* have supplementary interaction with an ITS?

If the correct answer to these questions is the sanguine "There's no reason why they can't!", it follows immediately that tomorrow's AI systems, specifically ITSs, will somehow obtain a capacity for understanding natural language and for understanding infinite sets and structures. However, the hope that such capacities will be acquired by tomorrow's computing machines is unsupported by any empirical evidence on hand today. Today, no AI system, and hence no ITS, can genuinely understand the natural-language sentences we routinely use; nor can such a system understand the infinitary nature of even our elementary mathematics. Both plane geometry and calculus, the two branches of mathematics touched upon most previously, are irreducibly infinite in nature in that the key structure they presuppose is one and the same: the continuum—that is, the reals, which are not only infinite but breathtakingly so.[32] In light of this daunting situation, there is certainly much work to be done, and that work will need to be paid for.

NEXT STEPS

We view the present chapter as a prolegomenon to and a call for research. There are at least two trajectories such research must take. The first is to climb toward a seamless integration between administrators on the one hand and other educators "on the ground" on the other hand. Making this climb requires that BD and B³D must themselves be seamlessly integrated. It is not enough to be able to pinpoint that failure to graduate in certain majors can be predicted by a failure to secure a strong grade in calculus. We must reach a time when, having pinpointed such things, we can in response simulate a range of educational interventions, personalized for each particular student, to find those that lead to mastery of Big-But-Buried Data. Implementing those interventions will in turn lead back to improvement signaled at the BD level, for instance, higher graduate rates across a university, a university system, a state, or across the United States as a whole. The second trajectory is, of course, research and development devoted specifically to providing the availability of these implementations, such as the design and engineering of ITSs with the kind of unprecedented power we have described.

NOTES

1. R is free and can be obtained at: http://www.r-project.org. To start having fun with R in short order, we recommend (Knell, 2013). With R comfortably on hand, those wishing an introduction to basic statistical techniques essential for analytics of BD can turn to the R-based (Dalgaard , 2008).

2. The limit of the function that takes some real number x, multiplies it by 2, and subtracts 5 (i.e., f is $2x - 5$), as x approaches 3, is 1. This very short statement, which also appears in figure 3.2, rather magically holds within it an *infinite* number of buried data points (e.g., that 2 multiplied by 1, minus 5, is not equal to 1). But no high school student understands limits without first understanding general 10-symbol-long schematic statements like this one. We return to this topic later.

3. While invented by Pascal, probability was still fundamentally obscure until Kolmogorov (1950; originally published in 1933) used precious few symbols to provide a classic big-but-buried axiomatization of all of probability (at the level of the propositional calculus).

4. A sign that the integration is missing is perhaps that there continues to be widespread tension between administrators and faculty members, since the former live and die, these post–Great Recession days, by how well they obtain, analyze, and act on BD in the increasingly tight-money environment of today's academy, while the latter, if still providing face-to-face instruction to physically co-located students, must be focused on teaching mastery of B^3D.

5. Our points in this section could be based on any of the crucial Big-But-Buried Data that future data scientists ought to master (e.g., decision theory, game theory, formal logic, search algorithms, R, programming languages and theory, etc.), but calculus, occupying as it does a pivotal place in STEM education within the academy, and—for reasons we herein review—in a general, enlightened understanding of our world, is particularly appropriate given our objectives. In addition, calculus provides the ultimate sobering subject for gauging how math-advanced U.S. students are or are not now and in the future. We assume our readers are acquainted with the brutal fact that in math K–12 U.S. students stack up horribly against their counterparts in many other countries. A recent confirmation of this long-standing fact comes in the form of the PISA 2012 results, which reveal that of 34 OECD countries, the United States is below average—ranking a dismal 26th despite the fact that the United States spends more per student on math education than most countries (Organisation for Economic Cooperation and Development, 2012).

6. Or *datum*, a definition of which could, of course, be used to define the plural case.

7. That which *expresses* a fact is, of course, readily compressible. Here is probably as good a place as any for us to point out that the hiding that is part and parcel of Big-But-Buried Data has nothing to do with data compression. In data compression, some bits that are statistically redundant are removed. By contrast, in B³D, nothing is removed and nothing is redundant: Usually all the bits or symbols, each and every one, are indispensable, and what is hidden is not found by adding back bits or symbols but rather by human-level semantic reasoning.

8. Alert readers may protest that, technically speaking, there are such things as *analog data* and *analog computation*, but this quarter of modern information processing is currently a minuscule one, and students trained in data science at universities, as a rule, are taught precious little to nothing about analog computers and analog data. A readable, lively overview of computation and intelligence, including the analog case, is provided by Fischler and Firschein (1987).

9. Those wanting to go deeper into the nature of information are encouraged to study Floridi (2011).

10. Of course, we give here an extremely simple example, but the principles remain firmly in operation regardless of how much BD one is talking about, and regardless of how multidimensional the BD is. The mathematical nature of BD and its associated analytics is in fact ultimately charted by working at the level of running algorithms over binary alphabets, as any elementary, classic textbook on the formal foundations of computer science will show (e.g., Lewis & Papadimitriou [1981]).

11. The example was originally given to Selmer Bringsjord by Professor Philip Johnson-Laird as a challenge.

12. But we supply the justification here: Since everyone likes anyone who likes someone, and Alvin likes Bill, everyone likes Alvin— including Bill. But then since Bill likes Alvin, and—again—everyone likes anyone who likes someone, we obtain (d) everyone likes Bill. QED

13. Our purposes in composing the present essay do not include delivery of designs for technology that can process BD and/or B³D.

Readers interested in an explanation of techniques, whether in the human mind or in a computer, able to answer queries about Big-But-Buried Data, and supply justifications for such answers, can begin by consulting Bringsjord (2008).

14. This is perhaps the place to make sure the reader knows that we know full well that mastery isn't always permanent. Reeducation is very important, as is the harnessing of mastery in support of ongoing work, which serves to sustain mastery. In fact, the sometimes fleeting nature of mastery only serves to bolster our case. Due to space limitations, we leave aside treatment of these topics herein.

15. As even non-cognoscenti will be inclined to suspect, Euclid only really kicked things off, and the B³D-oriented portion of the human race is still making amazing discoveries about plane geometry. For an example, see the positively wonderful and award-winning article by Greenberg (2010).

16. Lest it be thought the wonders of B³D are seen only in mathematics, we inform the reader that *physical* science is increasingly being represented and systematized in Big-But-Buried Data. For instance, half a page of symbols are needed to sum up all the truths of relativity theory (see Andréka et al. [2011]).

17. In principle, any recording can be faked and doctored.

18. Bertrand, if successful, will have shown command over (at least some aspects of) what is known as *recursion* in data/computer science, and the rules of inference known as *universal elimination* and *modus ponens* in discrete mathematics.

19. Analytics applied to nonburied data generated from relevant activity at individual universities is doubtless aligned strikingly with what the College Board's AP-based analysis shows. For instance, at Rensselaer Polytechnic Institute (RPI), grades in the first calculus course for first-year students (Math 1010: Calculus I) are highly predictive of whether students will eventually graduate. Of course, RPI is a technological university, so one would expect the predictive power of calculus performance. But, in fact, such performance has more predictive power at RPI than a combination of broader factors used for admission (e.g., high school GPA and SAT scores).

20. By "calculus" here we have meant and mean elementary versions of both the differential and integral calculi, invented

independently three centuries ago by Leibniz (whose ingenious and elegant notation is still used today in nearly every calculus course) and Newton, which are united by the Fundamental Theorem of Calculus, a result traditionally presented to students in their first calculus course. (While today calculus is taught to the world's students through the starting "portal" of the concept of a limit [a contemporary tradition echoed, of course, in the present chapter], this pedagogical approach is historically jarring, since, instead, *infinitesimals* [infinitely small numbers] formed the portal through which Newton and [especially] Leibniz seminally passed to find and provide calculus to humanity. Today, we know that while Leibniz was long lampooned for welcoming such a fuzzy thing as an infinitesimal, his approach has been fully vindicated, through the groundbreaking work of Robinson [1996; originally published in 1966], who continued the seminal work of Norwegian logician Thoraf Skolem [1934], and one can even find an occasional textbook today that gives an infinitesimal-based approach to teaching calculus.) There are many other calculi of great importance in our increasingly digital world. For instance, the λ-calculus, introduced by Church (1936), occupies a seminal and—often through much-used-today formalisms to which it is mathematically equivalent—still-central place in the history of data science.

21. Of course, some of the natural sciences are not all that intimately bound up with calculus; biology would be a case in point. We are saying that the *cognition* required to learn and apply calculus is what transfers across learning in data science and STEM, not all the B^3D particulars of calculus. By the way, while largely ignored, the idea that biology itself can be expressed in just a few symbols in an axiomatic system was rather long ago seminally presented by Woodger (1962).

22. For example, see the intriguing case in favor of Keynesian spending articulated by Woodford (2011), in which economies are modeled as infinitely lived "households" that maximize utility through infinite time series, under, for instance, the constraint that the specific, underlying function u, which returns the utility produced by the consumption of a good, must be such that its first derivative is greater than zero, while its second derivative is less than zero. Without understanding the differential calculus,

one could not possibly understand Woodford's case. And note that in how Woodford models an economy he is hardly idiosyncratic, since he follows a long-standing neoclassical approach articulated, for example, by Barro and King (1984).

23. Any of the theorems explicitly presented and employed in early calculus courses (where students are typically *not* asked to prove them) would do. In his NSF-sponsored, seminal approach to engineering computers able to assist humans in their learning of calculus, Suppes (see, e.g., Suppes & Takahasi [1989]) asked students to prove, for example, the Intermediate Value Theorem.

24. The vast majority of Zeno's direct writings are unfortunately not preserved for us living in the Big-Data era. We know of Zeno's reasoning primarily via Aristotle's (certainly compressed) presentation of it. The Paradox of the Arrow is presented by Aristotle in *Physics*, 239b5-32, which can be found in McKeon (1941). The titles given to Zeno's paradoxes (with "Paradox of the Arrow" no exception) have been assigned and affirmed by commentators coming after him. Zeno himself wrote in the fifth century B.C.; Aristotle about two centuries later. Would-be scholarly detectives with an interest in intrigue, we promise, will be nicely rewarded by searching out what is written/known about both Zeno the man and his work, beyond Aristotle as source.

25. Put with brutal brevity, one learns in calculus that the escape from Zeno's otherwise valid reasoning is that motion is formally defined in terms of what occurs at "nearby" moments. An arrow simply cannot be at motion in or during a particular moment, but thanks to calculus, we know precisely that it can certainly and easily have *instantaneous velocity* (formally defined early in a first calculus course using derivatives), since a traveling arrow is at different positions at moments before or after the instant in question. Zeno's reasoning stood rock-solid and (assuming honesty on the part of those courageous enough to confront it) compelling, despite rather desperate attempts to refute it (Aristotle struck out first), for millennia, until the advent of calculus.

26. Among the many fallacies committed by Baker (2013) is this prominent one: *reductio ad absurdum* deployed in the absence of any absurdity. All serious students of mathematics are taught that when deploying this rule of inference, one must obtain the absurdity or contradiction in question, at which point one is then free

to reject the proposition that implies the absurdity. Baker, apparently having never been taught this, blithely quotes (out of context, by the way) snippets from algebra textbooks, taking it for granted that the absurdity is thereby made plain (so that, in turn, the required teaching of these textbooks is shown to be a very bad idea). For instance, we are supposed to instantly perceive the absurdity in the following, which is word for word in its entirety a specimen of what Baker confidently presents and assumes to be self-evidently absurd: "A rational function is a function that you can write in the form $f(x) = \frac{P(x)}{Q(x)}$, where $P(x)$ and $Q(x)$ are polynomial functions. The domain of $f(x)$ is all real numbers except those for which $Q(x) = 0$" (Baker, 2013, p. 32).

27. For a superlative introduction to ITSs, and BD analysis regarding their effectiveness, see VanLehn (2011).

28. That framework is Unstructured Information Management Architecture (UIMA; see Ferrucci & Lally [2004]).

29. It's important to note, and concede, that human communication makes extensive and routine use of diagrammatic information (pictures, videos, diagrams, images, etc.), and that the AI challenge of engineering intelligent machines able to genuinely process such content is a severe one. Along these lines, see Bringsjord and Bringsjord (1996). In figure 3.3, we used a diagram to represent Big-But-Buried Data. There is currently no foreseeable set of AI techniques that would allow a computing machine to understand what even bright middle schoolers grasp upon study of the remarkably rich diagram in question.

30. Some automation has been, and is being, pursued. See, for example, Bringsjord et al. (2007) and Fan, Ferrucci, Gondek, & Kalyanpur (2010). But such automation falls far short of what the human reader is capable of.

31. It is possible, subsequent to the publication of the present chapter (since it will then end up being frozen for future consumption and available on the internet), that the very text you are reading might happen to end up being "digested" by Watson, in which case Watson might in fact return "1." But obviously a question along the same line, but never asked in the history of our race, could be devised, and posed to Watson. And besides, Watson could be asked, as the aforementioned Johnny was, to prove the answer returned correct.

32. The reals are larger than the natural numbers (0, 1, 2, . . .) and larger, too, than the rational numbers (natural-number fractions). For a readable explanation and proof, see Boolos, Burgess, and Jeffrey (2002).

REFERENCES

Andréka, H., Madarász, J. X., Németi, I., & Székely, G. (2011). A logic road from special relativity to general relativity. *Synthese* *186*, 1–17. doi:10.1007/s11229-011-9914-8

Ante, S. E. (2014, January 9). IBM set to expand Watson's reach. *Wall Street Journal*. Retrieved from http://online.wsj.com/news/articles/SB10001424052702303754404579308981809586194

Baker, N. (2013, September). Wrong answer: The case against Algebra II. *Harper's Magazine* 31–38.

Barro, R. J., & King, R. G. (1984). Time-separable preferences and intertemporal-substitution models of business cycles. *Quarterly Journal of Economics 99*, 817–839. doi:10.2307/1883127

Boolos, G. S., Burgess, J. P., & Jeffrey, R. C. (2002). *Computability and logic* (4th ed.). New York, NY: Cambridge University Press.

Bringsjord, S. (1998). Chess is too easy. *Technology Review 101*(2). Retrieved from http://www.technologyreview.com/featuredstory/400154/chess-is-too-easy/

Bringsjord, S. (2008). Declarative/logic-based cognitive modeling. In R. Sun (Ed.), *The handbook of computational psychology* (pp. 127–169). Retrieved from Rensselaer Polytechnic Institute website: http://kryten.mm.rpi.edu/sb_lccm_ab-toc_031607.pdf

Bringsjord, S., Arkoudas, K., Clark, M., Shilliday, A., Taylor, J., Schimanski, B., & Yang, Y. (2007). Reporting on some logic-based machine reading research. In *Proceedings of the 2007 AAAI spring symposium: Machine reading* (Technical Report SS–07–06, pp. 23–28). Retrieved from Association for the Advancement of Artificial Intelligence website: http://www.aaai.org/Library/Symposia/Spring/ss07-06.php

Bringsjord, S., & Bringsjord, E. (1996). The case against AI from imagistic expertise. *Journal of Experimental and Theoretical Artificial Intelligence 8*, 383–397. doi:10.1080/095281396147384

Church, A. (1936). An unsolvable problem of elementary number theory. *American Journal of Mathematics 58*(2), 345–363.

Dalgaard, P. (2008). *Introductory statistics with R* (2nd ed.). New York, NY: Springer.

Ebbinghaus, H.-D., Flum, J., & Thomas, W. (1994). *Mathematical logic* (2nd ed.). New York, NY: Springer-Verlag.

Eicholz, R. E., O'Daffer, P. G., Charles, R. I., Young, S. I., Barnett, C. S., Clemens, S. R., Gilmer, G. F., Reeves, A., Renfro, F. L., Thompson, M. M., & Thornton, C. A. (1995). *Addison-Wesley mathematics: Grade 7*. Reading, MA: Addison-Wesley.

Fan, J., Ferrucci, D., Gondek, D., & Kalyanpur, A. (2010). PRISMATIC: Inducing knowledge from a large scale lexicalized relation resource. In *Proceedings of the NAACL HLT 2010 first international workshop on formalisms and methodology for learning by reading* (pp. 122–127). Retrieved from Association for Computational Linguistics website: www.aclweb.org/anthology/W10-0915

Ferrucci, D., Brown, E., Chu-Carroll, J., Fan, J., Gondek, D., Kalyanpur, A., Lally, A., Murdock, J. W., Nyberg, E., Prager, J., Schlaefer, N., & Welty, C. (2010). Building Watson: An overview of the DeepQA Project. *AI Magazine 59*–79. doi:10.1609/aimag.v31i3.2303

Ferrucci, D., & Lally, A. (2004). UIMA: An architectural approach to un-structured information processing in the corporate research environment. *Natural Language Engineering 10*, 327–348. doi:10.1017/S1351324904003523

Fischler, M. A., & Firschein, O. (1987). *Intelligence: The eye, the brain, and the computer*. Reading, MA: Addison-Wesley.

Floridi, L. (2005). Is semantic information meaningful data? *Philosophy and Phenomenological Research 70*(2), 351–370. doi:10.1111/j.1933-1592.2005.tb00531.x

Floridi, L. (2008). Data. In *International Encyclopedia of the Social Sciences* (2nd ed., pp. 234–237). Detroit, MI: Macmillan.

Floridi, L. (2010). *Information: A very short introduction*. Oxford: Oxford University Press. doi:10.1093/actrade/9780199551378.001.0001

Floridi, L. (2011). *The philosophy of information*. Oxford: Oxford University Press.

Glymour, C. (1992). *Thinking things through*. Cambridge, MA: MIT Press.

Greenberg, M. J. (2010). Old and new results in the foundations of elementary plane Euclidean and non-Euclidean geometries. *American Mathematical Monthly 117*(3), 198–219. doi:10.4169/000298910X480063

Knell, R. (2013). *Introductory R: A beginner's guide to data visualisation and analysis using R* [Kindle version]. Retrieved from Amazon.com

Kolmogorov, A. (1950). *Foundations of the theory of probability*. (N. Morrison, Trans.). New York, NY: Chelsea.

Lewis, H., & Papadimitriou, C. (1981). *Elements of the theory of computation*. Englewood Cliffs, NJ: Prentice Hall.

Mattern, K., Shaw, E., & Xiong, X. (2009). *The relationship between AP exam performance and college outcomes*. New York, NY: College Board.

McKeon, R. (Ed.). (1941). *The basic works of Aristotle*. New York, NY: Random House.

Minelli, M., Chambers, M., & Dhiraj, A. (2013). *Big Data, big analytics: Emerging intelligence and analytic trends for today's businesses*. Hoboken, NJ: Wiley. doi:10.1002/9781118562260

Newell, A. (1973). You can't play 20 questions with nature and win: Projective comments on the papers of this symposium. In W. G. Chase (Ed.), *Visual information processing* (pp. 283–308). New York, NY: Academic Press.

Organisation for Economic Co-operation and Development. (2013). *PISA 2012 results—United States*. Retrieved from http://www.oecd.org/unitedstates/PISA-2012-results-US.pdf

Potter, M. (2004). *Set theory and its philosophy: A critical introduction*. Oxford: Oxford University Press. doi:10.1093/acprof:oso/9780199269730.001.0001

Robinson, A. (1996). *Non-standard analysis*. Princeton, NJ: Princeton University Press.

Sayood, K. (2006). *Introduction to data compression* (3rd ed.). Amsterdam: Elsevier.

Skolem, T. (1934). Über der Nichtcharaterisierbarkeit der Zhalenreihe mittels endlich oder abzahlbar unendlich vieler Aussagen mit ausschlisslich Zahlenvariablen. *Fundamenta Mathematica 23*, 150–161.

Suppes, P., & Takahasi, S. (1989). An interactive calculus theorem-prover for continuity properties. *Journal of Symbolic Computation 7*, 573–590. doi:10.1016/S0747-7171(89)80041-0

VanLehn, K. (2011). The relative effectiveness of human tutoring, intelligent tutoring systems, and other tutoring systems. *Educational Psychologist 46*(4), 197–221. doi:10.1080/00461520.201 1.611369

Woodford, M. (2011). Simple analytics of the government expenditure multiplier. *American Economic Journal: Macroeconomics 3*(1), 1–35. doi:10.1257/mac.3.1.1

Woodger, J. H. (1962). Biology and the axiomatic method. *Annals of the New York Academy of Sciences 96*(4), 1093–1116. doi:10.1111/j.1749-6632.1962.tb54121.x

Part II

ACCESS, COMPLETION, SUCCESS

4

BIG DATA'S IMPACT ON COLLEGE ADMISSION PRACTICES AND RECRUITMENT STRATEGIES

JAY W. GOFF AND CHRISTOPHER M. SHAFFER

ABSTRACT

This chapter considers the opportunities for developing a Big Data approach to improve U.S. college admission, recruitment, and enrollment management practices by drawing from current technology industry trends of using massive data resources to build stronger congruence and satisfaction between consumers and service organizations. The authors provide an overview of current student choice trends, enrollment management data applications, and student developmental research that indicates improvement in the student-college match, or fit, should increase student retention and degree completion rates. The chapter concludes that an enterprise feedback management (EFM) system approach could provide the planning framework and development processes needed to help colleges and universities utilize Big Data in improving the college selection experience.

INTRODUCTION

The drive for Big Data systems to improve the efficiency and effectiveness of colleges' and universities' admission and recruitment efforts is not a new venture. Since the 1970s, leaders in the enrollment management (EM) field have consistently pushed to make data-informed and information-driven decisions a core operating principle of strategic enrollment management (SEM) programs. Fundamentally, many dedicated administrators and faculty members have concluded that the more institutions know about and respond to students' interests, background, abilities, prior performance, and aspirations, the more likely students are to enroll in the appropriate school and successfully complete a degree program. This conviction is driven by the idea that well-organized and relevant information can be used to help a student make suitable college choice decisions, while also assisting institutions in the alignment of resources to best match students' learning and developmental needs. Ultimately, the best SEM plan uses a wide variety of data to help an institution attract, enroll, and graduate a well-defined student population. The entire process should involve continual improvement efforts that result in activities to build a stronger student-institutional congruence.

The concept of engaging Big Data in EM involves moving beyond the current data mining and analytical practices that can be performed with existing relational databases and the use of predictive enrollment models. Those "small data" activities can provide deep details in terms of *what* activities they engage in during the college selection process and *who* enrolls in specific colleges. Current systems allow schools to collect aggregate student data and develop model profiles of specific populations that are likely to select a particular school and succeed with current institutional services. When the profiles are compared with national data sets, schools can also determine market position, competitors, and ways to tailor services to better meet the needs of specific student populations. Most of these analytical models are based on historical data, use a limited number of available data sets, and take many years to develop. However, a Big Data EM approach would build upon the established predictive models by collecting and interconnecting vast amounts of student assessment and feedback data. It would help answer the questions of *why* students select institutions and choose to engage institutional support structures. The approach should push analysts to collapse the feedback data into real-time, actionable institutional intelligence. Ultimately, the effort should assist colleges in creating almost immediate prospective student response systems and propelling prompt changes in institutional support services designed to meet individual students' genuine needs and goals.

It is the authors' belief that Big Data applications could improve a number of student and institutional choice paths. A well-designed enterprise feedback management (EFM) system should further strengthen the outreach, new student recruitment, admissions, and student-college match processes.

DEFINING BIG DATA IN THE COLLEGE ADMISSIONS AND ENROLLMENT MANAGEMENT CONTEXT: EXTREME INFORMATION MANAGEMENT TO IMPROVE STUDENT ACCESS AND SUCCESS

The best college and university admissions programs use student, market, and institutional information along with broad communication systems to engage prospective students and help them understand how the institution can meet their educational, personal, and career goals. Using a variety of data sources to improve students' college awareness, readiness, and selection has been a long and ongoing objective for college admissions deans. Hossler and Bean (1990) noted the strategic need for enrollment managers to closely study student activity patterns and use data to improve practices:

> Organized by strategic planning and supported by institutional research, enrollment management activities concern student college choice, transition to college, student attrition and retention, and student outcomes. These processes are studied to guide institutional practices in the areas of new student recruitment and financial aid, student support services, curriculum development, and other academic areas that affect enrollments, student persistence, and student outcomes from college. (p. 5)

As noted in other chapters in this volume, defining Big Data is difficult and largely depends on the context of the data and desired outcomes for the resulting information. Data analyst consultants McKinsey and Company frame the concept in an operational definition that generally describes most U.S. colleges' analytical challenge:

"Big Data refers to datasets whose size is beyond the ability of typical database software tools to capture, store, manage and analyze" (Manyika et al., 2011, p. 1).

It is the complexity and resource-intensive nature of extreme information management that often allows institutions to not adopt Big Data concepts to understand actual institutional competencies (e.g., what they do really well). These competencies, along with a wide variety of student enrollment patterns and barriers, if addressed, have the potential to improve student persistence and success levels. In other words, Big Data is like art—it has the ability to bring new viewpoints to the foreground and create an image, or understanding, which did not previously exist.

Over the past decade, enterprise resource program (ERP) implementations and developments have promised to address the significant challenge of managing enormous amounts of information. Often, new institutional reporting and assessment plans will focus on collecting additional data when existing data are not utilized. Even without detailed data collection plans, millions of student transactions occur each day that could provide insight into students' engagement and productivity levels. Copeland (2012) observed that most universities already collect vast amounts of discrete and activity data that are

> already available from existing learning platforms (e.g., logins, content engagement), portal activity (e.g., enrollment, payment) and campus behavior (e.g., dining halls, library usage and building access). Most colleges are sitting on literally mountains of data, yet they have not aligned the resources to analyze and translate these data into actionable information for decision makers.

ETHICS AND STANDARDS ARE A FIRST PRIORITY OF ANY STUDENT DATA ENDEAVOR

Institutions of higher learning must always make safeguarding student data a top priority. Today's students are very willing to share information with organizations for a variety of services deemed essential in the digital age. Information is freely given and constantly updated when gaining access to online social networks, using a smart phone, and registering for e-mail. In all cases, students must be made aware of their rights and, if data are used, how they could assist them in receiving services and making more informed choices.

Any discussion of deep data mining and uses of personal information results in visions of "Big Brother" tracking technologies and the obvious potential for innocent people to be harmed. Although the authors assume any use of Big Data in higher education and enrollment management will be carried out with the strongest ethical considerations and in strict compliance with federal and state laws, we are not naïve concerning the abuses likely to happen when data conclusions are misunderstood or the conclusive applications or policies potentially violate civil rights for the sake of efficiency.

Many laws exist to protect student privacy, including the Family Educational Rights and Privacy Act (FERPA). Failure to comply with the regulations could harm students personally and financially, plus lead to severe institutional financial penalties. However, the possibility of using Big Data to find and recruit a student with a high probability for success is not only a noble activity, it is also a relatively new capability and expectation. The data protection and enforcement mechanisms must have many self-regulated, stop-gap measures built into the storage and sharing processes. Any of these new capabilities will require an investment of time to ensure safeguards are followed to the fullest extent.

STRONG ENROLLMENT MANAGEMENT HAS ALWAYS BEEN DATA DRIVEN

"To the organized, go the students."
—Jack Maguire

Today's college admissions and retention programs rely on deftly organized and personalized multimedia campaigns (e.g., direct mail, telephone, e-mail, internet homepages, mass media, social media, and mobile media). The institutional activities and expenditures supporting these efforts can be extensive. A recent study estimated private colleges and universities spend an average of $2,433 for every matriculating freshman, while public four-year institutions invest about $457 per new student enrolled (Noel-Levitz, 2013). The methods for effectively managing these activities have significantly developed over the past four decades.

The enrollment management (EM) concept formally materialized in the 1970s among private colleges and universities seeking to have stronger, more sustainable student enrollment cycles. Jack Maguire and his colleagues at Boston College are largely credited with developing constructs and systems that now help colleges attract and enroll their desired quantity, quality, and diversity of students (Black, 2001, p. 6). In 1976, Maguire's team recognized the need to have data guide the core enrollment management components. They categorized the five components as: "marketing admissions; research and information flow; market prediction; financial aid strategies; and retention and transfer programs" (Epstein, 2010, p. 4).

As access to richer data increased, so did enrollment-related information and predictive programs. Analytic and statistical models have been developed to predict students' interest levels, travel and mobility ranges, likelihood for successfully passing courses, financial need levels, and likelihood of persisting to graduation. Hoover (2011) stressed the heavy emphasis on today's admission and enrollment leaders to be statistically competent when he noted: "A profession (college admissions) that once relied on anecdotes and descriptive data now runs on complex statistical analyses and market research. Knowing how to decipher enrollment outcomes is a given; knowing how to forecast the future is a must" (Hoover, 2011).

Today's typical admission application information, secondary school transcripts, and college enrollment patterns can provide EM leaders and institutional researchers with hundreds of unique and comparable data points. The ACT college entrance/placement exam alone can provided over 265 data fields through detailed cognitive student demographic (age, gender, family income, etc.) and psychographic (lifestyle activities) information (ACT, 2013).

Coupled with institutional performance trends, college admissions exam data offer insights to students' academic development needs, college selection preferences, and career aspirations. The test and profile data can also indicate students' aptitude to succeed in first-year classes and thus the likelihood to fit in or match well with the academic rigor of a particular school. A number of studies have established the strong correlation between higher ACT or SAT composite scores and positive college persistence levels (Burton & Ramist, 2001; Bettinger, Evans, & Pope, 2013).

SEM: RECRUITMENT AND RETENTION ARE TWO SIDES OF THE SAME COIN

The strategic enrollment management concept of designing admission programs to recruit *future graduates* has long existed. For over 30 years, higher education research has recognized the ability for admissions programs to improve student retention and graduation levels. Seidman (1989) noted that early student persistence research indicated students were more likely to be retained and graduate if they experienced a strong alignment, or congruence, between their goals, values, and attitudes and those of a college (Creamer & Atwell, 1984; Crockett, 1984; Forrest, 1982; Lenning, Beal, & Sauer, 1980; Pantages & Creedon, 1978; Pascarella, 1982; Pascarella, Smart, & Ethington, 1986; Tinto, 1975, 1987). Seidman also highlighted that Tinto and Wallace (1986) and Grites (1979) believed student-institutional congruence could be established during the college search and admission selection process.

Prior to the online information age, Tinto and Wallace (1986) proposed that college admissions officers and recruitment communication efforts had the ability, and responsibility, to assist prospective students in developing reasonable expectations regarding how their goals and needs could be met by a college's degree programs and campus experiences after enrolling. Bean (1985) determined, "Regardless of its source, a feeling of belonging or fitting in at the institution was most important during the freshman year, but also remained important during the sophomore and junior year" (p. 55). More recent ACT research on EM trends (ACT, 2012) supports these findings. The research found strong linkages between a student's college choice, a student's level of fit with the school's degree programs, and a student's resemblance to other students in the selected college major (ACT, 2012, p. 9). The study measures "fit" as a level of similarity between a student's career and academic interests, level of college readiness skills, and top choice degree program. The report highlights recent findings that indicated that students with high first college choice and interest-major fit levels are more likely to reenroll and persist in a college degree program (Allen & Robbins, 2008; Tracey & Robbins, 2006), remain in their selected major (Allen & Robbins, 2008), complete their degree in a timely manner (Allen & Robbins, 2010), and earn higher college GPAs (Tracey, Allen, & Robbins, 2012).

SMALL DATA EXPOSING STUDENT CHOICE FACTORS: CURRENT ENROLLMENT TRENDS EMERGING FROM DEEP DATA SHARING AND ANALYTICS

Most U.S. colleges and universities have not primarily recruited students based on their probability of succeeding. Admissions and enrollment goals are different for each college and university. Mission, service regions, and strategic visions largely dictate the types and numbers of students colleges try to attract and enroll. Thus, preferred student profiles and enrollment patterns, and the data related to them, can vary widely depending on the institution.

U.S. media focus heavily on college admissions topics related to the most highly selective colleges and universities. Most admissions and student recruitment programs at selective colleges are designed to attract or match prospective students to colleges based on their prior academic performance in high school and the college's current student population or aspirational student academic profile. Efforts to diversify the incoming student class—by geographic region, gender, race/ethnicity, religious affiliation, economic status, and so on—generally are secondary targets or goals in attracting the desired mix of students. Effectively, these recruitment efforts focus on enrolling students with a high probability of success. However, the vast majority of U.S. colleges and universities focus on serving a mission-directed population. Thus, they have not recognized a capability to recruit solely based on a student's probability of graduating.

Traditional student studies indicate freshmen are selecting colleges largely because the institution offers their desired academic program and the perceived quality of the institution's reputation (Higher Education Research Institute, 2007).

CURRENT TRENDS IN TRADITIONAL STUDENT ENROLLMENTS AND COLLEGE CHOICE

Not surprisingly, recent studies of student college choice and enroll-ment patterns indicate student-institution fit is often ignored in favor of factors of convenience or cost. In 2012, ACT and the National Student Clearinghouse (NSC) combined their substantial data sys-tems to track and measure 1.6 million college-bound U.S. students who had completed the ACT college admission assessment (ACT, 2012). The data included students' background characteristics, time of testing, ACT scores, college preferences, and students' participa-tion in releasing their contact information to colleges and scholar-ship organizations. This enrollment pattern research confirms that student-college match or fit is often unaligned. Rather, most students are more likely to select a school based on its geographic distance from their home and their initial interest in a college. The research reaffirmed the following five dominant choice trends.

1. *Most traditional students choose to enroll at a college within an hour of their home.* An EM market analytical tool for determin-ing a college's primary student market (the geographic area from which approximately 80% of the total enrolled students live) and market penetration has been referred to as the "golden circle" prin-ciple (Goff, 2009). Over the past two decades, just over 80% of U.S. students have selected a college or university within their home state (National Center for Education Statistics, 2011) and have primarily considered colleges within a two-hour driving radius of their home (STAMATS, 2004). The ACT and NSC research indicates that stu-dents' mobility is limited and most colleges' "golden circle" is much smaller than previously assumed. For example, while the percentage of ACT-tested college freshmen in 2011 attending an institution in their home state remained about 80%, the median distance between home and their selected college was only 51 miles (or about an hour from home) (ACT, 2012). The data (see figure 4.1) indicated that students with higher test scores were more likely to choose a college a greater distance from their home.

Figure 4.1. Median distance from enrolled students' home to college by ACT composite score, 2011

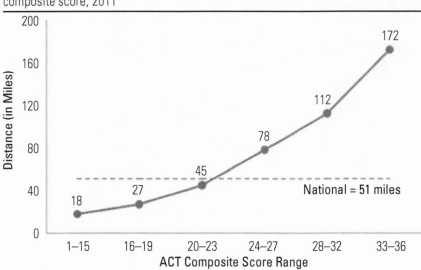

Source: ACT, 2012.

2. College-ready students tend to enroll at their first college of choice. The same study (ACT, 2012) also demonstrated that students, regardless of their exam scores, most often attended their first-choice college and the type of college that they planned to attend (two-year/four-year, public/private) prior to completing the college entrance exam. With the exception of students scoring in the upper 2%, the research shows a trend of enrollments at first-choice colleges increasing for students earning higher composite exam scores (see figure 4.2). The results suggest that schools will need very compelling recruitment programs to alter students' early college choice inclinations (ACT, 2012).

3. Colleges and universities choose to focus recruitment efforts on students who complete early college entrance exams. The data (ACT, 2012) indicate that students who test early and have higher test scores are recruited most heavily. It is not surprising that prospective students who test in their junior year, score well, and release their contact information to colleges and scholarship services are most heavily recruited (see figure 4.3). These data also indicate, however, that colleges' current recruitment plans are not flexible or

Figure 4.2. Enrollment of ACT-tested students by college choice number and composite score, 2011

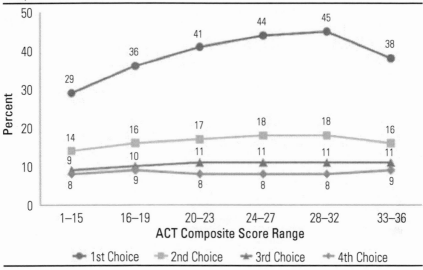

Source: ACT, 2012.

Figure 4.3. Average number of times ACT-tested students with contact data release were selected by first testing and ACT composite score, 2011

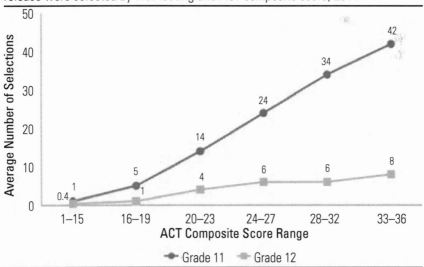

Source: ACT, 2012.

Figure 4.4. Full-time student enrollment at four-year colleges and universities by tuition and fee level

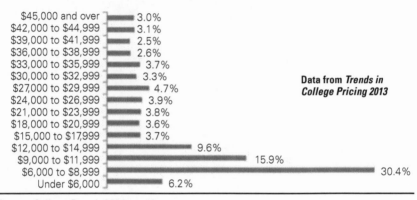

Distribution of Full-Time Enrollment at 4-Year Public and Private Nonprofit Institutions, 2013-2014, by Published Price for Tuition and Fees

Source: College Board, 2013, p. 12.

do not adjust well to attract talented students who test later in their senior year of high school (ACT, 2012).

4. *Most students only consider schools with "affordable" tuition and fee levels.* The overall student enrollment distribution by colleges' nondiscounted tuition and fee levels (see figure 4.4) supports the College Board's data, which indicate enrollment distribution by tuition and fee levels (College Board, 2013). Just over 60% of U.S. undergraduates are choosing to enroll at lower-cost community colleges and public universities, while less than 18% of all college-bound students select an institution with a total tuition cost exceeding $30,000 (College Board, 2013).

5. *Student loan debt has not dissuaded many students from attempting higher education.* Media and government attention to student loan debt has never been greater. About two-thirds of students who earned bachelor's degrees in 2012 graduated with student loan debt. The Institute for College Access and Success estimated the average debt to be $29,400 of students who borrowed. Even with the daunting forecasts, college-bound students have continued to apply and enroll at rather consistent levels (Reed & Cochrane, 2013).

BIG DATA'S POTENTIAL TO MORE CLEARLY SEGMENT STUDENT POPULATIONS AND IDENTIFY EARLY NEEDS

Today's prospective college students are sophisticated users of the latest internet programs and tools. They want a clear portrayal of how an institution will uniquely enable them to achieve what they want, articulated in life in terms that are logical, compelling, and succinct. Accessibility to this information must be immediate and direct, not buried within the content of a school's website and communications.

The challenge for colleges and universities to identify students' needs or problems early in the college selection process, and to apply timely interventions, has often been derailed by college counselors' and advisers' limited access to meaningful information. Solutions have been considered too costly and complex to implement. As multidimensional analytical computing becomes more affordable and easier to use, recent "small data" applications have been discovering meaningful patterns and relationships previously inaccessible in standard predictive modeling efforts. Such progress is particularly prevalent within desktop business intelligence and analytical platforms such as Tableau, Clear Analytics, or Microsoft's SharePoint. These new analytical tools can help to equip Big Data EM processes with the mechanisms necessary to build richer student and institutional competency profiles in the hope of enhancing the student-institution match or congruence.

Attracting new customers, developing stronger and longer lasting relationships, and meeting each customer's individual needs, have been the "secrets" of many companies' recent growth successes. Psychographic and geodemographic marketing researchers, such as the Nielsen PRIZM system, have long focused on using a variety of data to develop segmentation models for understanding and predicting behaviors of various populations (Mancini, 2009). This work has resulted in systems designed to forecast a population's needs or choices when voting, shopping, and choosing recreational and entertainment programs or the magazines and websites they engage for self-learning and personal development. When the PRIZM system started in the mid-1970s, they recognized 14 dominant consumer populations. Over the past three decades their models have vastly expanded their data sources to identify over 66 dominant clusters in just the United States (Golumbia, 2009). The company now believes more than

200 dominant population subcategories exist, but, similar to college choice research, their ability to identify and analyze these groups has been limited by data sources and analytical computing capacity—until recently. With perseverance, Big Data is likely to help schools develop a better understanding of their smaller or more refined student population segments and their unique needs. Existing assessment tools and applications will need to be reevaluated, expanded, and in some cases eliminated.

BIG DATA'S POTENTIAL TO BUILD STRONGER RELATIONSHIPS AND IMPROVE STUDENT-INSTITUTION MATCH

Although some researchers have tried to provide an expansive factor analysis of the variables in the college choice process, many readily recognize that most students' choice considerations are limited through a set of very personal filters (Braxton, 1990; McDonough, 1997; Terenzini, Cabrera, & Bernal, 2001). The college decision can be compared to other important and stressful life decisions: choosing a spouse/life partner or buying a home. The similarities in all three decisions are striking: they are all long-term commitments, they each demand a significant investment of time and money, and they can deeply impact one's future and satisfaction with life. The other similarity is the multiple variables of consideration and preference for each decision. It is rare for a single decision metric to exist in most complicated life choices. In honest and deep reflection, many individuals cannot pinpoint a single reason for deciding to marry someone or choosing a specific school—often it just "feels right."

Tackling the idea of finding fit in successful personal relationships has been studied for decades. With the internet and more robust data management systems, human mate selection and personal relationship science has boomed over the past decade. One of most highly recognized and regarded relationship science firms is eHarmony. Founded in 2000, eHarmony pioneered the science of matching singles seeking long-term relationships. The company now boasts over 40 million registered users in more than 150 countries around the world. In 2012, eHarmony estimated the program resulted in just under 200,000 marriages in the United States alone (Chang, 2012).

Much of the company's success has come from harnessing a Big Data approach in their principal mate-matching operations and marketing efforts (eHarmony.com, 2013). Regularly, the company makes sure that it is collecting deep amounts of data needed to achieve member-matching goals. Its standard 200-subject questionnaire results are blended with other relevant information sources. To be effective in creating a strong fit, a wide variety of elements must be factored into eHarmony's algorithms, which vary from country to country and among different cultural populations.

Analysts of eHarmony report the ability to capture millions of data sets or change events that are generated every hour each day. Most of these change events have no relational source database (such as homepage logins, number of content posts, or activity on their website) and are hard to assign to a single individual or membership cohort. Early on, the company regularly struggled with creating reports that could find trends from the large amounts of unaligned feedback. It developed a strategy to create analytical "data stacks" and layered software so as to process large amounts of data and find meaningful connections between their clients (Miller, 2011). The connections were designed to have real-time reporting efforts, while providing richer communications among eHarmony members. The analytical strategy eventually shaped eHarmony's marketing efforts by instructing the company on the best times to send specific messages to current and prospective clients.

The company believes the constant improvements in the analytics will increase the dependability of the fit in the partner matches and could potentially lower the nation's overall divorce rate (eHarmony, 2013).

USING BIG DATA TO DISCOVER "WHY": AN EHARMONY MODEL TO IMPROVE STUDENT RECRUITMENT?

Is it really possible to make sophisticated data mining and student needs research simple to access and use in the recruitment and retention processes? Until recently the answer was no, but with cloud-based, data warehouse, and multipoint analytical systems, new solutions are developing quickly.

In today's competitive enrollment environment, it is not enough to claim that your college is "student-centric" and knows your students' aggregate profile in terms of sociodemographics and entrance scores. Much like commercial organizations, universities must increasingly get to know their students, and the students whom they desire to enroll, as individuals—most students expect this level of familiarity. They are used to data clustering applications that help companies move quickly and proactively to meet their needs. Many students now expect all organizations, including higher education institutions, to respond in an almost hyper-personalized manner.

Currently, most students receive communications primarily focusing on a college's general benefits with little about how a school would uniquely meet a specific student's needs and wants. Many prospective search letters read like the following:

Dear Raina,

Thank you for inquiring about Mega College. A brochure about our psychology program is enclosed.

Mega offers more than 150 outstanding degree programs. We believe you should take a serious look at Mega. For decades we have been known for our world-class faculty, beautiful campus, and student-focused support programs. With more than 200 student activities and clubs to consider, we expect you will find your place very quickly—over 100,000 of alumni did, and they say it changed their lives forever.

If you are searching for a college of our quality, please consider visiting campus and applying to Mega before December 1. If you would like more information, please visit our homepage at www.mc.edu or call our Admissions Office at 1-800-MEGAC4U.

Best wishes for a successful senior year.

Raj Smith
Dean of Admissions, Mega College

Big Data could dramatically change and enhance the introduction to the student-institution relationship. Potentially, the day may arrive when a prospective student would receive a college search letter that reads:

Dear Raina,

After learning more about your chosen career and academic aspirations in Psychology, we have prepared for you the attached analysis of how Mega College is uniquely capable of providing you with the living-learning environment that best meets your preferred learning styles and educational environment. We believe you will also enjoy participating in our environmental remediation club and the alternative spring break service trip to Honduras.

Professor Stronghold has scheduled a video conference to provide you with a sample schedule and list of competencies you will benefit from if you choose to enroll at Mega College. Our research has shown that students with your interests and preparation levels are thoroughly satisfied with this path and college learning model, and over 90% complete their degrees on schedule.

Additional information about Mega's ability to support your learning and career aspirations are posted on your personal Mega portal at www.mega.edu/RainaJones and are networked to your social media page.

I look forward to seeing you online and on campus.

Raj Smith
Dean of Admissions, Mega College

This approach is similar to eHarmony's effort to segment messages to very specific individuals in an attempt to increase compatibility matches among members by specific beliefs, skills, and values. In this case, by focusing on the student's likely match or fit to the institution, the letter demonstrates the college's strong focus on student success and awareness of institutional competencies. It is rare for an institution to intentionally articulate the profile of a successful student and effectively "reverse engineer" the characteristics and related activities to a prospective student.

The ability to communicate to a prospective student's specific pathway to success and congruence with the institution could be a powerful tool, especially if the practice is replicated in all communications and personnel interactions. The process of defining success itself presents the institution with the opportunity to determine the exact data needed to engage students with a multilayered communication process. Without the ability to constrict the data, organizations may become paralyzed with too much information or can spend too much time looking for a perfect answer.

USING EFM TO EMBRACE BIG DATA IN ADMISSIONS AND ENROLLMENT MANAGEMENT

The grand challenge is to know "everything" about a student's needs and abilities as well as have the ability to quickly react accordingly. Successful organizations, like Nordstrom, Amazon, and Netflix, are finding that they must continuously ratchet up individualized experiences—whether in their stores, while providing a service, or even during online interactions. These organizations are challenged to bring together customer data from many sources: social media, point-of-purchase locations, opinion surveys, and interactions through all forms of digital channels—especially the growing feedback data from mobile devices.

Colleges and universities recognize similar business needs and have invested heavily in systems for storing and reporting on student transactions (ERPs), analyzing and mining student data, communicating to mass audiences on a regular basis (customer relation management systems, or CRMs), human resources systems, and student market research. Each system often performs its designed operations well, but these systems do not provide much insight into how particular students make decisions. Transactional systems are designed for recording profile details (age, gender, degree program, etc.) and what actions happened but not *why* the action happened.

ERP and CRM systems are simply not designed to record students' opinions, attitudes, and preferences, or to integrate these types of data when they are available. Although both are robust and essential to building a Big Data environment, they were created as

Figure 4.5. ERP and CRP Independent and Integrated Operations Models

Typical Small Data Flow for Driving Admissions and Recruitment Activities

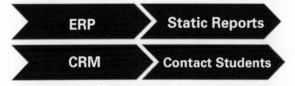

Potential Big Data Flow for Segmenting and Enhancing Admissions and Recruitment Activities

Source: Figure by Jay W. Goff and Christopher M. Shaffer.

separate data collection systems with independent operations (i.e., ERPs collect data on core business processes and produce static reports, CRMs integrate prospective contact data with established content to execute multichannel communications to students). The interpretation of data and strategy execution must come from the system users, otherwise an established set of reports, data loads, and communications will be executed as scheduled (see figure 4.5). To integrate the systems with a wide array of student data and feedback, schools would need systems that continually collect and integrate student feedback of many types and from many data sources. Over the past few years, companies have started creating new ways to integrate customer preference data from multiple locations—and use those data in real time to meet customers' needs and improve their overall experience.

The process of systematically collecting, analyzing, consolidating, and then using all sources of feedback to improve business operations in industry is commonly called enterprise feedback management (EFM). EFM is "a system for centralizing the collection, management, and use of feedback throughout an organization. It enables the organization to fully engage with people through targeted feedback programs or by asking questions during naturally occurring interactions" (SPSS, 2012, p. 2). The approach streamlines

Figure 4.6. EFM Model for Engaging Big Data in College and University Admission Practices

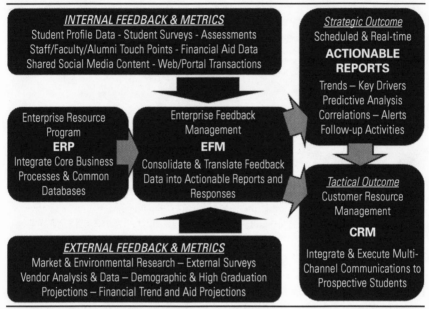

Source: Infographic concept adapted from Hanks (2013, p. 5).

the collection, management, and use of customer insight so as to optimize an organization's resources. EFM systems would allow colleges and universities to integrate student feedback with a variety of transactional data, student assessments, surveys, and demographic and psychographic information to create collective understandings of how outreach, counseling, and advising systems influence students' decisions and actions.

Hanks (2013) has explained that EFM is a Big Data management process that enables organizations to collect feedback in real time through multiple channels and multiple data sources; consolidate feedback from customers, employees, and other stakeholders; integrate that feedback with other important financial transactional data; use intelligent analytics to turn those data into actionable information; and distribute that information to the right person at the right time for follow up. In other words, EFM is about collecting, consolidating, and managing feedback from numerous sources—then immediately acting on that feedback to quickly and accurately demonstrate how the business can meet a specific customer's needs (see figure 4.6).

EFM APPROACH TO IMPROVE ADMISSIONS AND ENROLLMENT MANAGEMENT SERVICES?

Organized feedback on its own is not that useful; it only becomes useful when it is informational and provides insights that drive some type of action. As noted previously, Big Data companies are quickly moving beyond organizing passive feedback and are increasingly mining insights from unstructured, unsolicited feedback from comments on surveys, call-center conversations, inbound e-mails, social media sites, and customer feedback comments.

An EFM program would systematically collect and analyze student feedback from multiple channels in real time, with the goal of using that information to create changes that improve response times, service, and ultimately admit to enroll yields and student persistence to graduation rates. The feedback can come from multiple sources including conversations with admissions counselors, website actions, social media networks, and online chat rooms. The process should develop simple and intuitive reports that ensure the entire organization, from the president's office to the admissions counselors, understand the perspective of current students and how to take action to improve.

The end result could allow schools to more clearly understand their students at each stage of the college choice process and more reliably meet their expectations. Admissions counselors would be able to immediately understand students' preferences and concerns and explain how the institution's programs and services can address those issues. Staff members who rarely interact with prospective students would be able to more clearly understand students' preferences and meet their expectations. By providing more effective student interactions through the college's existing systems and channels, the EFM could help the institution increase student satisfaction, connectivity, and higher enrollment yield rates. Throughout the process, the university collects a central repository of student insights, which could be mined in many productive ways and used to reengineer business processes.

An EFM approach would allow admissions officers to understand questions such as:

- Why do various student segments choose certain colleges or degree programs?
- What precollege student activities are most useful to build a strong student-institution relationship?
- How do we build a solid student pipeline program for each targeted population segment?
- Why are we losing students to our competitors?
- What would make the institution more competitive in attracting our preferred student body?
- Could we obtain meaningful prospective student information from other sources at a lower cost?

GETTING STARTED: PREPARING TO USE BIG DATA IN ADMISSIONS AND ENROLLMENT MANAGEMENT

Colleges and universities rarely suffer from having too little information from the students they serve and want to serve, but they often lack the overall system for managing data and related feedback. It is important to be clear about the questions that need to be answered. Valuable information is often isolated in campus databases and information collection systems. The inaccessibility of data forces decision makers to have a limited view of students and a partial understanding of how the institution can best serve them. This situation potentially negatively affects both strategic planning efforts and daily, tactical decision making.

The following principles are an overview of the activities intended to provide a phased development plan for embracing an EFM admissions environment:

1. *Set data use standards.* Establish clear and documented ethical and legal standards for all student data collection

and uses. Initiate formal annual and quarterly reviews of the policies and practices.

2. *Establish clear enrollment goals.* Define the desired student profile, enrollment challenges, and related research questions for the EFM. This exercise should include an expanded institutional research plan to determine methods for improving students' match/fit with the institution.

3. *Inventory all student assessment and data resources.* Create a data inventory and reporting portfolio of all current data and information sources. Make sure to include faculty and staff feedback after they interact with a student.

4. *Consolidate data and feedback storage.* Develop an information technology plan to consolidate, cleanse, and centralize the data and report sources. This process should include plans for broad data storage and data saving capabilities through cloud arrangements and consortiums.

5. *Add missing feedback sources and set goals to manage data sources.* Annually review the research questions and identify any gaps in the available data needed to address the questions. Also, the review process should establish targets for supporting any additional feedback assessments and data gathering achievements.

These fundamental planning objectives will provide an incremental pathway to developing a Big Data plan and information technology environment that can support an EFM system.

CONCLUSION

The most effective college admissions and enrollment management systems will continue to use data-informed strategies to improve students' fit or congruence with their college of choice. The effort increases the likelihood that students will be successful in completing their degree and satisfied with their college experience. Most colleges and universities that desire to gain a competitive advantage through greater enterprise insight will need to consider a platform for embracing broader data analytics and deep information management throughout the student life cycle. Solid planning will be needed for these efforts to be successful.

Any Big Data admissions system should aspire to engage students in the "right way" at the "right time" so as to help them understand how a school can best assist them in meeting their goals. A Big Data effort should focus on discovering *why* each student population segment makes decisions and *how* they develop the most meaningful bond with an institution. Through system development and implementation processes, institutions should fully expect to find new trends in micro-populations and institutional barriers that need to be addressed. EFM systems appear to be emerging as a best practice option to establish planning efforts and help synchronize the wide variety of data collected across the many touch points of a student's college selection and enrollment journey.

REFERENCES

ACT. (2012). Enrollment management trends report 2012. Retrieved from http://www.act.org/emtrends/12/pdf/EMTrendsReport2012.pdf

ACT. (2013). *The condition of college and career readiness*. Retrieved from http://www.act.org/readiness/2013

Allen, J., & Robbins, S. (2008). Prediction of college major persistence based on vocational interests, academic preparation, and first-year academic performance. *Research in Higher Education 49*, 62–79. doi:10.1007/s11162-007-9064-5

Allen, J., & Robbins, S. (2010). Effects of interest-major congruence, motivation, and academic performance on timely degree attainment. *Journal of Counseling Psychology 57*, 23–35. doi:10.1037/a0017267

Bean, J. P. (1985). Interaction effects based on class level in an explanatory model of college student dropout syndrome. *American Educational Research Journal 22*(1), 35–64

Bettinger, E. P., Evans, B. J., & Pope, D. (2013). Improving college performance and retention the easy way: Unpacking the ACT exam. *American Economic Journal: Economic Policy 5*(2). Retrieved from http://cepa.stanford.edu/sites/default/files/ACT%20Paper%20(final).pdf

Black, J. (2001). *The strategic enrollment management revolution.* Washington, DC: AACRAO.

Braxton, J. M. (1990). How students choose colleges. In D. Hossler & J. P. Bean (Eds.), *The strategic management of college enrollments* (pp. 57–67). San Francisco, CA: Jossey-Bass.

Burton, N. W., & Ramist, L. (2001). *Predicting success in college: SAT studies of classes graduating since 1980* (College Board Report No. 2001-2). Retrieved from http://research.collegeboard.org/publications/content/2012/05/predicting-success-college-sat-studies-classes-graduating-1980

Chang, A. (2012, December 13). eHarmony founder has his heart set on reviving the dating site. *Los Angeles Times.* Retrieved from http://articles.latimes.com/2012/dec/13/business/la-fi-eharmony-20121214

College Board (2013). *Trends in college pricing.* Retrieved from http://trends.collegeboard.org/sites/default/files/college-pricing-2013-full-report-140108.pdf

Copeland, T. (2012). Big data enrollment: Higher ed lessons from the 2012 election. Retrieved from http://www.enrollmentmarketing.org/highereducation/2012/11/big-data-enrollment-higher-education-election-2012.html

Creamer, D. G., & Atwell, C. A. (1984). The great debate: Academic advising. *Community and Junior College Journal 54*(8), 18–20.

Crockett, D. S. (1984). *Advising skills, techniques, and resources.* Iowa City, IA: ACT National Center for the Advancement of Educational Practices.

eHarmony. (2013, June 3). *eHarmony ranks #1 for most online marriages and marital satisfaction in groundbreaking marriage data published in Proceedings of the National Academy of Sciences (PNAS).* Retrieved from http://www.eharmony.com/press-release/57/

Epstein, J. (2010). *The creation of enrollment management at Boston College: A history as told by the original enrollment management team.* Retrieved from Maguire Associates website: http://www.maguireassoc.com/wp-content/uploads/2012/03/Creation-of-Enrollment-Management.pdf

Forrest, A. (1982). *Increasing student competence and persistence: The best case for general education.* Iowa City, IA: ACT National Center for the Advancement of Educational Practices.

Goff, J. (2009). *Building a SEM organization.* Presentation at the annual ACT Enrollment Planners Conference, Chicago, IL. Retrieved from http://enrollment.mst.edu/presentations/

Golumbia, D. (2009). *The cultural logic of computation.* Cambridge, MA: Harvard University Press.

Grites, T. J. (1979). Academic advising: Getting us through the eighties. *AAHE-ERIC Higher Education Research Report No. 7.* Washington, DC: American Association of Higher Education.

Hanks, R. D. (2013) *Are you ready for enterprise feedback management?* Retrieved from mindshare Technologies website: http://www.mshare.net/white-papers/images/pdf/are_you_ready_for_enterprise_feedback_management.pdf

Higher Education Research Institute. (2007). *College rankings and college choice: How important are college rankings in students' college choice process?* (HERI Research Brief). Retrieved from http://www.heri.ucla.edu/PDFs/pubs/briefs/brief-081707-CollegeRankings.pdf

Hoover, E. (2011, June, 26). Those tweedy old admissions deans? They're all business now. *The Chronicle of Higher Education.* Retrieved from http://chronicle.com/article/The-Evolution-of-the/128035/

Hossler, D., & Bean, J. P. (1990). *The strategic management of college enrollments.* San Francisco, CA: Jossey-Bass.

Lenning, O. T., Beal, P. E., & Sauer, K. (1980). *Retention and attrition: Evidence for action and research.* Boulder, CO: National Institute for Higher Education Management Systems.

Mancini, M. (2009). Segmentation and customer loyalty: Using segmentation to increase customer loyalty. Retrieved from Nielsen Company website: http://www.nielsen.com/content/dam/corporate/us/en/newswire/uploads/2009/06/segmentation-and-customer-loyalty-white-paper.pdf

Manyika, J., Chui, M., Brown, B., Bughin, J. Dobbs, R., Roxburgh, C. and Byer, A. H. (2011). *Big Data: The next frontier for innovation, competition and productivity.* Retrieved from McKinsey Global Institute website: http://www.mckinsey.com/insights/business_technology/big_data_the_next_frontier_for_innovation

McDonough, P. M. (1997). *Choosing colleges: How social class and schools structure opportunity.* Albany, NY: State University of New York Press.

Miller, R. (2011, June 10). *eHarmony switches from cloud to atom servers*. Retrieved from Data Knowledge Center website: http://www.datacenterknowledge.com/archives/2011/06/10/eharmony-switches-from-cloud-to-atom-servers/

National Center for Education Statistics. (2011). Youth indicators 2011. America's youth: Transitions to Adulthood. Retrieved from NCES website: http://nces.ed.gov/pubs2012/2012026/tables/table_17a.asp

Noel-Levitz. (2013). *2013 cost of recruiting an undergraduate student report*. Retrieved from https://www.noellevitz.com/papers-research-higher-education/2013/2013-cost-of-recruiting-an-undergraduate-student-report

Pantages, T. J., & Creedon, C. F. (1978). Studies of college attrition: 1950–1975. *Review of Educational Research 48*(1), 49–101.

Pascarella, E. T. (Ed.). (1982). *Studying student attrition*. San Francisco, CA: Jossey-Bass.

Pascarella, E. T., Smart, J. C. & Ethington, D. A. (1986). Long-term persistence of two-year college students. *Research in Higher Education 24*(1), 47–71.

Chang, A. (2012, December 21). *eHarmony founder has his heart set on reviving the dating site*. Retrieved from http://phys.org/news/2012-12-eharmony-founder-heart-reviving-dating.html

Reed, M., & Cochrane, D. (2013). *Student debt and the class of 2012*. Retrieved from Institute for College Access and Success website: http://projectonstudentdebt.org/files/pub/classof2012.pdf

Ryan, C. L., & Siebens, J. (2012). *Educational attainment in the United States: 2009*. Retrieved from U.S. Census Bureau website: http://www.census.gov/prod/2012pubs/p20-566.pdf

Seidman, A. (1989). Recruitment begins with retention: Retention begins with recruitment. *Colleague*. Retrieved from Center for the Study of College Student Retention website: http://www.cscsr.org/article_recruitment_begins.htm

SPSS. (2012). Maximize customer insight to achieve your goals: What enterprise feedback management offers your organization. SPSS Executive Brief. Retrieved from http://www.techrepublic.com/resource-library/whitepapers/maximize-customer-insight-to-achieve-your-goals/

STAMATS. (2004, March 12). Teens TALK: A review of college-bound teen trends, attitudes, lifestyles, and knowledge.

PowerPoint presentation by Steve Kappler. Missouri ACT Council Conference. Columbia, MO.

Terenzini, P. T., Cabrera, A. F., & Bernal, E. M. (2001). *Swimming against the tide: The poor in American higher education* (College Board Research Report No. 2001-1). Retrieved from http://research.collegeboard.org/publications/content/2012/05/swimming-against-tide-poor-american-higher-education

Tinto, V. (1975). Dropout from higher education: A theoretical synthesis of the recent literature. *Review of Educational Research 45*, 89–125.

Tinto, V. (1987). *Leaving college: Rethinking the causes and cures of student attrition.* Chicago, IL: University of Chicago Press.

Tinto, V., & Wallace, D. L. (1986). Retention: An admission concern. *College and University Journal 61*, 290–293.

Tracey, T. J. G., Allen, J., & Robbins, S. B. (2012). Moderation of the relation between person-environment congruence and academic success: Environmental constraint, personal flexibility and method. *Journal of Vocational Behavior 80*, 38–49. doi:10.1016/j.jvb.2011.03.005

Tracey, T. J. G., & Robbins, S. B. (2006). The interest-major congruence and college success relation: A longitudinal study. *Journal of Vocational Behavior 69*, 64–89. doi:10.1016/j.jvb.2005.11.003

5

WHO IS THE BIG DATA STUDENT?

FRED FONSECA AND
MICHAEL MARCINKOWSKI

ABSTRACT

In online education today, the rise of MOOCs has highlighted the importance of Big Data for education. While a surface appeal to Big Data provides only a totalizing and averaged picture of users, Big Data can also be used to provide individual students with a personalized and authentically individual learning experience. Developing a conceptual approach for the use of Big Data in education, we utilize a Heideggerian framing in addressing the question of the individual student in order to lay out a path for the meaningful use of Big Data in education. By establishing means for student data to feed back into the design of each individual student's learning path, Big Data can be seen as more than just a static representation of student activities. As a tool for designers, Big Data is able to take on ontological import of its own and offer designers a view toward the individual student.

> Perhaps when Dasein addresses itself in the way which is closest to itself, it always says "I am this entity", and in the long run says this loudest when it is 'not' this entity.
> —Martin Heidegger, *Being and Time*

IT'S BIG DATA TIME FOR EDUCATION

As students engage with an online class, they leave a trail of data behind them. Simply by logging in, downloading an assignment, or taking a quiz, students provide an indication to course designers about what they think should be done at any particular moment. At each moment in a course, we are able to see what is commonly done (by individual students) in this or that situation. We can know if a significant group of students would read one text before another, watch a video before taking a quiz on the content, and so on. Independently, though in unison, each student makes his or her own choices that, brought together, might give precious information to course designers. It is with this knowledge that a baseline of student activity might be developed, one that provides an account of average and ordinary interactions with a course.

For instance, an online course with 25 students at the Pennsylvania State University had an average of 2.5 student interactions a day for 14 weeks. This course generated around 6,000 data collection points—6,000 data points in a class that was designed with no intentions of data collection and enrolled only 25 students. Companies such as Coursera, which might have data collection as one of its main revenue streams, collect data about student interactions at a much higher rate. If we consider a Coursera offering with an average class size of 50,000 students and a completion rate around 10%,[1] in a 14-week course we might have between 1.3 million and 12 million data collection points. This is Big Data for education.

In such a sea of data, a constant duality is in play between an image of the individual learner and the collective image of all the students in the class. The designer knows that a course is created for many students, but it is taken by each student individually. Ultimately, the experience of the learner is the experience of the individual student. However, the (Big) data collected is about the many. After all, the possibilities found in the sheer volume of the numbers are what make Big Data so appealing today. The challenge is to make the journey from the individual student—who is, for example, generating each interaction, taking each quiz, and clicking each link—to the larger group (or groups) of students—which, perhaps, spends the same amount of time on reading #3 or achieves 80% on quiz

#4—and then back to future individual learners who will take the course and benefit from a better-designed learning experience.

While a course is taken by individuals who approach learning in a subjective fashion, only objective points of data can be collected. The "I," the individual student taking the course, is more than just what may be objectively known. All students bring to bear in their work in a course their past experiences, their present engagement, and expectations for the future. The student and his or her learning experience need to be understood from a fundamentally ontological perspective. That is, instead of being understood simply in terms of the signals and surface characteristics that can be immediately identified, it is necessary to look at the more fundamental conditions, motivations, and engagements upon which student performance is founded. While data collected about student performance provides an account of the present activities of the student, it does not, in its initial and immediate form, provide the whole story of the student. A rigorous engagement with the data on the part of the educational designer is necessary in order to approach the more fundamental aspects of the individual student. What such an ontological understanding of a student provides is a holistic account of his or her engagement with the world. Rather than a factual account of each student's activities, it includes the trajectory of his or her possibilities and active engagements with the world.

This chapter develops a picture of how we can understand individual students by using Big Data. We aim to provide a theoretical and conceptual schema through which the needs of individual users can be identified through an analysis of data concerning a set of multiple users.

FINDING ONE STUDENT AMONG THOUSANDS: A HEIDEGGERIAN PERSPECTIVE

One thing that is obvious in the development of massive open online courses (MOOCs) and the data that are generated from them is the large number of students involved. In traditional classrooms, or even in more traditional modes of online education, it is relatively easy for course designers and instructors to attend to the needs of individual students in a direct way. With MOOCs, however, the scale of the courses makes this practice impossible, and it is necessary to develop new approaches to understand students through the data generated by their engagement in their courses. In this chapter, we propose a way to understand individual students within the thousands who may be taking a course.

While Big Data provides a snapshot of what is going on at any moment (or over a series of moments) during a student's learning, it is not able to capture the ontological character of each student's individual experience of online learning. This ontological perspective of the individual is what Heidegger (1962) called *Dasein*. Taken literally, Dasein means "being there" (from the German *da*, "there," and *Sein*, "being"). In colloquial German, Dasein means "existence," but Heidegger used it specifically to refer to individual human beings. He was not saying that humans have Dasein, however. Rather, he asserted that each of us is Dasein.

> We are a Dasein because of the way we exist in the world. Heidegger deliberately chose the term because of its literal connotations—Dasein always has a "there", a place in which it understands how to comport itself, and within which it has meaningful relationships to other entities. No other philosophical name for human beings—names like "subject" or "rational animal"—is quite so good at capturing what Heidegger thinks is distinctive about us: that we always find ourselves surrounded by particular objects and items of equipment, and caught up in particular activities and goals, all of which contribute to making up a particular situation. (Wrathall, 2005, p.19)

In discussing the concept of *Dasein*, Heidegger (1962) noted that it is not about what the person is in terms of actuality but what his or her ontological possibilities are. Dasein is predicated on an involved engaged interaction with the world. It is the total course of involvement of an individual's life—his or her cares, concerns, and interactions over his or her whole life toward death. Dasein is not concerned with the simple facts of any individual person; it is about the temporal relationships that are built up over the course of individuals' lives and the ways in which these progressions and relationships have a distinctly human character. The mode of human involvement with the world is distinct from that of a rock or a dog. While each has its own way of being in the world, humans have a particular way of caring about and being concerned with the world. It is this invested sense of care that provides Dasein's unique character.

In building our conceptual schema, we are posing this question to course designers about their use of student interaction data in their work: Are they using the data only as simple representations of actual occurrences, or are they able to understand the data in an ontological fashion toward an expansion of the possibilities of online learning?

To understand the difference between what Big Data is capturing through the recording of each student's interactions within a course and the extended view of the data that we are proposing, it is necessary to use two of Heidegger's concepts—the *ontic* and the *ontological*. For Heidegger, the ontic refers to the plain facts of the description of a state of affairs. Ontically, a student may be male or female, old or young. He or she may take this class or that one, perform well or poorly in either. He or she may be from Canada or Uganda, speak Persian or Italian, have graduated from high school or not. These characteristics are all ontic facts of a student.

In the classic example, ontically, a hammer is (or was) made from a piece of wood of a certain shape with a piece of metal attached at one end. When viewed as such, in Heidegger's terms, the hammer is considered to be only *present-at-hand*. Ontologically however, a hammer brings forward the possibility of the activity of hammering. When in use, the hammer is considered to be *ready-to-hand*. The ontological is not just a description of actuality but of possibility. The ontological possibilities of the world are what make the ontic actualities possible, or in Heidegger's (1997) words: "What makes the comporting towards beings (ontic knowledge) possible is the preliminary understanding of the constitution of being, ontological knowledge" (p. 7).

To draw out this ontological perspective, we propose to explain the potential of Big Data through Heidegger's concept of *Das Man*, or the collective of our ideas, norms, and ways of doing things that are so important to human understanding. First, however, we must introduce Heidegger's question regarding the "authenticity" of Dasein's actions, which lays out the ontological relation between Das Man and Dasein.

Heidegger's question of authenticity concerns the way in which Dasein may or may not engage with a situation in an authentic manner. For Dasein, acting authentically means that Dasein approaches the possibilities of a situation in such a manner that Dasein's decisions within that context are made on the basis of Dasein's own experiences and personal trajectory through the world over time. If Dasein does not act in this manner, it is said to have fallen into averageness. While the exact relationship of (and ultimate implications for) this movement between averageness and authenticity has been (and remains to be) a point of contention (Carman, 1994; Dreyfus, 1995; Olafson, 1994), what is important here is that Heidegger gives a name to that which steps in for Dasein as it falls away from authenticity and into averageness: Das Man.

Alternatively translated as "the One" or "the They," Das Man functions to relieve Dasein of its decision-making responsibility, providing an account for what *should* be done in any given situation so that Dasein need not make its own choices. In relying on Das Man rather than its own, uniquely situated faculties, Dasein falls into averageness and away from authenticity. In ceding the opportunity to make authentic choices, Dasein simply follows along with what "one" would do in any given situation. Instead of following its own unique path, Dasein acts in an average fashion and does what "they" would do in any situation. Das Man does not function as a universal subject that actually makes decisions. Rather, it is a necessary constituent part of Dasein that makes social interactions possible. By laying out average approaches to the world, Das Man pushes Dasein away from authentic action and authenticity but also provides necessary insight into how others approach the world. To what degree such averageness is necessary for social action is open for debate, but what is clear is that in Dasein's authentic decisions, there is nevertheless a reliance on the kind of shared meaning that Das Man provides.

UNDERSTANDING THE STUDENT AS DASEIN

Central to the question of how to engage individual students in online education is the question of how we should understand online learners themselves. Instead of approaching users as simply represented in points of data, in this chapter we develop a fuller picture of the online learner, one that is based on the Heideggerian conception of the human being, Dasein. A more robust understanding of human beings is called for, particularly in that online learners are much more than just individuals who are engaged in an online class: They all have reasons and motives for engaging with the material of the course that extend well beyond their interactions in the course itself.

It is useful to contrast a rigorously developed picture of Dasein (as defined in Heidegger's work) with a simplified caricature of human activity that, while ultimately inaccurate, provides a sometimes necessary simplification of human beings and as such often remains as a pervasive ideological backdrop. This caricature presents a human being only in terms of its qualities, as a static collection of data points that may be accurately, and meaningfully, described. From this assertion it then follows that human behavior may be meaningfully and wholly understood through the analysis of data. At bottom, this atomistic and Cartesian understanding of individuals fails to offer a realistic picture of human activity (Dreyfus, 1991).

In contrast, we propose the ontological view of human beings as developed by Heidegger (1962), understanding the human being as Dasein. For Heidegger, Dasein is the existential possibility of human beings. Rather than being concerned with the ontic facts and details of the human being, Dasein is concerned with the ontological setting of the human being, the way in which the individual makes meaningful sense of the world in an engaged and situated fashion. In its constitution and in the accounting of what it is, Dasein is defined by its engagement with the world. This engagement with the world is one of a fundamental state of care and investment in the world. It is not possible to separate the individual from the context of its actions and the possibilities that accompany such a context. While we acknowledge that characteristics do exist, and individuals may be described by these characteristics with a certain modicum of accuracy, we assert that prior to the possibility of any such description there exists an ontological determination of the field of possibilities. That is, previous to a descriptive and ontic account of human beings is an ontological account of Dasein. As Heidegger (1962) explained:

Theoretically concocted "explanations" of the Being-present-at-hand of Others urge themselves upon us all too easily; but over against such explanations we must hold fast to the phenomenal facts of the case which we have pointed out, namely, that Others are encountered environmentally. This elemental worldly kind of encountering, which belongs to Dasein and is closest to it, goes so far that even one's own Dasein becomes something that it can itself proximally "come across" only when it looks away from "Experiences" and the "centre of its actions," or does not as yet "see" them at all. Dasein finds "itself" proximally in what it does, uses, expects, avoids in those things environmentally ready-to-hand with which it is proximally concerned. (p. 155)

As such, here we are concerned with this formulation of the human being: as Dasein, as that which is previous to, and ultimately determinate of, the ontic actuality of the student. After all, "[h]igher than actuality stands *possibility*" (Heidegger, 1962, p. 63). We are interested in the development of the possibilities contained in individual students as they are engaged in online education and so must look beyond an ontic description of each student.

BIG DATA IN EDUCATION

Online education produces a lot of data. Even traditional models of online education, when considered previous to the characterization of being "massive," produced a wealth of data about students and the ways in which they interact with courses. Now, MOOCs—with their ability to attract thousands of students to a single course—are able to generate tremendous amounts of data about how students learn, both in regard to the particular course and in general.

Having access to a large amount of user data allows instructors and designers to understand students' progress in courses, identify when a lesson is not being understood, and know which resources are being used and how. Online education offers the chance to understand how students engage with a course, compare the statistics generated from one course with another, and test different approaches, all the while obtaining empirical data about student behaviors and performance.

As has been shown in disciplines ranging from biology to climate science to astronomy (Frankel & Reid, 2008), Big Data has the potential to transform understandings and to revolutionize disciplines.

What is unique about the domain of online education is that the data collected provide a representation of human activities and understandings. In this context, Big Data is not about the natural world but about us.

In particular, what distinguishes online education's use of large-scale data from the natural sciences' use of them is that in the case of education, it is possible (and we will argue here, necessary) to intervene on the basis of conclusions drawn from the data. In the natural sciences, Big Data is particularly useful because once a data set is collected, it can be reused in a number of different areas (Lynch, 2008). For instance, in the case of the human genome, once a genomic data set has been established, its relative stability allows it to be used in other research projects. Data from online education, however, might not be so lasting. Different teaching approaches address different students at different times and thus yield different sets of data. As data collected from online education are analyzed, designers and educators will develop new education strategies that will produce new data sets. Unlike the data collected in the natural sciences, what online education data tell us changes with each intervention, and in online education, the perpetual goal is to develop new modes of educational intervention.

With this distinction, we must carefully and deliberately approach the picture of students that is developed through the data collected from online education. Specifically, we must explore how the unique aspects of human learners can be represented in Big Data and these aspects can be understood.

WHAT IS SO DIFFERENT ABOUT BIG DATA?

While there is no question of its impact, there is still "no clear consensus on what Big Data is" (Labrinidis & Jagadish, 2012, p. 2032). Despite this lack of agreement, it can be said for certain that the characterization of Big Data goes well beyond a simple account of the size of the data set. As the history of computing has shown, what may be defined as a large data set in one era appears insignificant in the next (boyd & Crawford, 2012).

Big Data is defined not just by the *volume* of the data but also by the *variety* and *velocity* of the data (Hendler, 2013; Laney, 2001; Russom, 2011). The volume of the data can be understood as a characteristic of sheer size: the tera-, peta-, or exabytes of data present (Hendler, 2013) or the size of database tables or number of records (Russom, 2011). The variety of the data refers to the way structured and unstructured data might exist alongside semi-structured data and each other (Russom, 2011), with text data mixed in with video data. Finally, the velocity of data refers to the way in which the data in Big Data are collected from constant streams from sensors and online interactions. Velocity is what provides Big Data with its dynamic power—that it is able to be understood as representative of changing conditions of human activity.

As useful as the "three Vs" of Big Data (volume, variety, velocity) are for expanding our understanding of Big Data beyond a simple account of the sheer size of the data sets involved, such a high-level definition obscures the analytic work that goes into Big Data. As boyd and Crawford (2012) observed, "Big Data is less about data that is big than it is about a capacity to search, aggregate, and cross-reference large data sets" (p. 663). Specifically, boyd and Crawford proposed that the real definition of Big Data comes from our technological ability to analyze large data sets to achieve a supposed "higher form of intelligence and knowledge that can generate insights that were previously impossible, with the aura of truth, objectivity, and accuracy" (p. 663). This assertion is consistent with the sentiment that "the greatest shared challenge was not only engineering Big Data, but also doing so meaningfully" (Bizer et al., 2012, p. 56).

In essence, Big Data "refers to enormous amounts of unstructured data produced by high-performance applications falling in a wide and heterogeneous family of application scenarios: from scientific computing applications to social networks, from e-government applications to medical information systems" (Cuzzocrea, Song, & Davis, 2011, p. 101). Just as there is an emphasis on the heterogeneity and volume of the data in Big Data, there is also an emphasis on the heterogeneity of uses and the different ways in which they may be leveraged and analyzed as they are put to work.

What needs to be emphasized here is that there is no one definition or characteristic of Big Data. All definitions, however, point to an amorphous set of conditions (an ever-changing definition of size, the kinds of analysis necessary, etc.) that are able to be called Big Data only by virtue of what we want to get out of them. Big Data is made, in effect, by our relation to it and is not anything ontological by itself. It comes into being through analysis. The task, therefore, is to look at Big Data as a tool that we use—and as nothing else.

BIG HUMAN DATA

Again, what is central to the present discussion of Big Data is that we are concerned with human data, which are distinct from the kind of data collected in the natural sciences. While one of the key advantages of Big Data in the natural sciences is that it is portable and once collected may be applied to numerous settings, Big *Human* Data— such as that collected in a MOOC—faces the same challenge as other sociological data: It is open to the recursive effect of the data on the subjects of the data. Especially in the case of design work, patterns of behavior that may be true today may not be true tomorrow following some intervention (Carroll, Kellogg, & Rosson, 1991). This challenge is particularly relevant to the role that Big Data can play in the design of online systems such as MOOCs.

While some relatively stable and generalizable insights into low-level patterns of learning behavior (Cooper & Sahami, 2013) may be developed out of data collected from students, Big Data's real value in education comes in how it can be brought directly to bear on the educational process. Through its dynamic nature (or velocity), Big Data informs the educational experience of the very students who are generating the data. When Big Data is introduced into the process of designing online courses, it becomes possible to build courses around students, based on their individual experiences and data. As the data can be used to modify a course as it is being run, it becomes part of the experience of the course. Big Data in education has a double nature: It simultaneously provides generalized insights concerning all students and offers specific insights into the progress and paths of individual students.

The fact that in these situations Big Human Data is tied to the historical progression and situation of its collection reinforces the need to account for it in an ontological manner. It does not just function as an ontic representation of the facts of the situation. Instead, it has the potential to play a dynamic and ontological role in the process of course design. Its importance is not in its ontic abstraction away from the wider world in which it is embedded but in the way in which it is ontologically integrated into the whole of the process of design and use as found in online education. In its temporal aspects (both in terms of its velocity and possibility of recursive application), Big Human Data can be leveraged by online course designers in an ontological fashion to alter students' experiences of education in a real and positive way.

TAKING THE ANALYSIS OF BIG DATA FROM THE ONTIC TO THE ONTOLOGICAL: FINDING DASEIN AMONG DAS MAN

By itself, data concerning an individual student cannot provide any ontological insight into the development of an individual student as Dasein. While information pertaining to individual students might be helpful for educators in a small class, extracting all student profiles from a course of 100,000 students would not facilitate the work of an education designer. At such a scale, the individual consideration of each student is simply unmanageable. Sampling a handful of profiles or concocting an averaged picture of the student population of 100,000 would not help the designer either, as such approaches would miss the individual student as Dasein.

However, more than just presenting students as a simple, aggregated, and nameless whole, Big Data gives us a representation of the student body as it is constituted of individual students and their individual interactions. What we see in the data are not students acting consciously together as a group but individuals acting independently within a common field of possibilities.

Looked at directly, the raw picture of students and their groups provided by Big Data is unable to provide an ontological view of either Das Man or Dasein. While Big Data is able to provide an aggregated snapshot of each student, this snapshot is not a representation of Dasein: Even though a student's individual activities can be seen in the data, his or her ontological intentions and motivations as Dasein are not. Similarly, even the understanding of Das Man offered through Big Data is not able to achieve an ontological status since it only has a tenuous relationship to the lived experiences of individuals, however average Das Man may appear.

Big Data is, however, able to give a limited, ontic representation of Das Man by virtue of the way Dan Man functions as a collective orientation toward the world. Specifically, it offers a picture of what individual students do in this or that situation given the possibilities presented by an online course. It is possible to see the way in which students, while acting independently, still share common approaches to the materials in a course. In this way, an ontic representation of Das Man can be understood: To a certain degree, students all interact with a course as it *should* be interacted with. Here, Big Data does not give an ontological account of what the students do, only an ontic one that traces an outline of the ways their behaviors signal a common and shared understanding. At the same time, Big Data is also able to give a series of retrospective ontic snapshots of the ontological activities of Dasein. The wholly individual and historically situated actions of Dasein, however, remain opaque to any data-driven analysis, even as students' activities may be considered on an individual level.

As was noted previously, the picture of Das Man found in the data "is not something like a 'universal subject' which a plurality of subjects have hovering above them" (Heidegger, 1962, p. 166), nor is it simply a larger category or "the genus to which the individual Dasein belongs" (Heidegger, 1962, p. 166). Das Man and the picture given by Big Data are constituted by the actions of individuals as seen in aggregate. To understand Das Man and Big Data in this way is to have "an ontology of the present-at-hand" (Heidegger, 1962, pp. 166–167) rather than the deeper ontological view that makes understanding Dasein possible. It is this deeper, ontological view of Dasein and Das Man that we are looking for in order to be able to design authentic learning experiences. In particular, beyond gaining an ontological insight, we look toward the question of how to distinguish Dasein from any understanding of Das Man.

The limited and ontically representative view found in Big Data is, of course, anathema to the fundamentally temporal and situated way in which Dasein functions. In Big Data, we are only given glimpses into the activities of Dasein, while to really understand Dasein what is needed is a constant and holistic understanding of Dasein as it *carefully* navigates the possibilities offered to it by the world. Dasein—and the insight into it that might be found in Big Data—can only be understood in the specific situation of its immediate context. To look at it any other way distorts this fundamental understanding of how we are to conceive of human beings.

To establish a means by which to draw from Big Data an understanding of the Dasein of students, it is useful to consider the way in which Dreyfus (1991) approached the positive role of Das Man, albeit from a different direction. For Dreyfus, rather than seeing Das Man as purely a limiting image that functions to only drag Dasein down into averageness, Das Man also constitutes the field from which Dasein is able to reach up toward authentic and creative action. For Dreyfus (1991), that Das Man gives everyday guidance to Dasein does

> not mean . . . that the roles, norms, etc., available to Dasein are fixed once and for all. New technological and social developments are constantly changing specific ways for Dasein to be. Nor does it mean that there is no room for an individual or political group to develop new possibilities, which could then become available to the society. But it does mean that such "creativity" always takes place on a background of what one does—of accepted for-the-sake-of-whichs that cannot all be called into question at once because they are not presuppositions and in any case must remain in the background to lend intelligibility to criticism and change. Just as it is possible to find something occurrent and then give it a use, but only on the background of shared practical activities, so here too we have a case where ontic activity can create a new role or meaning, but only against an ontological background that is not subject to willed change. This sociocultural background too can change gradually, as does a language, but never all at once and never as the result of the conscious decision of groups or individuals. (p. 161)

In considering Big Data, however, we are faced with the inverse problem. Rather than being interested in understanding forward-looking creativity, we are looking backward at how, out of a fixed background of ontic information (the data), we might be able to reconstitute, in some form, the ontological movements of Dasein. Instead of refiguring ontic cultural activities against "an ontological background that is not subjected to willed change," we are faced with the question of how to draw Dasein out from the obfuscation of a mass of ontic data.

Toward this end, two insights are particularly powerful. The first comes in the way in which Heidegger (1962) characterized Dasein:

> Dasein is an entity which does not just occur among other entities. Rather it is ontically distinguished by the fact that, in its very being, that being is an *issue* for it. But in that case, this is a constitutive state of Dasein's Being, and this implies that Dasein, in its Being, has a relationship towards that Being—a relationship which itself is one of Being. And this means further that there is some way in which Dasein understands itself in its Being, and that to some degree it does so explicitly. It is peculiar to this entity that with and through its Being, this being is disclosed to it. Understanding of Being is itself a definite characteristic of Dasein's Being. Dasein is ontically distinctive in that it is ontological. (p. 32)

In other words, "Dasein's activity—its way of being—manifests a stand it is taking on what it is to be Dasein" (Dreyfus, 1991, p. 15). Dasein is what it is in the way that it is self-interpreting (Dreyfus, 1991). For us, what this assertion indicates is that a purely data-centric view of Dasein cannot be achieved. We must always have the input from Dasein in order to recognize Dasein. There will never be an objective set of data in which it is possible to see Dasein.

The second insight comes in the way in which Dasein can be "ontically distinguished by the fact that, in its very being, that being is an *issue* for it" (Heidegger, 1962, p. 32). The relationship between Dasein and the world is one of care. Dasein, in whatever it does, rests on the condition of possibility of a caring engagement with the world. This is not an ontic care, such as whether my favorite baseball team has a winning season this year but rather an ontological care, one that without which I would not be able to say whether baseball even exists. Dasein's care for the world is indicative of its involvement with the fundamental issue of the Being of the world. To distinguish Dasein from the ontic representation of Das Man in Big Data, it is necessary to, in some way, engage Dasein so as to reveal its caring orientation toward the world.

Combining these insights, a direction for understanding the Dasein of students through Big Data begins to develop, one centered on the designer's active engagement with the data in the design process.

If designers (each in their own Dasein) interact with the ontic representations provided by the data in such a way that they are able to engage the caring nature of students' Dasein, students' Dasein begins to be distinguished from the ontic representation of Das Man so evident in the data.

BIG DATA IMPLICATIONS FOR THE DESIGN OF EDUCATION

Such a representation of Das Man, taken as just a representation, does not, however, provide an ontological account of the student. In order to achieve an ontological account, one that considers the possibilities of individual students, it is necessary to use Big Data captured from MOOCs in a way that affects students' experiences within the online learning context. Big Data is understood ontologically through the way it is meaningfully put to use (Bizer et al., 2012; boyd & Crawford, 2012). Through this meaningful use, Big Data becomes doubly ontological. First, as designers engage the data as resources with which they interact and integrate into their work—rather than as simply theoretical information that provides a descriptive understanding—Big Data reveals its ontological character as something in the world. In this way, as in Heidegger's (1962) example of working with a hammer, Big Data is not limited to being descriptive data; it becomes enmeshed in the possibilities of the intent of the designer's work. To an extent, the designer forgets the data as data, and they are instead just part of their work as a designer, creating systems for education. To use Heideggerian terminology, Big Data becomes "ready-to-hand" for designers as they enter into the kind of seamless engagement described earlier.

Second, through the designer's ready-to-hand use of it, Big Data collected from students exceeds the purely ontic description of Das Man that it initially provides, and, through the designers' integration of the data into the experiences of students, the initially ontic descriptions of Das Man take on an ontological character. That is, as designers use Big Data to intervene in the progress of a course (making changes to the course in medias res), and the data, as reflections of student action, become entangled in the ways in which students are confronted with possibilities in a course, the data come to play, in a meta-ontological sense, a role in the emerging possibilities of student action. Key here is the kind of velocity that Big Data is able to attain and how designers are able to tap into the data as ready-to-hand tools and effect change in the progress of a course.

For individual students, as the Big Data collected about their activities (as ontic representation of a collective impulse) is put to use, the effect of the designers' work with their data comes to function as a sort of call and response. In this way, there is a sort of inverse of the relationship that designers have with the data. As designers approach the data in a ready-to-hand fashion, using them as tools to make active interventions in the course, the students feel these effects in a substantive way. From the perspective of the designer, it is not the individual student who is subject to the changes, nor is it the individual student who responds to the changes and whose activities are altered by the new possibilities offered in the design. Neither is it the individual student who is seen in the data. Rather, designers find themselves engaged only with Das Man. While individual students, in their own private actions, confront the new possibilities offered by changes in a design, these responses are only seen by designers when individual students, through their autonomous action, come to shape Das Man.

In looking beyond this exchange for the possibility of an ontological approach to student data, one that addresses Dasein more so than just the Das Man of the students, Descartes's (2001) example of a blind man's use of his cane as an extension of his sensory apparatus is helpful. In grasping the cane and running it along the ground, a person without sight, despite the cane's artificial mediation, still receives ontological signification of the ground through the cane, without being concerned with the ontic representation. The cane does not provide a picture of the ground for the person walking along; it simply provides an understanding of the terrain. In Heideggerian terms, the cane, as being ready-to-hand, comes into proximal being with the person using the cane. In a sense, the cane becomes an extension of the person feeling his or her way along, providing the linkage between the sensing subject and the object of touch.

Placing this metaphor within a Heideggerian unification of subject and object in Dasein, when students are, in a sense, poked through the interventions of the designer (as their work is based on the Big Data collected from students), students' reactions, however they may fall under the guidance and rubric of Das Man, become temporalized along the continuum of the data collection. This relationship is the case no matter how small a slice of the total appreciation of the historical and personal tradition and experience of students is at stake. No matter the scale, when all are brought together into this temporal circuit of monitoring and effect, the students, the data, and the designers all coalesce into an ontological picture of activity in the truest sense: They are neither individual designers, bits of data, nor students. Instead, they constitute the body of ontological online education. In this way, the ontic representation of Das Man is able to be turned into an important and ontological part of the system of online education, one that brings individual students to confront the implications of Das Man in a way rarely made more overt. The "stick" of the data concerning the ontic representation of Das Man gives designers a chance to come into an ontological relationship with the students.

This outcome is achieved through the studied and skillful work of the designers as they modulate the collection of data, as it pertains to all students, with an attention toward the function of the data of each individual student. In this manner, the larger set of data concerning the whole of the student-user base is, through the intuitive work of the designer, applied in a sparing manner to the design in ways that allow for the picture of Das Man represented in the data to fulfill its positive role of enabling a coherent social communication and an intelligibility of use. That is, there are some aspects of online education that would be common to all students, such as the size of buttons or the organization of course information. Data from individual students, though still contributing to the wider picture of the representation of Das Man, are also simultaneously approached as indicating toward the path of the individual student and are seen as ontically representative of only the individual student.

However, when the data are used as ready-to-hand tools, a subtle transformation takes place in the way in which the representation of the individual student is able to function. Instead of being an abstracted and reduced representation of their activities, the information can be tied back into their interaction with a MOOC and the whole of their experience of online education in such a way that it plays a real and ontological role in their development as a student. By establishing means for the data to feed back into the design of each individual student's learning path, the data are no longer simply a representation but something with ontological import of its own. As Big Data is utilized to modify the course, and additional data are collected and the cycle of data collection is repeated, the data take on a lived relation to the Dasein of the student and become bound up with him or her. As Heidegger (1962) described it:

> In our "description" of that environment which is closest to us—the work-world of the craftsman, for example,—the outcome was that along with the equipment to be found when one is at work, those Others for whom the "work" is destined are "encountered too." If this is ready-to-hand, then there lies in the kind of Being which belongs to it (that is, in its involvement) an essential assignment or reference to possible wearers, for instance, whom it should be "cut to the figure." Similarly, when material is put to use, we encounter its producer or "supplier" as one who "serves" well or badly. (p. 153)

For designers, the online student has the double relation of both "those Others for whom the 'work' is destined" and the "producer or 'supplier'" of the data used in the work of design. Used as such, the Big Human Data collected from students brings designers to encounter the Being (the Dasein) of the students.

Through this process, what could be taken as an ontic representation of the collective sense of Das Man, as an index of what should be done at any point in an online course, is made into a living, ontological engagement with the Dasein of individual students—one that addresses the individual learner as an ontological entity. What is central in this approach is that the Big Data collected from users is not viewed as a symbolic representation of the state of affairs as it is but rather as a derivative representation that, as a tool for designers, is itself part of the experience of the learner. The representative stance of the data undergoes an ontological shift when it is understood and used as such. It is the task of the designer to approach and work with Big Data in such a way that the data are handled as part of the extended possibility of students—that the data are not something distant from the students but that are connected to their online interaction, able to flow back to them in the form of a reshaped and changing course.

CONCLUSION: GIVING STUDENTS THE POSSIBILITY OF AN AUTHENTIC COURSE

When students are understood as individuals, with unique trajectories in the world, the data collected from their online course interactions presents a unique opportunity for designing online education. Imagine what is seen as the gold standard of education: one-on-one personal instruction from a qualified instructor. In this context, designers and instructors are able to respond to a student's developing needs, offer suggestions and assistance as it is needed, and give the student enough space to learn on his or her own. In this way, the student is allowed to respond to the lessons totally from his or her own perspective, in an authentic manner through which each response opens up new possibilities for learning.

At first glance, MOOC education seems to be radically different from this picture of one-on-one education. Not only are instructors and designers dealing with thousands of students, but their interactions are dependent on the large sets of data generated by student activity. For us, the goal is to understand how to use Big Data in online education in such a way that the developing possibilities for students, as individual learners, are addressed. The Big Data generated through MOOCs should not be seen as only providing a static snapshot of what is going on in a class or with an individual student. The data need to be understood as giving a keyhole view into the full experience of a student, one that is predicated on the opening horizons of possibility rather than one that limits and averages students' possibilities. The negative aspects of the collective representation in the data that limits students to an average path should be avoided, and the possibilities of each student's individual trajectory need to be taken seriously. The data need to be understood as tools by which designers can appreciate the authentic choices made by students as they interact with an online course. If the designers use the data as instruments with which they can engage with the varied and developing situations in which students find themselves, they can better offer students authentic learning experiences. A set of a thousand test scores alone is not able to give instructors and designers deep insight into students, but when those scores are coupled with other scores over time, and this larger set is understood in relation to the reflective activities of the designer, deep insight into the students can begin to emerge. By approaching the data itself as an active part of the design process and establishing connections between the causes of design and the effects seen in the data, students can over time be brought into a dialogic engagement with courses.

There are two directions for online education. In the first, students are kept to prescribed paths and courses that remain static. Here, data are understood as representing students as they are and only how they are seen in aggregate with other students. In the second, individual paths through dynamic courses are open to students. Here, through a proper understanding of the way in which Big Data gives an averaged representation of the student activity as a whole, designers are able to approach an ontological account of individual students as Dasein.

NOTES

1. See http://www.katyjordan.com/MOOCproject.html for MOOC completion rate data.

REFERENCES

Bizer, C., Boncz, P., Brodie, M. L., & Erling, O. (2012). The meaningful use of Big Data: Four perspectives—four challenges. *SIG-MOD Record 40*(4), 56–60. Retrieved from http://www.sigmod.org/publications/sigmod-record/1112/pdfs/10.report.bizer.pdf

boyd, d., & Crawford, K. (2012). Critical questions for Big Data: Provocations for a cultural, technological, and scholarly phenomenon. *Information, Communication & Society 15*(5), 662–679. doi:10.1080/1369118x.2012.678878

Carman, T. (1994). On being social: A reply to Olafson. *Inquiry 37*(2), 203–233. doi:10.1080/00201749408602349

Carroll, J. M., Kellogg, W. A., & Rosson, M. B. (1991). The task-artifact cycle. In J. M. Carroll (Ed.), *Designing interaction: Psychology at the human-computer interface* (pp. 74–102). Cambridge, UK: Cambridge University Press.

Cooper, S., & Sahami, M. (2013). Reflections on Stanford's MOOCs. *Communications of the ACM 56*(2), 28–30. doi:10.1145/2408776.2408787

Cuzzocrea, A., Song, I.-Y., & Davis, K. C. (2011). Analytics over large-scale multidimensional data: The Big Data revolution! In *Proceedings of the ACM 14th international workshop on data warehousing and OLAP*. New York, NY: ACM. doi: 10.1145/2064676.2064695

Descartes, R. (2001). *Discourse on method, optics, geometry, and meteorology*. Indianapolis, IN: Hackett.

Dreyfus, H. L. (1991). *Being-in-the-world: A commentary on Heidegger's "being and time," division I*. Cambridge, MA: MIT Press.

Dreyfus, H. L. (1995). Interpreting Heidegger on Das Man. *Inquiry* 38(4), 423–430. doi:10.1080/00201749508602398

Frankel, F., & Reid, R. (2008). Big Data: Distilling meaning from data. *Nature 455*(7209), 30. doi: 10.1038/455030a

Heidegger, M. (1962). *Being and time*. (J. Macquarrie & E. Robinson, Trans.). New York, NY: Harper. (Original work published 1927.)

Heidegger, M. (1997). *Kant and the problem of metaphysics* (5th ed.). (R. Taft, Trans.). Bloomington, IN: Indiana University Press. (Original work published 1929.)

Hendler, J. (2013). Broad data: Exploring the emerging web of data. *Big Data 1*(1), 18–20. doi:10.1089/big.2013.1506

Labrinidis, A., & Jagadish, H. (2012). Challenges and opportunities with Big Data. *Proceedings of the VLDB Endowment 5*(12), 2032–2033.

Laney, D. (2001). 3D data management: Controlling data volume, velocity, and variety. Retrieved from Gartner website: http://blogs.gartner.com/doug-laney/files/2012/01/ad949-3D-Data-Management-Controlling-Data-Volume-Velocity-and-Variety.pdf

Lynch, C. (2008). How do your data grow? *Nature 455*(7209), 28–29. doi:10.1038/455028a

Olafson, F. A. (1994). Heidegger à la Wittgenstein or "coping" with Professor Dreyfus. *Inquiry 37*(1), 45–64. doi:10.1080/00201749408602339

Russom, P. (2011). *Big Data analytics: TDWI best practices report, fourth quarter*. Renton, WA: TDWI Research.

Wrathall, M. A. (2005). *How to read Heidegger*. New York, NY: W. W. Norton.

6

NUDGE NATION

A New Way to Use Data to Prod Students into and through College[1]

BEN WILDAVSKY

ABSTRACT

There is increasing interest in the power of digital nudges to influence how we shop, think, behave, and educate. While online education and software-driven pedagogy on college campuses have received a good deal of attention, a less visible set of technology-driven initiatives also has gained a foothold: behavioral nudges designed to keep students on track to succeed. Just as e-commerce entrepreneurs have drawn on massive troves of consumer data to create algorithms for firms such as Netflix and Amazon to personalize and influence the shopping experience of their customers, architects of campus technology nudges also rely on data analytics or data mining to improve the student experience. This chapter explores the ways in which digital nudges can help students persist through college and strengthen their ability to be academically successful.

When Harvard law professor Cass Sunstein took his teenage daughter to the Lollapalooza music festival during a Chicago heat wave some years ago, the huge electronic displays that typically show performance schedules also flashed periodic admonitions:

DRINK MORE WATER. YOU SWEAT IN THE HEAT: YOU LOSE WATER. "The sign was a nudge," wrote Sunstein and his coauthor Richard Thaler, one of many described in their bestselling book, *Nudge* (Thaler & Sunstein, 2008, pp. 243–244). Without coercing concertgoers to behave in a certain way, the sign provided information designed to prompt them to make wiser decisions—increasing their water intake to prevent dehydration.

Thanks in part to Thaler and Sunstein's (2009) work, the power of nudges has become well established—including in higher education. While online education and software-driven pedagogy on college campuses have received a good deal of attention, a less visible set of technology-driven initiatives also has gained a foothold: behavioral nudges designed to keep students on track to succeed. Just as e-commerce entrepreneurs have drawn on massive troves of consumer data to create algorithms for firms such as Netflix and Amazon—which unbundle the traditional storefront consumer experience through customized, online delivery—architects of campus technology nudges also rely on data analytics or data mining to improve the student experience. By giving students information-driven suggestions that lead to smarter actions, technology nudges are intended to tackle a range of problems surrounding the process by which students begin college and make their way to graduation.

New approaches are certainly needed. Just 59% of full-time, first-time college students at four-year institutions complete a degree within six years (National Center for Education Statistics, 2013). Among Hispanics, blacks, and students at two-year colleges, the figures are much worse. In all, more than 400,000 students drop out every year (Selingo, 2013, p. viii). At a time when postsecondary credentials are more important than ever, around 37 million Americans report their highest level of education as "some college, no degree" (Kamenetz, 2012).

There are many reasons for low rates of persistence and graduation, including financial problems; the difficulty of juggling nonacademic responsibilities such as work and family; and, for some first-generation students in particular, culture shock. Academic engagement and success are also major contributors, which is why colleges are using behavioral nudges, drawing on data analytics and behavioral psychology, to focus on problems that occur along the academic pipeline such as:

- Poor student organization around the logistics of going to college
- Unwise course selections that increase the risk of failure and extend time to degree
- Inadequate information about academic progress and the need for academic help
- Unfocused support systems that identify struggling students but do not directly engage with them
- Difficulty tapping into counseling services

These new ventures, whether originating within colleges or created by outside entrepreneurs, are doing things with data that just could not be done in the past—creating giant databases of student course records, for example, to find patterns of success and failure that result when certain kinds of students take certain kinds of courses. Like many other technology initiatives, these ventures are relatively young, and much remains to be learned about how they can become most effective. Already, however, nudge designers are having a good deal of success marrying knowledge of human behavior with the capacity of technology to reach students at larger scale, and lower cost, than would be possible in person.

COOLING "SUMMER MELT"

For education researcher Benjamin Castleman, the idea of using technology nudges to keep teenagers on track to college was a logical extension of his thinking about adolescent cognitive development. For several years he and his colleagues had conducted experiments gauging the effectiveness of various interventions designed to prevent "summer melt," the troubling phenomenon in which high school graduates, who have been accepted to a college and plan to attend, never show up in the fall. Summer melt affects 10% to 20% of teens nationally, and the numbers are higher among low-income, first-generation college teenagers. After counselors in the summer melt experiments reported that texting was by far the most effective way to set up counseling sessions with students, Castleman, who is finalizing his Harvard Graduate School of Education doctoral dissertation and recently joined the faculty of the University of Virginia, realized that making even greater use of texting would capitalize on adolescent impulsiveness.

As a one-time high school teacher, Castleman said in an interview, he knew that if students are given the choice between "wading through a bunch of [college-entry] paperwork they find confusing, without any help," or hanging out with friends and working at summer jobs, they tend to put off important precollege tasks until too late in the summer. Why not turn teenage impulsiveness into an asset by allowing students to complete key precollege tasks immediately from their mobile phones?[2] Castleman did just that in a 2012 summer experiment with his collaborator Lindsay Page, a researcher at Harvard's Center for Education Policy Research. In randomized experiments involving thousands of low-income students in the Dallas Independent School District and districts in the Massachusetts cities of Boston, Lawrence, and Springfield, researchers sent personalized texts to recent high school graduates in the treatment groups to remind them about tasks such as registering for freshman orientation and placement tests. The texts offered help with deciphering financial aid letters and more. The project was coordinated with the colleges that most district graduates attend, so the reminders and accompanying web links took students to the right places to complete tasks and were tailored to specific deadlines and requirements of each student's intended school. Interestingly, although each text offered the option to connect students to live counselors for personalized assistance, relatively few students (just 6% in Dallas) sought this help. Results were striking. Just 10 to 12 text messages sent to low-income students over the summer raised college enrollment by more than four percentage points among low-income students in Dallas and by more than seven percentage points in Lawrence and Springfield. Castleman noted that the texting intervention had no impact in Boston, where students can access a wide range of college-planning support services both during the school year and during the summer after graduation. The total cost of this technology nudge was $7 per student, including the cost of counselors' time.

Why was the intervention so effective? "The summer is a uniquely nudge-free time in students' educational trajectory," said Castleman. Given that so many college-intending adolescents receive few reminders about completing key tasks—and that so many are prone to procrastination—well-designed prompts can fill a void. According to Castleman, "The text intervention has the potential to be several times more cost-effective at increasing college entry among students from disadvantaged backgrounds than other comparable interventions," such as additional college counseling during the summer after high school graduation.

Castleman's study surely will not be the last word on summer melt. Many factors prevent disadvantaged students from enrolling in college; Castleman, Page, and many other researchers continue to explore numerous ideas for tackling those barriers. As policy makers seek to improve college-going rates, however, a cheap, scalable, personalized, technology-based intervention such as the Castleman-Page texting campaign seems to have a lot of appeal.

CHOOSING THE RIGHT COURSES

Getting students through the campus gates is just the first step. New undergraduates must make course-selection decisions that have significant implications for their future persistence and success, yet they do not always receive the best advice. Many low-income and first-generation students cannot rely on guidance from family members, and all undergraduates must rely on faculty and staff advisers who do not necessarily do a good job helping them puzzle through the course catalogue to discern which classes, taken in which order, make the most sense on the way to fulfilling requirements and maximizing the likelihood of academic success.

These problems, according to Tristan Denley, provost and vice president for academic affairs at Austin Peay State University in Tennessee, are among the reasons that nationwide on average bachelor's degree students take 14% more courses than they need to graduate. This practice wastes resources, leads to a longer time to degree, and puts students at risk for not graduating at all. Denley, a mathematician who arrived at Austin Peay in January 2009 from the University of Mississippi (and is now vice chancellor for academic affairs at the Tennessee Board of Regents), set out to tackle the course-selection challenge as part of a broader look at how Austin Peay could make better use of data to maximize student success.

The idea for a new system came to Denley while he was traveling in Europe and reading three books: *Super Crunchers* (Ayres, 2007), which describes how bodies of data can shed light on decision making across disciplines; *Moneyball*, the Michael Lewis (2003) book about how Billy Beane, the general manager of the Oakland A's, used a revamped statistical analysis of the optimal way to assemble a successful team; and *Nudge* (Thaler & Sunstein, 2008). He realized, Denley said in a telephone interview, that "data-informed choice architecture" could help students make better course selections. "Every campus is sitting on terabytes of historical grade data. It's just a matter of . . . can you take that data, analyze it in the right kind of way, and communicate it?"

Denley did just that, creating the Degree Compass system, which combines data mining and behavior nudges to match students with "best-fit" courses. It draws on data from hundreds of thousands of past students, scrutinizing their classes, grades, and majors. Then it gives current students—and their advisers—course recommendations based on how well similar undergraduates with similar course-taking histories have performed in the past. In certain respects, it is similar to the you-might-also-like choices on Netflix, Amazon, and Pandora. But, Degree Compass is less concerned with students' likes and dislikes than with predictive analytics—calculating which course selections will best help undergraduates move through their programs of study most successfully and most expeditiously. Information generated by Degree Compass also goes to department chairs as "enterprise-scale" reports, which allow them to intervene with students who are having difficulty and need extra tutoring or mentoring.

Students are not forced to take any of the recommendations generated by Degree Compass, which is why the system is a technology nudge rather than a more directive tool. There is reason to believe that students should take the nudges seriously, however. While it is too soon for any extensive retention and graduation data to be available, there is already some evidence that Degree Compass can accurately predict grades. Initially, the system correctly predicted whether students would earn a C grade or higher 90% of the time. Now, Denley said, more recent research has found that Degree Compass can predict grades in a given class with 90% accuracy.

The next step for Degree Compass is MyFuture, launched in November 2012, to match students not just with individual classes but with entire majors. Again, the goal is to look at an individual student's academic record and predict future grades, match that history against the trove of data on a university's servers, and recommend academic specialties most likely to successfully lead that student to a degree. Moving beyond major recommendations, MyFuture also gives students links showing possible career options for a given major, as well as average salary data, and current job prospects in the field.

GETTING THE ACADEMIC GREEN LIGHT

The need for better information, of course, does not end when students pick their classes. On the contrary, undergraduates moving through their coursework often do not know as much as they should about their academic progress, which means that struggling students do not seek out help early enough to make a difference in their class performance. Here, too, technology nudges using data analytics are proving to be valuable tools for letting students know when they are at academic risk.

Probably the best known of these nudges is Purdue University's Course Signals program, which was piloted in 2007 and has reached nearly 30,000 students in 122 courses and 246 course sections. Created by John Campbell, Purdue's associate vice president for academic technologies (who recently moved to West Virginia University as associate provost and chief information officer), Course Signals relies on the kind of large data set mining now common in the corporate world. Its proprietary algorithm predicts students' risk status in the classroom by drawing on a wide range of data, including:

- Class performance, based on marks earned to date
- Effort, measured by how often students interact with Blackboard Vista, the learning management system used by Purdue
- Previous academic history, including high school grades and standardized test scores
- Student characteristics, such as age and number of credits taken

Students who log on to the learning management system—or who receive a personalized e-mail from their professors asking them to log on—see one of three traffic signals: red (stop and get help), yellow (caution, you are falling behind), or green (keep on going). By clicking on the signal, students facing difficulties can receive specific feedback from the instructor, including guidance about which tutoring or study resources they can access to improve their academic progress. If they wish, they can do this on the go: Signals is available through the Blackboard mobile application.

The program has encouraged students to seek out academic support, thus improving retention rates, according to Purdue officials. When Signals was used for some sections of a large biology course, for example, students who received messages from the Signals system were much more likely to visit the biology resource center than their counterparts in non-Signals classes. Overall, the Signals students received better final grades. The four-year retention rate for the 2007 cohort of Purdue undergraduates who used Signals at least once was 87.4%, compared to 69.4% for those who did not—an impressive 18 percentage point difference (Willis, Campbell, & Pistilli, 2013).

The spike in student retention, at 93%, was even higher for students who took two or more Signals courses. That is particularly noteworthy given that those students were less prepared for college than their non-Signals counterparts, as measured by SAT scores that were 50 points lower. "In short," wrote Campbell and two former Purdue colleagues, James E. Willis III and Matthew D. Pistilli, in a May 2013 *EDUCAUSE Review* article, "by receiving regular, actionable feedback on their academic performance, students were able to alter their behaviors in a way that resulted in stronger course performance, leading to enhanced academic performance over time." The program's impressive results, they conclude, stem from "using big data to offer direct feedback."

That said, initial graduation rate results for Signals participants have been more mixed. Students from the 2007 cohort who took one Signals class saw a four percentage point boost in their four-year graduation rates, to 45%, compared to those never enrolled in a Signals course. But those who took two or more Signals courses saw a 2.5 percentage point decline in their four-year graduation rates. There is an explanation for this counterintuitive finding, according to Purdue officials. Students taking more than one Signals class often are academically weaker than their peers, who may have tested out of large "gateway" courses by taking Advanced Placement classes in high school. Thus, students who take two or more Signals courses often take longer to earn their degrees because of the time they must spend taking required courses. Moreover, many Purdue majors are designed as five-year programs. For these reasons, Purdue officials predicted that five-year graduation rates for undergraduates who have taken two or more Signals classes would surpass those of their peers. They turned out to be correct. The five-year graduation rate for non-Signals students in the 2007 cohort was 61%. Undergraduates who took two or more Signals classes, despite average SAT scores that were 50 points lower than their non-Signals peers, had a 71% graduation rate—a 10 percentage point difference (Pistilli, Arnold, & Bethune, 2012).

However, the retention-boosting powers of the Course Signals initiative came into question in the fall of 2013 when researchers at Washington State University and McGraw-Hill Education separately scrutinized Purdue's claims and found them wanting. In essence, the critics argued that Purdue officials had demonstrated only a correlation between taking Signals courses and higher retention rates but not causation. Students who stay longer in college are more likely to take more Signals courses, which doesn't by itself provide that the courses improved retention, the critics argued. The criticism suggests that additional, rigorous research will be required for retention nudges to prove their worth. At the same time, the critics of Course Signals did not fault the core approach of Purdue's early-warning approach itself, which seems at a minimum to offer the crucial benefit of helping students improve their performance in class.

Technology nudges that rely on algorithms created by analyzing large volumes of student data might seem likely to prompt privacy concerns. Among students taking Signals classes, however, that has not been the case, according to Campbell. "I was always in genuine fear that I'd have my picture on the front of the student newspaper with the caption 'Big Brother Is Watching,'" he said in an interview. However, he added, in the age of social media and pervasive Googling, "students have a very different sense of privacy and how data can be used." Among some faculty members, by contrast, there has been apprehension that giving students a high number of yellow and red signals could be viewed as a sign of deficient teaching. Says Campbell, "I get more Big Brother questions from the faculty than I do from students."

COPING IN CLASS AND LIFE

The technology nudges described here—texting to reduce summer melt, help with course selection, and warnings about problematic course performance—are targeted at specific moments in a student's educational trajectory. Another initiative, a for-profit start-up called Persistence Plus, aims to provide more general behavioral interventions throughout undergraduates' academic careers. Calling itself the "Weight Watchers of college completion," Persistence Plus provides students with regular personalized nudges either via text message or through iPhone and Android applications. Using data from partner universities' data management systems, the company sends undergrads messages about time management and class deadlines, offers help coping with setbacks, and connects students to their peers in social networks organized around academic goals.

The Boston-based firm was founded in late 2011 by Jill Frankfort and her husband Kenny Salim, who is now superintendent of the Weymouth School District. Incubated in part at the Ewing Marion Kauffman Foundation's labs program for education start-ups, Persistence Plus has begun a series of pilot projects to test its model in different settings. In one partnership, Persistence Plus worked with the University of Washington, Tacoma, to nudge students in online introductory math classes. The goal was to see whether behavioral intervention could help lower-division undergraduates who are studying online, a population that often performs poorly. Students received daily reminders, often requesting a response. Behavioral research shows that students are more likely to complete a task when they commit to doing it not only at a specific time but at a specific place as well. So the Persistence Plus iPhone application might text this message: "Students who pick specific times to finish assignments do better. Your personal essay is due soon. When and where will you finish it up?" To which a student might reply, "Tuesday at the library" (Frankfort et al., 2012).

Text messages also ask students about their sense of well-being: "The beginning of the semester can sometimes feel overwhelming. How are you feeling?" If an undergraduate's response indicates that he or she is having personal difficulties, Persistence Plus sends the student messages geared toward the challenge that he or she faces, or it can connect students who have larger needs to campus counselors for individual support. For now, the firm's behavioral interventions combine what it calls "machine and human intelligence, and manual and automated process" (Frankfort et al., 2012). Along with differentiating the messages it sends based on what students report about their experiences, Persistence Plus staff members can also become personally involved. (On one occasion, Frankfort said via e-mail, a student told Persistence Plus—but not any faculty or staff—that she was about to fail all her classes because of a medical problem. The firm was able to help her arrange a medical withdrawal.) But over time it plans to automate and personalize the experience in a way that can be scaled "to an unlimited number of students" (Frankfort et al., 2012).

The Tacoma pilot found that students who received nudges performed better academically than those who did not. The company is still in a data-gathering, start-up stage—it is developing pilot projects with several universities in 2013–2014. In this experimental spirit, Persistence Plus has asked students to design their own motivational messages in an effort to find out which are most effective. (One student's message: "Stick with it, sit down and study your ass off, you brilliant bastard" [Frankfort et al., 2012].) Over time, the company plans to assess the effectiveness of the range of messages students design, then tailor its nudges to different student personalities.

Perhaps even more than some other technology nudges, the Persistence Plus model shows that worries about the potentially dehumanizing effects of technology in an educational setting are misplaced. The firm's model, while still a work in progress, may show just the opposite—that technology can be used to personalize student support through outreach of a kind that simply is not possible using traditional face-to-face methods. Frequent messages keyed to course deadlines and personal well-being give students the message, both literally and figuratively, that the university cares about them and their success.

COUNSELING BY PHONE

An underlying philosophy behind behavioral nudges, though rarely stated directly, is that nudges are paternalistic—they tell students what to do (albeit without coercion) rather than assume that they can figure out pathways to academic success on their own. That is a good thing, according to Stanford University economist Eric Bettinger. Together with a PhD student, Rachel Baker, Bettinger conducted a study for the National Bureau of Economic Research assessing the effectiveness of another for-profit service, InsideTrack, which provides telephone counseling to undergraduates in a directive way that seems to be good for them. As Bettinger and Baker asserted:

> Oftentimes in higher education, we assume that students know how to behave. We assume that they know how to study, how to prioritize, and how to plan. However, given what we know about rates of college persistence, this is an assumption that should be called into question. (Bettinger & Baker, 2011, p. 18)

The largest coaching firm in the country, InsideTrack, works with more than 40 colleges, including public, private, and for-profit institutions. It advises students, many of them nontraditional undergraduates enrolled in online programs, about issues that can get in the way of their academic progress. The company's philosophy is to try to connect students' life goals with their schoolwork. Practical advice to students addresses common problems such as academic time management. But counselors (the firm employs more than 300, located primarily in Portland, Oregon; San Francisco; and Nashville) also spend significant time on practical, life-management skills that can make a big difference in whether students stay enrolled—helping students deal with challenges from financial problems to working around job schedules to childcare responsibilities.

The results of the Bettinger and Baker (2013) study, originally released in March 2011, were striking. After just six months of coaching, 8,000-plus students in the test group were five percentage points more likely to stay in school than the 5,500 in the control group. After one year, when the coaching program ended, a dismaying number of students—more than half—had dropped out, but the five percentage point spread between the coached and noncoached students remained, diminishing only slightly by the 24-month mark. Coaching had an impact regardless of a student's SAT or ACT scores,

Pell Grant status, or age, though male students were more likely to benefit than female students (Jaschik, 2011).

While phone calls are not as cutting edge as texts or smart phone applications, they share the key characteristic that makes technology nudges appealing: scalability. In-person counseling is more expensive—and in some cases less convenient for students—than advice delivered over the phone. A key finding of the Bettinger-Baker study is that the cost per student of telephone-coaching intervention was $500 per semester—not trivial but a figure that compares favorably to the modest retention effects achieved though measures such as paying undergrads to attend campus counseling or boosting need-based financial aid by $1,000 or more annually (Jaschik, 2011).

The cost savings of phone counseling are possible not just because of technology but because of specialization. Counseling typically is part of a large bundle of services offered on a college campus (though rarely in the systematic, intense form provided by InsideTrack). Like Persistence Plus, InsideTrack unbundles one slice of counseling. By specializing, by focusing on the nudges most likely to influence student behavior, by using technology (including, at times, texting and e-mail in addition to phone calls), and by taking its services to scale, the company is able to offer less expensive counseling than the traditional model. Based on the evidence to date, that combination is producing clear benefits for students.

BUILDING POLICIES FOR SUCCESS

The examples cited here are by no means the only instances of colleges or companies giving students technology-driven prompts to persist to graduation. However, many colleges and universities continue to use more traditional—and less effective—student support methods. What might be done to encourage more widespread use of technology nudges—whether to combat summer melt, promote better course selection and scholarly progress, provide more effective coaching with personal and academic challenges, or to give students personalized digital encouragement simply to persist through college?

Louis Soares, a Center for American Progress senior fellow, has offered several policy recommendations for expanding personalized higher education technology in an October 2011 report. He suggested the U.S. Department of Education could create competitive grants to promote the use of technology tools with a special focus on low-income students. The government could try to integrate existing data collected by the Education Department with user-generated data from colleges to inform and improve student decision making, and the department could generate guidelines for how these data could be shared "in a social environment" while protecting student privacy (Soares, 2011).

These are worthwhile ideas, but ultimately the promise of behavioral nudges delivered via technology seems unlikely to be unleashed first and foremost through public policy. Colleges themselves need to recognize the value of these new tools and move to adopt them as they prove their worth. This process will happen more quickly on some campuses than on others. Nudge initiatives, like other educational technology ventures—from digital textbooks to customized, computer-driven teaching modules—are going through a period of trial and error. Early results seem good, and some high-quality assessments have begun, but advocates who want nudges to spread will need to ensure that they are studied rigorously by outside analysts.

If nudges are not as effective as they should be—and they will not always be—their creators will need to be willing to make course corrections. In an increasingly data-driven world, this is healthy and should become routine. If behavioral nudges continue to become more effective, and if they become part of the internal culture of more universities, they should become an increasingly important tool for promoting student success.

NOTES

1. An earlier version of this chapter appeared on the Education Sector website http://www.educationsector.org/publications/nudge-nation-new-way-prod-students-and-through-college. This revised version is reprinted here with permission.
2. All quotes attributed to Benjamin Castleman, Tristan Denley, and John Campbell are drawn from telephone interviews and e-mail exchanges with the author from February 2013 to May 2013, unless otherwise noted.

REFERENCES

Ayres, I. (2007). *Super crunchers: Why thinking-by-numbers is the new way to be smart.* New York, NY: Bantam.

Bettinger, E. P. & Baker, R. B. (2011). The effects of student coaching: An evaluation of a randomized experiment in student advising. *Educational Evaluation and Policy Analysis.* doi: 10.3102/0162373713500523.

Frankfort, J., Salim, K., Carmean, C., & Haynie, T. (2012, July 18). Analytics, nudges, and learner persistence. *EDUCAUSE Review Online.* Retrieved from http://www.educause.edu/ero/article/analytics-nudges-and-learner-persistence

Jaschik, S. (2011, March 10). The power of the nudge. *Inside Higher Ed.* Retrieved from http://www.insidehighered.com/news/2011/03/10/study_finds_value_in_coaching_college_students_on_academic_and_life_issues

Kamenetz, A. (2012, December 5). Dropouts: College's 37-million-person crisis—and how to solve it. *The Atlantic.* Retrieved from http://www.theatlantic.com/business/archive/2012/12/dropouts-colleges-37-million-person-crisis-and-how-to-solve-it/265916/

Lewis, M. (2003). *Moneyball: The art of winning an unfair game.* New York, NY: Norton.

National Center for Education Statistics. (2013). *Fast facts: Graduation rates.* Retrieved from U.S. Department of Education website: http://nces.ed.gov/fastfacts/display.asp?id=40

Pistilli, M., Arnold, K., & Bethune, M. (2012, July 18). Signals: Using academic analytics to promote student success. *EDUCAUSE Review* Online. Retrieved from http://www.educause.edu/ero/article/signals-using-academic-analytics-promote-student-success

Selingo, J. (2013). *College (un)bound: The future of higher education and what it means for students.* New York, NY: New Harvest.

Soares, L. (2011). The "personalization" of higher education: Using technology to enhance the college experience. Retrieved from Center for American Progress website: http://www.americanprogress.org/issues/labor/report/2011/10/04/10484/the-personalization-of-higher-education/

Thaler, R., & Sunstein, C. (2008). *Nudge: Improving decisions about health, wealth, and happiness.* New Haven, CT: Yale University Press.

Willis, J., III, Campbell, J., & Pistilli, M. (2013, May 6). Ethics, Big Data, and analytics: Model for application. *EDUCAUSE Review Online*. Retrieved from http://www.educause.edu/ero/article/ethics-big-data-and-analytics-model-application

7

Unanticipated Data-Driven Innovation in Higher Education Systems

From Student Success to Course Equivalencies

TAYA L. OWENS AND DANIEL J. KNOX

ABSTRACT

The drive for more data-driven decision making has led campuses and systems to implement new technologies that can gather and analyze student-level information. For the State University of New York (SUNY) system, the gathering of such information was motivated by the need to provide students with information that would allow them to more easily pursue and complete their educational goals. An analysis of a system-wide data tool, DegreeWorks, indicates that administrative capacity was increased by the new data being collected and played an important supportive role in the creation of strategic policy. However, analysis suggests an additional dimension. Rather than merely playing a supportive role, an increase in administrative data capacity at the system level appears to have influenced new policy innovations not previously considered. This chapter explores how the largest comprehensive system of higher education in the United States implemented a system-wide degree-audit tool and how the new data resulted in unanticipated policy impacts.

Two notable trends in college attendance in recent decades have been the overall increase and complex enrollment patterns of

159

student transfers. Alongside broad increases in student enrollment, there has been much more movement of students between campuses. Students have shifted the ways in which they use higher education, swirling between all campus types—and with more frequency— cross-registering at multiple campuses at the same time. Meanwhile, the undergraduate student body has become more diverse, requiring different scheduling options and program offerings, as well as raising concerns about affordability. Systems are uniquely positioned to address these new student mobility and diversity patterns, thinking beyond a single college to how students use multiple institutions throughout their academic careers.

Let us take the State University of New York (SUNY), the public multi-campus system in New York, as an example. As a university system of 64 campuses, SUNY was conceived with transfer in mind. Beginning with the master plans of the 1960s and reiterated by subsequent boards of trustees in 1972, 1980, 1987, and 1990, the commitment to seamless transfer remained consistent (O'Brien, 2011). On the ground, however, principle often conflicted with practice for transfer students. At four-year campuses, faculty maintained the authority to accept individual courses for transfer credit. Faculty at the community colleges added a diverse array of courses that in some cases mirrored upper-level courses in baccalaureate programs. In addition to variation between campuses, the system lacked a curriculum framework.

Beginning in 1998, the board of trustees introduced a system-wide faculty review process that ultimately developed a transfer structure for general education courses. Known as the General Education Requirement, this policy allowed for a wide degree of student flexibility and exploration in foundational courses, while simultaneously providing some consistency in requirements between all the campuses (O'Brien, 2011). However, while recognizing a system framework, this policy did not fully embrace the potential power of a system. Much of the policy focused on individual campus implementation; as such, system administration academic affairs staff relied heavily on local databases to keep track of transfer activity. SUNY campuses and administration needed to bridge the gaps between student needs and existing data infrastructure. The arrival of a new chancellor in 2009 provided this bridge in the form of a new perspective, systemness: "the ability of a system to coordinate the activities of its constituent campuses so that, on the whole, the system behaves in a way that is more powerful and impactful than what can be achieved by individual campuses acting alone" (Zimpher, 2013, p. 27).

In her 2012 State of the University address, "Getting Down to Business," SUNY chancellor Nancy L. Zimpher laid out plans to drill down on core infrastructure issues, including seamless transfer, a comprehensive policy designed to streamline student mobility across the system. In providing an update of progress-to-date, she highlighted a new mobility website and other data-based transfer tools, including a system-wide degree planning and audit tool. She recognized the pivotal role of faculty participation, through the Faculty Council of Community Colleges and University Faculty Senate, in building the new transfer system. Calling it "systemness at work," the chancellor hailed the progress on seamless transfer as a roadmap for college completion (Zimpher, 2012).

This roadmap for college completion depends on successfully engaging technologies and communications across a state-wide system of public colleges and universities. Linking student transfer information for over 420,000 undergraduate students across 64 campuses is no small task. Rather, it is one that requires sophisticated data infrastructure and, more importantly, a perspective larger than any one academic program, department, or campus. The following story of a degree planning and audit solution, DegreeWorks, at SUNY is a story of a shift in perspective from the campus as a discrete entity to a system as a complex organization where students flow among multiple institutions. This is also a story of how technology, specifically data tools, can fundamentally alter the way that higher education approaches student success and service delivery. This chapter highlights the critical role these data, combined with a system perspective, have played in assisting unanticipated policy innovations among SUNY's colleges and universities.

STRATEGIC POLICIES AND ADMINISTRATIVE CAPACITY: THE RELATIONSHIP BETWEEN POLICY AND DATA

For the last several decades, higher education institutions have been increasing their capacities to collect and analyze data, but institutions' individual focus can make it difficult to track the flow of students, many of whom now often move among multiple institutions (Hossler et al., 2012). At the same time, there have been several failed attempts to collect and share student data at the national level to provide a more accurate picture of trends within national higher education. One of the important intervening entities often overlooked in the data collection movement is the multi-campus higher education system, a collection of public campuses that tend to act semi-autonomously but often serve many of the same students and are coordinated by a central administrative structure (Lane & Johnstone, 2013).

This study analyzes the relationship of a system-wide data tool that was developed to support an overarching strategic policy to enhance the mobility of students among the 64 campuses in the SUNY system. This study is based on policy analysis, a methodology with a rich history of emphasizing tools of agency action as key variables in policy implementation (Salamon, 1981, 1989). Known as *policy instrument studies*, these analyses distinguish between substantive and procedural instruments (Eliadis, Hill, & Howlett, 2005). *Substantive* instruments are designed to effectuate a behavior change in the production, distribution, and delivery of goods and services in society. Examples include mechanisms designed to alter or monitor social behavior: regulation, grants, loans, registration and reporting, census taking, user charges, licenses, training, polling, and surveys (Hood, 1986). This toolbox represents a broad set of activities that governments or public agencies can use to translate policy intent into action.

Procedural instruments are designed to ensure support for agency actions. These tools are thought to affect the manner in which implementation unfolds but without predetermining the results of substantive implementation activities (Howlett, 2011). Initial research around procedural instruments has focused on the use of information to influence policy implementation: training, interest group participation, hearings, and commissions (Bressers & Klok, 1988; Lynn, Heinrich, & Hill, 2000). Prior research has suggested that administrative capacity is also a procedural tool. Administrative capacity can be considered the sum total of tools under agency discretion, including leadership, planning, management, or autonomy (Boschken, 1988; Milio, 2007). The following story of DegreeWorks is also a study of policy instruments, specifically the relationship between

Figure 7.1. Two-way relationship between instrument types

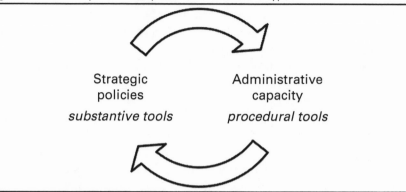

Strategic
policies

substantive tools

Administrative
capacity

procedural tools

Source: Figure by Taya L. Owens and Daniel J. Knox.

strategic policy (substantive tools) and administrative capacity (procedural tools).

This study deepens our understanding of the role of administrative capacity in the policy implementation process. Furthermore, this study illuminates the role of procedural instruments with regard to substantive policy instruments (see figure 7.1). For the purposes of this study, *administrative capacity* is defined as a procedural instrument under agency discretion that represents the ability of the agency to manage the implementation of a substantive policy. This ability can be identified as *commitment* (coordination or alignment with other policy priorities), *resources* (money, training, expertise), and *support* (facilities, equipment, infrastructure). While recent studies based on institutional and network theories have emphasized the role of external actors and contexts in policy implementation (Sabatier, 2007), an emphasis on administrative capacity highlights the continuing importance of internal agency attributes.

ANALYTIC METHOD AND DATA

An investigation of a degree planning and audit tool allows us to think through the unanticipated administrative and policy consequences of introducing new data structures into a system context. We consider the implementation of a system-wide degree audit software program across the 64 colleges and universities of the SUNY system. Specifically, this analysis considers how a strategic policy necessitated the development of administrative capacity, and in turn how this new capacity enabled the design of further strategic policies. This study asks: How does strategic policy drive data-tool development, then in turn, how does new data infrastructure drive new policy?

To investigate this question, this analysis makes use of the process-tracing method. The emphasis of process tracing is to investigate causal mechanisms within or between case studies (George & Bennett, 2005). That is, rather than emphasizing the causal effects of a variable on an outcome, this study uses concepts identified in prior policy literature to investigate the processes and mechanisms that might contribute to variation in outcomes. Furthermore, this particular study employs an inductive, theory-building approach (Beach & Pedersen, 2013), designed to ask, "What is the causal mechanism between X and Y?" where in this case study, X is strategic policy and Y is policy implementation. Theory-building process tracing is guided by both preexisting theory and the particular events of a complex case study. In the case of policy analyses, the methodological emphasis of process tracing is therefore on mid-range processes rather than on individual human behavior or institutional structures.[1]

DEGREEWORKS: FROM STUDENT SUCCESS TO COURSE EQUIVALENCIES

Since its inception in 1948, the State University of New York's identity as a public multi-campus university has been inexorably linked to the capacity of the system to provide broad access to higher education that reflects the opportunity for individual choice and the needs of society (Clark, Leslie, & O'Brien, 2010; Zimpher, 2013). This multifaceted identity is captured in the SUNY motto: "To learn, to search, to serve." Student success, defined as broad access and timely completion, is the ultimate SUNY strategic policy. Through the years, SUNY system administration and individual campuses have refined discrete strategic policies to better achieve this overall commitment to student success. Organizational and structural differences between campuses and system administration have allowed each to develop

Figure 7.2. From student success to course equivalencies

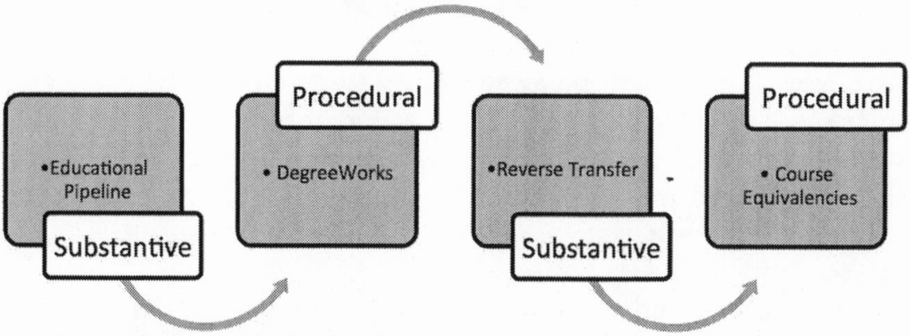

Source: Figure by Taya L. Owens and Daniel J. Knox.

various approaches to the same end. While campuses have focused on student success as retention and persistence at the local level, the system vision of student success has historically included an explicit emphasis on student mobility.

This study traces the relationship between strategic policies designed to increase student success through a seamless educational pipeline and the administrative capacities developed to support these strategic policies. Using process tracing, we explore how SUNY moved from student success to course equivalencies in three distinct phases, identified through major relationships between policy and capacity (see figure 7.2). These phases capture the action emphasis at a given point in time in the evolution of student mobility. In other words, these phases highlight the perspectives that drove the policy processes and the resulting strategies and capacities.

Phase I: Student-Driven Strategy

The first policy action phase considers the relationship between an identified strategic plan, educational pipeline goals, and the administrative capacities (i.e., degree audit software) selected to implement this plan.

Strategic policies. In 2010, SUNY unveiled *The Power of SUNY* strategic plan, a directional document that introduced six big ideas intended to "revitalize the economy of New York and enhance the quality of life for its citizens" (SUNY, 2010, p. 6). Among the six big ideas, the Seamless Education Pipeline was introduced to "find ways to close the gaps that impede success" (p.10). Educational pipeline goals were broadly defined as increasing student mobility and degree completion. The agency decision of which administrative capacities to develop to implement this policy rests on three critical organizational perspectives: (1) a shift from campus to system-based initiatives, (2) an emphasis on data-driven needs assessment, and (3) incorporating student opinions.

Historically, student success has played a significant role as a major strategic goal within the system, but prior to 2010, system master plans focused on academic excellence at the campus level, based on each campus's mission, strengths, and identity (SUNY, 1996, 2000a, 2004). The shift from a campus-based perspective to an inclusive system-based perspective (i.e., systemness) reoriented administrative decisions with regard to organizational conceptualization. Rather than developing discrete initiatives for each campus, administrators decided to develop a comprehensive educational pipeline program, a portion of which would eventually become known as *seamless transfer*.

An additional two organizational perspectives, an emphasis on data-driven needs assessment and the incorporation of student voice, had already provided campus and system administrators with substantive information on which to base institutional effectiveness decisions. Since 1991, the Office of Institutional Research has administered the Student Opinion Survey to undergraduate students at the four-year campuses once every three years. In the 2000 survey, some campuses reported that students wanted to see improvement in academic advising services (SUNY, 2000b). Administrators on these campuses convened a series of town halls and ad hoc surveys to further understand the problem: Faculty and students identified an information gap as the major impediment in advising services (State University College at Potsdam, 2000, 2006). Students, and at times faculty, did not clearly understand graduation requirements, resulting in a small number of cases of bad degree auditing every year. Additionally, at times department chairs, registrars, or even individual faculty advisers were allowed to authorize specialized waivers and course substitutions, introducing inconsistency to degree audits. Several campuses began to invest in degree planning and audit tools, software that enables students to map and monitor their progress toward graduation.

As such, the use of degree planning and audit tools originated at the campus level as a tool intended to facilitate student, faculty, and institutional planning for increased student success (Degree Audit Design Team, 2010). This goal translated into a system-level Degree Planning and Audit Initiative. However, the system perspective identified an additional use for this administrative tool: to facilitate student mobility and ease of transfer. It could so clearly facilitate several system-level policies that had been under development in stages over several years, leading to the Trustees' Resolution 2012-089, *Seamless Transfer Requirements*, and the Memorandum to Presidents, vol. 13, no. 3, *Policy and Guidance: Seamless Transfer Requirements*. Ultimately, campuses that had resisted adoption were convinced to fully participate.

Administrative capacities. The organizational ability to implement the educational pipeline goals listed previously (student mobility and degree completion) bears a relationship to the administrative capacity under agency discretion to manage the implementation. This ability can be identified as commitment, resources, and support.

Administrative commitment to student mobility initiatives aligned with several other strategic priorities, namely Memoranda of Understanding (MOUs) between campuses and the SUNY system intended to aid underrepresented minority, financially disadvantaged, and first-generation community college students in degree completion, as well as to advance the systemness paradigm. Campus MOUs were derived from two cycles of mission reviews (2001 and 2006) that were intended to encourage campus responsibility for higher levels of distinctiveness, performance, efficiency, and system-wide collaboration (SUNY, 2000a, 2004). Diversity initiatives emphasized the need to create seamless transfer opportunities for students to move from community colleges to four-year institutions (SUNY, 2012c). The systemness paradigm outlined in the *2012 Master Plan* (SUNY, 2012a) reflected these aligned educational pipeline goals under three umbrellas: controlling costs (systems integration initiatives), increasing productivity (developing a P-20 data system), and ensuring access and completion (connecting the transfer dots).

Considerable administrative resources were acquired through the New York State (NYS) Race to the Top grant awarded from the U.S. Department of Education in 2010. This federal initiative provided direct funding and specialized training on the degree audit software. Of the monies allocated to New York State for data systems, approximately $9.7 million were awarded to SUNY for the purpose of tracking students throughout their academic lives (NYS, 2010). Of the $9.7 million, approximately $6 million were invested in the purchase, licensing, and maintenance of DegreeWorks, a degree auditing software tool developed by Ellucian, a proprietary technology firm. This large-scale, federally funded grant allowed SUNY to implement degree planning services online, across almost all two- and four-year campuses (the statutory campuses at Cornell and Alfred do not participate in this initiative). Furthermore, funds for additional implementation services covered the knowledge transfer and setup of the technology solution for each campus. These resources allowed for initial expert training by Ellucian staff on every participating campus.

Finally, the major administrative support for educational pipeline initiatives was developed specifically to advance these policies through the system-wide implementation of DegreeWorks (discussed later) by previously established information support centers. The Information Technology Exchange Center (ITEC) at Buffalo State University had been created in 1988 to support computer-related activities targeted at improving the quality, quantity, and cost-effectiveness of services across the system (ITEC, 2006). Additional support for DegreeWorks came from the Student Information & Campus Administrative Systems (SICAS) center, established at SUNY Oneonta in 1990 to provide software, services, and training to higher education institutions throughout the state.

Phase II: Data-Driven Innovation

The second policy action phase analyzes the relationship between administrative capacities selected to implement an initial policy and the processes of capacity building that influence subsequent policies that emerge from these newly developed capacities.

Administrative capacities. As a supportive administrative capacity, degree audit software provides the infrastructure to solve a key logistical challenge for student success: locating essential academic planning information. On most campuses, degree requirements are stored in one location, course schedules are in a second location, and course descriptions are detailed in yet a third location. The logistical challenges presented by separated databases are often compounded by insufficient access to advising. The problem is primarily one of resources, as often there are simply not enough advisers to address the needs of students adequately (Carlstrom, 2013). Taken together, the lack of accessible academic planning information and resource constraints on advising can present significant barriers to timely degree completion, particularly for transfer students (Moore & Shulock, 2009).

To address these challenges, the system administration launched the *Degree Planning and Audit Initiative* (SUNY, 2011a). Following a comprehensive review of available degree planning software, Ellucian was contracted to license and install DegreeWorks software for all nonstatutory SUNY campuses and extend the functionality of the software to include the ability for students to run degree audits across SUNY campuses. DegreeWorks pulls a student's academic history from the campus student information system and allows the user to map his or her history onto degree requirements, course schedules, and course descriptions within a common, interactive platform. In this way, students are able to engage in academic planning at their own campus, while potential transfer students can gauge progress to degree at any other SUNY campus.

One of the primary implementation challenges involved "scribing" each campus's program requirements from natural language in course catalogs to scribe code, a proprietary programming language used by DegreeWorks's audit engine. The production of scribe code data involves two main processes: standardization and centralization. The standardization of program requirements into scribe code necessitated a translation process from natural language, or everyday language, to detailed logic statements. Program requirements were previously conveyed to students through natural language either via course catalogs or in-person advising. Natural language allowed for substantial ambiguity or variation in communicating program requirements.

For example, a student might be instructed to "take a natural science class next fall" to fulfill a program requirement. The instructions assume a knowledge base, where the student understands what "natural science" is, how to find courses, check scheduling, and so on. However, students often do not possess the basic knowledge necessary to navigate the college "decision context," particularly students from lower socioeconomic backgrounds without college-educated parental support (Scott-Clayton, 2011). In practice, terminology at SUNY campuses tended to vary widely, and program requirements were often vaguely described. In contrast, software code requires precise logic statements and detailed decision trees to represent programs accurately. During the scribing process, every detail of the academic programs was documented and coded in a standard terminology. As a result, practices that were previously informal or undocumented became apparent through the scribing process.

As scribing progressed, the resulting data revealed the tremendous variability and complexity of program requirements across the system. For example, one four-year campus's general education program alone required over 3,100 lines of code to complete, as compared to an average of 784 lines for other campuses' general education programs. As the complexity of individual campuses' general education programs came into stark relief (both within and between campuses), this newly identified knowledge informed aspects of transfer policy discussions that were simultaneously taking place between SUNY system administration and campuses. The results of these discussions are reflected in Trustees' Resolution 2012-089, *Seamless Transfer Requirements*, adopted on December 17, 2012. Among other policy reforms, the resolution standardized the SUNY general education requirements across the system so that 30 credits of coursework in 7 of 10 content areas are required in the first 60 credits of all associate's and bachelor's degrees. In this way, "seeing" the curriculum standardized through software code created a new understanding of the complexity of general education requirements placed on students, which in turn informed further policy innovations in the seamless transfer resolution.

The second scribing process involves centralization. After scribing, the code for all campus programs is stored within the data center at ITEC in Buffalo. Prior to DegreeWorks's implementation, campuses submitted minimal information about academic programs to the central SUNY program database. While the annual data surveys on student enrollment, outcomes, and finances have collected detailed information regarding student behavior, the program data survey has historically requested simple descriptive information such as program name, level and award type, and disciplinary codes. Going forward, the scribe code database brings together all undergraduate program requirements at all campuses into a central location in a common language—historically unprecedented detail in data. Finally, due to the nature of DegreeWorks's data collection, ITEC servers are updated nightly, providing access to live student program and course data rather than the data delay due to surveys that are typically submitted at the end of each term. The centrality of program-level data allows for innovation in analytics for policy development.

Strategic policies. Scholarly and institutional research on student mobility has indicated that transfers are very common among students, either before or after receiving an associate's degree. As shown in a recent report by the National Student Clearinghouse Research Center, approximately one-third of all U.S. undergraduate students transferred at least once between 2006 and 2011 (Hossler et al., 2012). Similar trends appear prevalent within the SUNY system. In 2010–2011, 46.4% of all baccalaureate degrees and 27.1% of associate's degrees were awarded to students who entered as transfers. Among all students who transfer within SUNY on a per-semester basis, only 35.3% move vertically from a two-year campus to a four-year campus, while 38.5% move laterally from either two-year to two-year campuses (16.6%) or four-year to four-year campuses (21.9%), and 26.2% reverse transfer from four to two-year campuses (SUNY Institutional Research Information System, 2013).

Additionally, a significant number of those transfer students who move from a community college to a four-year campus transfer without first having earned a credential (associate's degree or certificate). During fall 2011, 9,881 students transferred vertically, but only 4,049 (41%) had earned an associate's degree prior to transfer (SUNY, 2011b). While a portion of these students drop or stop out before completing bachelor's degree requirements, some of the students will meet associate's degree requirements while attending the receiving four-year campus, providing the credits may be transferred back to the community college. In other words, some transfer students are caught in a degree limbo—attending a four-year college with enough credits for an associate's but not enough for a bachelor's degree. If these credits could be "transferred in reverse" back to the community college, the student could then be awarded the associate's degree. A major implementation challenge to reverse transfer involves the automation of data mining to identify these students. Given the sheer numbers of students involved, examining each transcript by hand quickly becomes labor intensive and as such, infeasible for campuses to complete by themselves.

Identification of reverse transfer eligible students requires three essential sources of data: student transcript data, program requirements, and course equivalency data (which courses at the receiving campus are comparable to courses at the sending campus). By fall 2012, SUNY had built two of these essential data infrastructures. Since 2010, student transcript data have been centrally collected and stored at SUNY system administration's Oracle data warehouse through an automated data transmission system. With the implementation of DegreeWorks, now a centrally available data source for program information exists. But a third data infrastructure, course equivalency, was needed for reverse transfer implementation. New access to data mining encouraged system administrators to pursue a new and innovative strategic policy: tackling low associate degree achievement through reverse transfer.

Phase III: System Integration

The third policy action phase analyzes the relationship between an identified strategic plan, the reverse transfer initiative, and the administrative capacities selected to implement this plan.

Strategic policies. The reverse transfer initiative developed from a confluence of two intervening administrative capacities: coordination and alignment with other policy priorities as well as established equipment and infrastructure in the form of DegreeWorks. Reverse transfer developed on the back of a prior initiative designed to increase degree completion. Concurrent to all the policy activity related to establishing DegreeWorks, SUNY system administrators had begun to collaborate with national organizations on a small initiative intended to increase student success. In 2010, six SUNY community colleges joined a two-year project spanning 61 campuses across nine states (Adelman, 2013). Project Win-Win, a program designed to identify several paths to increasing associate's degree completion, was sponsored through several national organizations: the Education Trust, the Institute for Higher Education Policy (IHEP), the Lumina Foundation, the National Association of System Heads (NASH), the

State Higher Education Executive Officers (SHEEO), and the Kresge Foundation.

Project Win-Win was a campus-based effort designed to leverage student-level information from institutional, state, and national databases to help community college students complete associate's degree requirements. These students were identified as being within close range of degree completion but without having yet received an award. Particular attention was paid to transfer students, since independently they accounted for 42% (transfer-ins) and 60% (transfer-out) of the student population. Project Win-Win did identify some pathways to increase associate's degree completion, but more pertinently this project identified some of the considerable problems that exist in sharing data among institutions and between institutions and state central databases. SUNY administrators working with DegreeWorks had begun to address this data coordination problem on campuses through the establishment of a large-scale student-unit database complete with course-level information defined through the scribing process.

Critical lessons learned from Project Win-Win combined with the infrastructural support provided by DegreeWorks enabled SUNY system administrators to launch the Reverse Transfer Initiative, a program that allows students who have transferred from a community college to a four-year school without completing their associate's degree to reverse transfer their credits from the four-year campus back to the sending community college to be awarded an associate's degree.

Administrative capacities. The organizational ability to implement reverse transfer again bears a relationship to agency commitment, resources, and support. With regard to administrative commitment, reverse transfer aligned with overall strategic initiatives old and new: student success, smooth student mobility, and increased degree completion. Furthermore, SUNY system administrators were able to take advantage of an external funding initiative to identify sufficient financial resources. The Lumina Foundation, alongside several other major national foundations, spearheaded the "Credit When It's Due: Recognizing the Value of Quality Associate Degrees" grant in April 2012. SUNY was awarded $500,000 to implement reverse transfer on a large scale, across all 64 two-year and four-year campuses (SUNY, 2012b). While SUNY was able to secure financial resources, the success of this project still depended on the development of a key administrative capacity: system-level data integration.

With regard to administrative support, the DegreeWorks implementation process produced a form of infrastructure surplus (data, in this example). That is, the goal of implementing a system-wide degree audit solution was not to build a comprehensive database of program requirements to facilitate reverse transfer; the database was a supportive administrative capacity developed out of the goal to deliver degree audit services across campuses. However, once detailed program and course-level data were centralized, new opportunities and challenges for integration became apparent. Taken together, the degree audit and reverse transfer initiatives exposed the need for a key infrastructural capacity in the process: a course equivalency system.

A key infrastructural component for determining transfer credit, course equivalencies are historically stored in campus student information systems. These tables show which transfer courses can be accepted for credit and which satisfy certain programmatic requirements. As such, these tables are the technical lynchpin that allows students to run degree audits across campuses, as well as enabling the data-mining techniques for identifying reverse transfer eligible students.

As part of the reverse transfer initiative, the implementation team performed site visits at all 30 community colleges to determine the current state of transfer process and technology needs. The analysis revealed that approximately one-third of all campuses visited did not maintain any course equivalency data. The issue appeared not to be technological, as nearly all student information systems have the capacity to store course equivalencies. Rather, the deficits appeared due to procedural inefficiencies (SUNY, 2013). Namely, campus staff did not input and maintain course equivalency data as they evaluated incoming transcripts from transfer students. In interviews and focus groups, staff members cited the lack of timely information and a heavy workload as the primary reasons that they did not maintain course equivalencies. At present, system administration has proposed a centralized database of course equivalencies between all SUNY campuses, along with accompanying integrated data tools, such as predictive modeling and web services for automated course equivalency updates. This system approach to data integration allows for a comprehensive approach to student, course, program, campus, and system-level information (see figure 7.3).

Figure 7.3. Integrated data systems: students, programs, courses, and systems

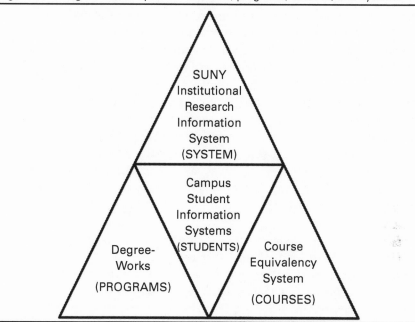

Source: Figure by Taya L. Owens and Daniel J. Knox.

DISCUSSION

Dr. David Lavallee, the serving SUNY system provost during these initiatives, has likened the policy process in higher education to pushing a string along a table. On one end of the string lies policy, in the middle procedures, and at the other end technology. When you push on a string, it does not all move at the same rate. When administrative energies focus on policies, technology does not immediately move forward with it. Similarly, advances in technology are not immediately coupled with progress in policy and procedure. That being said, because of the interconnectedness of policy, procedure, and technology on one string, they do affect reform and advances among themselves. Once energy is put into one area—say, policies—soon procedures and technologies will be developed to catch up to the policy goals.

Lavallee's string approach echoes the relationships between substantive and procedural tools: policy goals influence changes in administrative capacity. More so, this relationship appears to be two-directional, where changes in administrative capacity may affect new policy directions. In the processes traced earlier, there appears to be a relationship between the data surplus created by new technology infrastructure and a new policy initiative, reverse transfer. Furthermore, this second policy thrust also appears to have served as the impetus for yet another source of data innovation and system integration, the course equivalency system.

Interviews with administrators suggest that these new technological advances can impact several other initiatives related to educational pipeline goals, student mobility, and degree completion. Related applications include support for Open SUNY, an extensive distance-learning strategic initiative, which intends to bring all online courses offered at each of the system's 64 campuses onto a shared and comprehensive online environment. A smaller pilot program, Complete SUNY, intends to identify and support former SUNY students who wish to return to SUNY to earn a degree. This program is designed to increase graduation rates system-wide by offering students opportunities to complete their degrees online. Both these online initiatives, large and small, are directly and indirectly supported by the new data available through DegreeWorks and the course equivalency system.

The system perspective, complemented by centralized system data, has also encouraged policies that provide students access to almost any course in any institution, such as the Memorandum to Presidents, vol. 13, no. 1, *Policy and Guidance: Cross Registration of Full-Time Students*. This guiding document removes institutional barriers to students' completing courses by providing access to cross-registration in a course or courses not taught by the home institution. This policy hopes to facilitate student success by removing course scheduling conflict and by utilizing existing faculty, facilities, and resources more efficiently.

CONCLUSION

This analysis does not suggest that administrative capacity is the main issue that affects new policy designs, or said another way, that new substantive instruments are uniquely dependent on procedural instruments. In considering the role of administrative capacity in influencing strategic policy design, the results of this case study also reveal other processes that reflect the widely documented and influential roles of policy networks, interest groups, financial dependency, and political stability (Sabatier, 2007). The political phenomena through which public policy emerges are notably complex.

However, our analysis suggests a strong relationship between the internal process of an agency and its effectiveness or innovativeness. This case study reflects that administrative capacity plays a supportive role to strategic policy as traditionally envisioned: a system-wide degree audit system was conceived to address student success and mobility policy objectives. Rather than merely playing a supportive role, administrative capacity appears to have influenced the creation of new policy directions: the reverse transfer initiatives. These results dovetail with prior theoretical conceptions. In the now classic Kingdon (2002) multiple streams model, "technical feasibility" is identified as a contributing variable in the policy stream. That is, this model recognizes that for a policy alternative eventually to become a policy decision, policy makers must "[attend] to the feasibility of implementation, and [specify] the actual mechanisms by which an idea would be brought into practical use" (Kingdon, 2002, p. 31). The processes traced in this study lead us to argue that administrative capacities not only are selected in order to implement prior strategic policies but that they affect subsequent strategic policy design. By presenting a measurable definition of administrative capacity (commitment, resources, and support), we hope this single case study may contribute to further studies across cases, in a variety of policy contexts.

APPENDIX 1: GLOSSARY OF SUNY STRATEGIC POLICIES AND ADMINISTRATIVE CAPACITIES

Strategic Policies (in chronological order)

The Power of SUNY: Strategic Plan 2010 & Beyond. The result of Chancellor Nancy Zimpher's engagement tour across all 64 SUNY campuses, the plan commits SUNY to the realization of six areas of focus (Big Ideas): the Entrepreneurial Century, Seamless Education

Pipeline, Healthier New York, Energy-Smart New York, Vibrant Community, and SUNY and the World.

Master Plan 2012 & Beyond: Delivering on Our Promise. Under New York's Education Law, SUNY and CUNY are required to submit master plans on a four-year cycle. *Master Plan 2012* details the implementation process and progress to date on the blueprint established in *The Power of SUNY: Strategic Plan 2010 & Beyond.*

Trustees' Resolution 2012-089, Seamless Transfer Requirements. Passed on December 17, 2012, the resolution established principles to guide undergraduate curricula to assure seamless transfer within SUNY. Key reforms involved standardizing general education programs, establishing core coursework in the major, and instituting credit maximums for associate's and bachelor's degree programs.

Memorandum to Presidents, vol. 13, no. 1, *Policy and Guidance: Cross Registration of Full-Time Students.* Issued January 14, 2013, this memorandum modifies university policy on the cross-registration of students as of the fall 2013 semester. It establishes the method by which State University of New York campuses, including community colleges, can enter into cross-registration arrangements with other SUNY campuses.

Memorandum to Presidents, vol. 13, no. 3, *Policy and Guidance: Seamless Transfer Requirements.* Issued June 13, 2013, this memorandum provides detailed implementation guidelines for Trustees' Resolution 2012-089. Details are provided on five key areas: curriculum design; curriculum delivery; transfer guarantee and appeals; information for current and prospective students, faculty, and administrators; and, leadership and renewal.

Administrative Capacities (in alphabetical order)

"Credit Where Credit Is Due: Recognizing the Value of Quality Associate Degrees." The initiative expanded on work of Project Win-Win, which promoted 12 states' efforts to expand their approaches to reverse transfer. The initiative was funded by the Lumina Foundation, the Kresge Foundation, the Helios Education Foundation, USA Funds, and the Bill & Melinda Gates Foundation.

DegreeWorks. This web-based software application allows students to view their progress toward degree in the form of an electronic audit. The application maps the student's academic history against program requirements.

Ellucian. Based in Fairfax, Virginia, Ellucian Corporation markets a variety of technology solutions to the higher education sector. Ellucian was the result of the August 2011 merger of Datatel and SunGard Higher Education group.

Information Technology Exchange Center (ITEC), Buffalo. Established in 1989, ITEC provides software support and services, business continuity/disaster recovery, remote services, IT hosting services, and product installation and maintenance services for participating SUNY campuses.

Project Win-Win. The initiative, undertaken in a partnership of the Institute for Higher Education Policy and the State Higher Education Executive Officers, was funded principally by the Lumina Foundation for Education. The initiative involved 64 community colleges and four-year institutions. These institutions identified former students, no longer enrolled within the SUNY system and never awarded any degree, but whose records qualified them for an associate's degree, to award the degrees retroactively.

Race to the Top. The American Recovery and Reinvestment Act of 2009 provided $4.35 billion for the Race to the Top Fund, a competitive grant program designed to encourage and reward states that are creating the conditions for education innovation and reform. Specific areas of focus include standards and assessment, building data systems, recruiting and retaining effective teachers, and turning around the lowest-achieving schools.

Student Information & Campus Administrative Systems (SICAS), Oneonta. The SUNY SICAS program supports the administrative software, service, and training needs for campuses using offerings from SunGard Higher Education's (now Ellucian) product line. With various membership options, the program serves state-operated campuses, community colleges, and private institutions statewide.

NOTES

1. Data for this study were collected from published SUNY strategic plans, policies, and resolutions; internal SUNY policy papers and memoranda; and unpublished interviews with senior SUNY

system staff. These staff members include D. DeMarco, C. Hatch, R. Kraushaar, D. Lavallee, R. Miller, and D. Powalyk.

REFERENCES

Adelman, C. (2013). *Final report: Project Win-Win at the finish line*. Retrieved from the Institute for Higher Education Policy website: http://www.ihep.org/publications/publications-detail.cfm?id=166

Beach, D., & Pedersen, R. B. (2013). *Process-tracing methods: Foundations and guidelines*. Ann Arbor, MI: University of Michigan Press.

Boschken, H. L. (1988). Turbulent transition and organizational change: Relating policy outcomes to strategic administrative capacities. *Policy Studies Review* 7(3), 477–499. doi:10.1111/j.1541-1338.1988.tb00849.x

Bressers, H., & Klok, P. (1988). Fundamentals for a theory of policy instruments. *International Journal of Social Economics* 15(3/4), 22–41. doi:10.1108/eb014101

Carlstrom, A. (2013). *NACADA national survey of academic advising* (Monograph No. 25). Manhattan, KS: National Academic Advising Association.

Clark, J. B., Leslie, W. B., & O'Brien, K. P. (2010). *SUNY at sixty: The promise of the State University of New York*. Albany, NY: State University of New York Press.

Degree Audit Design Team. (2010). *Degree audit design team recommendations*. Retrieved from the Mohawk Valley Community College website: http://www.mvcc.edu/design-teams/degree-audit-design-team-2009-2010

Eliadis, P., Hill, M., & Howlett, M. (2005). *Designing government: From instruments to governance*. Montreal: McGill-Queens University Press.

George, A. L., & Bennett, A. (2005). *Case studies and theory development in the social sciences*. Cambridge, MA: MIT Press.

Hood, C. (1986). *The tools of government*. Chatham, NJ: Chatham House Publishers.

Hossler, D., Shapiro, D., Dundar, A., Ziskin, M., Chen, J., Zerquera, D., & Torres, V. (2012). *Transfer and mobility: A national view of pre-degree student movement in postsecondary institutions*

(Signature Report No. 2). Retrieved from National Student Clearinghouse website: http://nscresearchcenter.org/signaturereport2/

Howlett, M. (2011). *Designing public policies: Principles and instruments.* New York, NY: Routledge.

Information Technology Exchange Center. (2006). *Introduction and mission.* Retrieved from http://www.itec.suny.edu/info/itec_mission.htm

Kingdon, J. (2002). *Agendas, alternatives, and public policies* (2nd ed.). London, England: Longman.

Lane, J. E., & Johnstone, D. B. (Eds.). (2013). *Higher education systems 3.0: Harnessing systemness, delivering performance.* Albany, NY: State University of New York Press.

Lynn, L. E., Heinrich, C. J., & Hill, C. J. (2000). Studying governance and public management: Challenges and prospects. *Journal of Public Administration Research and Theory 10*(2), 233–261.

Milio, S. (2007). Can administrative capacity explain differences in regional performances? Evidence from structural funds implementation in southern Italy. *Regional Studies 41*(4), 429–442. doi:10.1080/00343400601120213

Moore, C., & Shulock, N. (2009). *Student progress toward degree completion: Lessons from the research literature.* Sacramento, CA: Institute for Higher Education Leadership and Policy.

New York State. (2010). *Race to the Top application: Phase 2.* Retrieved from http://usny.nysed.gov/rttt/application/criteriaapriorities.pdf

O'Brien, K. P. (2011, November). *SUNY, general education, and student transfer: Trying to get it right.* Paper presented the annual meeting of the American Association of University Professors, Washington, DC.

Sabatier, P. A. (2007). *Theories of the policy process* (2nd ed.) Boulder, CO: Westview Press.

Salamon, L. M. (1981). Rethinking public management: Third-party government and the changing forms of government action. *Public Policy 29*(3), 255–275.

Salamon, L. M. (1989). The tools approach: Basic analytics. In L. S. Salamon & M. S. Lund (Eds.), *Beyond privatization: The tools of government action* (pp. 23–50). Washington, DC: Urban Institute.

Scott-Clayton, J. (2011). *The shapeless river: Does a lack of structure inhibit students' progress at community colleges?* (CCRC Working Paper No. 25). Retrieved from the Teachers College, Columbia University, Community College Research Center website: http://ccrc.tc.columbia.edu/publications/lack-of-structure-students-progress.html

State University College at Potsdam. (2000). *Memorandum of Understanding: College at Potsdam and the State University of New York*. Office of the Provost. Albany, NY: SUNY.

State University College at Potsdam. (2006). *Memorandum of Understanding: College at Potsdam and the State University of New York*. Office of the Provost. Albany, NY: SUNY.

State University of New York. (1996). *Master plan: Rethinking SUNY*. Albany: Author.

State University of New York. (2000a). *Master plan 2000–2004*. Retrieved from http://www.suny.edu/provost/master_plan/index.cfm

State University of New York. (2000b). *Student opinion survey*. Office of Institutional Research. Albany, NY: Author.

State University of New York. (2004). *Master plan 2004–2008*. Retrieved from http://www.suny.edu/provost/master_plan/index.cfm

State University of New York. (2010). *The power of SUNY: Strategic plan 2010 & beyond*. Retrieved from http://www.suny.edu/powerofsuny/

State University of New York. (2011a). *Degree planning and audit initiative*. Retrieved from http://www.suny.edu/provost/academic_affairs/SUNYDPAI.cfm

State University of New York. (2011b). *Transfer patterns to SUNY campuses, fall 2011*. Office of Institutional Research. Albany, NY: Author.

State University of New York. (2012a). *Master plan 2012 & beyond: Delivering on our promise*. Retrieved from http://www.suny.edu/sunynews/sunyPublications.cfm

State University of New York. (2012b). *SUNY receives $500,000 grant for reverse transfer, degree planning services*. Retrieved from http://www.suny.edu/sunynews/News.cfm?filname=10.10.12SUNYGrantforReverseTransferDegree.htm

State University of New York. (2012c). *SUNY Replication Project*. Office of Diversity, Equity and Inclusion. Albany, NY: Author.

State University of New York. (2013). *SUNY course equivalency system*. Office of Information Technology. Albany, NY: Author.

SUNY Institutional Research Information System. (2013). *Student enrollment and outcome tables*. Office of Institutional Research. Albany, NY: Author.

Zimpher, N. L. (2012). *Getting down to business*. Retrieved from the State University of New York website: http://www.suny.edu/chancellor/speeches_presentations/SOU2012.cfm

Zimpher, N. L. (2013). Systemness: Unpacking the value of higher education systems. In J. E. Lane & D. B. Johnstone (Eds.), *Higher education systems 3.0: Harnessing systemness, delivering performance* (pp. 27–44). Albany, NY: State University of New York Press.

Part III

POLICY DEVELOPMENT AND INSTITUTIONAL DECISION MAKING

8

INTEGRATING DATA ANALYTICS IN HIGHER EDUCATION ORGANIZATIONS

Improving Organizational and Student Success

LISA HELMIN FOSS

ABSTRACT

Forces within and outside higher education are positioning data analytics as an organizational innovation with the potential to improve the quality of education, increase student success, and reduce costs. Successful implementation of innovations in general and data analytics programs specifically are a challenge for many institutions, however. This chapter describes an implementation framework that was developed through a critical analysis of existing innovation research and tested using survey data gathered during spring 2013 from deans and department chairs from a cross-section of U.S. higher education institutions. The chapter includes examination of current attitudes and usage patterns of data and analytics by academic leaders across the country and offers guidance for organizational leaders on how to structure and manage the implementation process in a way that increases the likelihood of success.

D ata analytics—the extensive use of data, statistical analysis, and modeling to drive organizational decisions and actions (Davenport & Harris, 2007)—has received significant coverage over the last few years as holding the promise of enhancing the productivity and success of higher education organizations. Proponents contend that it has the potential to simultaneously answer increasing calls for accountability from observers outside the academy, improve student learning and success, reduce costs, improve effectiveness, and promote the innovation of individual institutions and the higher education industry (Grajek, 2011; Petersen, 2012). Some have even called analytics the "killer app" or the "universal decoder" for education reform (Norris & Baer, 2013).

EDUCAUSE, an organization for information technology (IT) professionals in higher education, named data analytics one of its "Top 10" strategic initiatives for 2013,[1] and the 2012 *Horizon Report*, a joint publication of EDCAUSE and the New Media Consortium, identified "learning analytics" as one of the six technologies to watch, with a "time-to-adoption" horizon of the next two years (Johnson, Adams, & Cummins, 2012). Within the ongoing debate, critics warn that data analytics is simply a bureaucratic intrusion upon institutional autonomy (Petersen, 2012). They argue that data analysis is not new; colleges and universities have been engaged in the collection and reporting of data for years (Oblinger, 2012). Proponents counter that data analytics is different from data analysis and requires a shift in focus from applying analytical methods to solve individual problems to a broader view of developing analytical solutions characterized by the integrated use of data, processes, and systems (Liberatore & Luo, 2011). One university president, for example, asserted that to "address societal imperatives, higher education must begin by transforming its own culture, which is reflected in the questions we ask (and those we don't), the achievements we measure and highlight (and those we ignore), and the initiatives we support (or don't support)" (Hrabowski, Suess, & Fritz, 2011, p. 16) and identified data analytics as central to this transformation.

Current interest in data analytics is not unwarranted. Though data on the impact of analytics on higher education organizations is not available, a study of large U.S. corporations found that high-performing businesses are five times more likely than low-performing businesses to use analytics strategically (Davenport & Harris, 2007). A recent study by the McKinsey Global Institute (Manyika et al., 2011) found that U.S. health care could derive more than $300 billion in value every year from data analytics, two-thirds of which would be in the form of reducing national healthcare expenditures by about

8%. The authors of this study also estimated that in the developed economies of Europe, government administration could save more than $149 billion in operational efficiency improvements (Manyika et al., 2011). With all the interest in data analytics, however, it is clear that all organizations do not practice data-driven decision making. Indeed, one study found that 40% of major decisions in U.S. businesses are based not on facts but on the manager's instinct (Davenport & Harris, 2007), and according to a recent survey by *Inside Higher Ed*, only 36% of presidents, 31% of provosts, and 39% of financial officers said that their institutions were "very effective" at using data to aid and inform campus decision making (Green, 2012).

Within higher education, there remains little agreement on what data analytics is, and it appears that little progress has been made in implementation. In 2005 (Goldstein & Katz, 2005) and again in 2012 (Bichsel, 2012), the EDUCAUSE Center for Applied Research (ECAR) surveyed chief information officers at institutions of higher education across the United States in an attempt to understand the "state of the industry," highlight institutions that have made progress on analytics, and provide an overview of the opportunities for and challenges to implementation of a data analytics program. A comparison of the results indicates that over the seven years between surveys, some movement has been made to expand technology infrastructure to support data analytics, and a small increase in the percentage of institutions engaged in analytics efforts has occurred. At the same time, data analytics remains limited to the functional areas of admissions and enrollment management, business and finance, and student progression with little movement into the core academic functions of student learning, faculty productivity, cost to degree, and research administration. Similarly, the McKinsey Global Institute's investigation (Manyika et al., 2011) of the potential for data analytics and Big Data to positively impact productivity, competition, and innovation across different industries found that while all sectors will have to overcome barriers to capture value from the use of Big Data, barriers are structurally higher for the public sector, including education, in part because of a lack of a data-driven mindset and available data.

If higher education organizations are to implement a data analytics initiative successfully, especially one that touches the academic core, organizational leaders must understand how they might develop a more data-driven culture. In particular, they must understand academic leaders' (i.e., deans and department chairs) views of organization processes and decision points that would benefit from data analytics. Recently, both the American Council of Colleges and Universities (ACC&U) and the Council of Graduate Schools (CGS) urged colleges and universities to engage in more robust data-driven assessment practices to improve student learning and success outcomes, but they also identified "academic departments and faculty in particular as the key agents for how an institution changes its approach to implementing and evaluating intervention efforts to improve student success" (Hrabowski, Suess, & Fritz, 2011, p. 18). As individuals with substantial responsibility for data generation and operational decisions within higher education organizations, academic leaders have been surprisingly silent on the role of data analytics in higher education organizations, including the questions we ask, the achievements we measure and highlight, and the initiatives we support.

THE NEED FOR A DATA-DRIVEN CULTURE

Despite the apparent interest, the higher education sector is struggling to capitalize on data analytics. What can be done to facilitate colleges' and universities' use of data analytics, and how can their success and scope of data analytics be improved in the future? In 2012, EDUCAUSE identified the primary challenges to implementing data analytics as a lack of investment and not enough analysts to do the work (Bichsel, 2012). While acknowledging that all industries struggle to attract top analytical talent, the McKinsey Global Institute found that the educational sector is in the bottom quintile in IT investment and identified as the substantial barriers to be overcome the lack of data-driven decision making within education's culture and the absence of data on critical operational processes (Manyika et al., 2011). The 2012 EDUCAUSE study confirmed that a culture in which administrators, faculty members, and staff members fear or mistrust data is a significant barrier to a successful analytics program (Bichsel, 2012). The imposition of analytics on an organization that is not data-oriented can also result in ineffectual implementation or lead to fundamentally misinformed, inaccurate decisions (Stiles, 2012).

DATA ANALYTICS AS AN ORGANIZATIONAL INNOVATION

A fundamental challenge for senior administrators and change agents within higher education organizations is how to overcome these barriers to the successful implementation of data analytics at their own institutions. Data analytics is an example of an organizational innovation and as such may be best investigated through the theoretical framework of innovation adoption and diffusion. Throughout the extensive history of the study of innovation, many definitions have been developed. Most include the identification of an idea that is new to an individual, group, or organization and the implementation of that idea with the goal of organizational improvement (Dill & Friedman, 1979; Rogers, 2003; White & Glickman, 2007). Van de Ven, Polley, Garud, and Venkataraman (2008) added that an organizational innovation "entails a collective effort of considerable duration and requires greater resources than are held by the people undertaking the effort" (p. 22). An idea is not required to be new to the world to be defined as an innovation. It must simply be new to the organization that is attempting to implement it, even if others outside the organization perceive it as an imitation of an existing idea (Rogers, 2003).

Innovations can come from many places and many directions. Innovations can be developed by professionals based on their experiences and engagement in the core work of an organization, introduced to an organization through implementation by competitors, or forced upon the organization because of a change in the political or regulatory environment. To become an organization-level innovation, internal ideas must achieve currency among enough and the right people to reach organizational importance and attention (Van de Ven, 1986). Innovations that are introduced to the organization from the external environment require organizational responses that must be framed and refined to align with organizational values and identity (Rogers, 2003) before they can be adopted successfully.

Rogers (2003) proposed a five-stage model to describe the innovation process within organizations (figure 8.1). The model is split between the initiation phase and the implementation phase. During the initiation phase, the organization moves through an agenda-setting stage, in which a general organizational problem is identified, and a matching stage, in which the organization fits a problem from

Figure 8.1. Five stages in the innovation process in organizations

I. INITIATION		II. IMPLEMENTATION		
#1 AGENDA-SETTING	#2 MATCHING	Decision #3 REDEFINING/RESTRUCTURING	#4 CLARIFYING	#5 ROUTINIZING
General organizational problems that may create a perceived need for innovation	Fitting a problem from the organization's agenda with an innovation	The innovation is modified and re-invented to fir the organization, and organizational structures are altered.	The relationship between the organization and the innovation is defined more clearly.	The innovation becomes an ongoing element in the organization's activities and loses its identity.

Source: Rogers (2003, p. 421).

the organization's agenda with an innovation. At the point when the organization decides to adopt a specific innovation, the implementation phase begins.

The implementation phase contains three stages. The first is the redefining stage, in which the innovation is modified and reinvented to fit the organization and organizational structures are altered. The second is the clarifying stage, in which the relationship between the organization and the innovation is defined more clearly. Third is the routinizing stage, in which the innovation becomes an ongoing element in the organization's activities and loses its separate identity. Though Roger's model (2003) may appear linear, the actual process of implementing organizational innovations is a highly organic, nonlinear process (Rogers, 2003; Van de Ven et al., 2008) that requires organizational as well as individual change and a continual reframing to fit the local context and priorities. It is adaptive, meaning the organization adapts to the innovation, and the innovation is adapted to the organization (Fonseca, 2002).

The successful implementation of innovations (Rogers's stages 3–5) is influenced both by the process an organization uses to redefine and clarify the innovation to fit its context and by the support structures it provides to encourage individual adoption and integration of the innovation into ongoing, regular activities. Greenhalgh, Robert, MacFarlane, Bate, and Kyriakidou (2004) conducted a meta-analysis of innovation research in healthcare organizations and found that innovation implementation is not straightforward and that many of the standard variables are necessary but not sufficient to explain successful implementation of complex innovations in professional organizations. Overall, they found that attributes are neither stable features of the innovation nor sure determinants of successful implementation or routinization. Rather, it is the interaction among the innovation, the intended adopter(s), and a particular context that determines successful implementation and routinization. During the process, individual adoption results from the adaptation of the organizational innovation to align it with his or her professional practice. At the same time, adoption of the innovation changes the individual's professional practice. Over time, though the length of time can vary considerably, the innovation may build momentum as more and more professionals absorb the innovation into their professional practice until a point is reached when the innovation is no longer seen as separate from the day-to-day routines of the organization or its professionals. The innovation has been transformed from something that is done in addition to regular functions to something that is seen as integral to regular practices and operations of the individual and the organization. In this context, the successful implementation of a data analytics program may be related to a shift to a data-oriented organizational culture, which Stiles (2012) identified as critical to the success of any data analytics program.

ADOPTING DATA ANALYTICS IN COLLEGES AND UNIVERSITIES

The focus of the rest of this chapter is on the development of a framework for implementing the use of data analytics within higher education. I first discuss the key factors identified in previous research on innovation adoption (table 8.1). These factors were used to develop a survey that asked deans and department chairs from the disciplines of biology, management, English, nursing, political science, and education to identify their attitudes toward and personal use of data analytics.[2] I discuss the specific results of the study and then describe a model of individual adoption of data analytics, a model that can be used to help academic leaders integrate data analytics into their institutional culture.

Factors That Influence an Academic Leader's Choice of Adoption and Use of Data Analytics

The following factors were identified from existing literature as having high likelihood of influencing an academic leader's decision to use

Table 8.1. Factors that influence individual adoption of data analytics

Factor	Definition of Scales Used in the Study
Authenticity	The extent that the respondent perceives his/her organizational culture as data-driven
Collaboration	The extent of involvement of academic leaders in the development and implementation of data analytics
Ease of Use	The extent that the end user perceives the data analytics system as flexible and easy to use.
Functionality	The extent that the end user perceives the data and information available from data analytics is of good quality and is dynamic or flexible in use
Institutional Support	The extent to which the institution provides appropriate funding, tools, and staff to support and maintain data analytics
Integrated Use	The extent to which information from data analytics is integrated with other information within the institution and is used for multiple purposes, such as to inform strategic priorities or communication with external audiences
Legitimacy	The extent to which the end user perceives data analytics as an appropriate way to address organizational and industry opportunities and challenges
Training	The extent to which the institution provides training and professional development for the end user to successfully use data analytics
Usefulness	The extent to which the end user perceives data analytics as improving their professional performance.

data analytics. These factors are described here and their role in the overall model is described in a later section.

Authenticity. An organization's openness and ability to adopt specific innovations is inherently tied to the culture of the organization, especially if the organization has a significant number of professionals (Schein, 2004). It is believed that the norms of the organization affect the innovation decision, rate of diffusion, and role of opinion leaders and change agents in the adoption process (Rogers, 2003). An organization's culture can support increasing innovation and effectiveness if the change aligns with that culture, but pressure to behave in culturally acceptable ways may constrain innovation or attempts to do things differently (Schein, 2004). The concept of authenticity describes the shared understanding and agreement among members of the organization of the purpose of an innovation, the outcomes that it is designed to achieve, and the consistency between the innovation and the organizational culture and values (Eraut, 1975; Kezar, 2006; Rogers, 2003; Van de Ven, 1986). Innovations that radically differ from an organization's values have been found to be difficult to implement successfully (Rogers, 2003).

Collaboration. Research suggests that the innovation implementation process is a collective activity that requires attention, expertise, resources, and efforts from multiple individuals and groups (Heckscher & Adler, 2006; Rogers, 2003; Van de Ven, 1986). The relative autonomy of professionals within higher education organizations and the political nature of the organizational environment make collaboration and decentralized decision making important characteristics of the implementation process (Baldridge, 1980; Green, 2003; Greenhalgh et al., 2004; Rogers, 2003). Innovations in universities are often locally developed (Kozma, 1985) and begin with an individual or a small group of individuals. The innovation is altered through a dialectical process of negotiation and compromise as groups seek to modify the innovation to address their own unique needs and interests (Klein, 2010; Van de Ven & Poole, 1985). It evolves gradually through debate at all levels of the organization, improving quality and encouraging acceptance by all participants (Easterby-Smith, 1987). An innovation's eventual acceptance may have less to do with the particular innovation and more to do with the collaborative process by which it was developed and implemented (Kozma, 1985). As a result, the idea or innovation itself changes over time in a recursive fashion (Hargrave & Van de Ven, 2006). When successful, the collaborative mode is cooperative rather than confrontational and emerges from shared previous experience and values (Kozma, 1985).

Ease of use. Research on the adoption of technology and information systems points to the importance of the overall ease of use of the system in an individual's decision to adopt and continue to use an innovation (Davis, 1989; Wixom & Todd, 2005). The concept of ease of use indicates that a user finds the innovation to be simple to use and operate, and easy to manipulate so that it does what the end user wants it to do (Wixom & Todd, 2005).

Functionality. The concept of functionality means that the innovation being implemented actually solves a problem as defined by the user and provides a relative advantage compared to the program, tool, or technology that came before it (Rogers, 2003; Van de Ven, 1986). Innovations, however, can be created without a problem to solve or when no dissatisfaction with the current solution exists (Eraut, 1975). The challenge of problem solving in colleges and universities is that sometimes minimal problem assessment occurs prior to an adoption decision (Baldridge, 1980), or solutions are identified first and then organizational actors go looking for problems to solve (Cohen, March, & Olsen, 1972). The cause-and-effect relationship between the problem and the innovation or solution is often reversed (Van de Ven, 1986). In addition, faculty and professional staff members have explicit and tacit knowledge gained through education and professional and disciplinary affiliations that informs and influences what they see as an appropriate definition of the problem and acceptable solutions (Eraut 1975; Kozma, 1985). As a result, functionality may be defined differently by professionals within an organization than by the organization itself, requiring flexibility as a key component of the innovation. Flexibility is critical because it allows for innovations, particularly those that come from outside the organization, to be altered to more specifically address organizational problems or opportunities (Greenhalgh et al., 2004; Van de Ven, 1986). Flexibility in the innovation and implementation process creates an environment in which the end user can adapt to the innovation, and the innovation is adapted to the organization over time (Fonseca, 2002).

Institutional support. Institutional support includes dedicated organizational resources, both financial and personnel, to support ongoing implementation and use (Baldridge, 1980; Eraut, 1975; Rogers, 2003; Savenjie & Van Rosmalen, 1988), including the competence and connectedness of the innovator or local champion and his or her ability to navigate the political dynamics of the organization (Baldridge, 1980; Kozma, 1985; Van de Ven, 1986). Institutional support includes organizational leaders who actively and visibly support an innovation, are engaged in its use and implementation, and recognize and publicly reward adoption (Baldridge, 1980; Davis et al., 1982; Greenhalgh et al., 2004; Kezar, 2003, 2006). An important component of leadership support is accountability or the level at which organizational leaders are held accountable for organizational outcomes related to the innovation (Kezar, 2003).

Integrated use. The purposeful use of integrating structures and systems may be particularly important to higher education organizations because of their loosely coupled nature (Weick, 1976). Loose coupling is critical to the initiation of innovative ideas because the organization needs to be open to its changing environment and flexible enough to consider novel adaptations, but implementing an innovation requires a tight coupling around a best solution and singleness of purpose (Cameron, 1984). Loose coupling means it is likely that these novel solutions will remain local even if it is desirable for them to be standardized across the organization. Thoughtful integration of an innovation into existing organizational systems provides opportunities for the innovation to move across formal structural boundaries and allow for knowledge transfer about an innovation, its implementation, and success (Greenhalgh et al., 2004; Kezar, 2006; Rogers, 2003). Kezar (2006) found that one of the biggest obstacles in implementing innovative academic programs is the siloed bureaucratic departmental and administrative structures on most campuses. She argued that new structures, processes, and rewards need to be established that enhance group and cross-divisional work, including integrating mechanisms. Integration of the innovation into the organization may require feedback loops and novel data and information about the innovation, the organization, and the changing external environment (Greenhalgh et al., 2004; Kezar, 2006; White & Glickman, 2007) that reinforce the importance of adoption. Communication networks are critical in the management of perceptions and information about the innovation and implementation process and in guiding the organization's interpretation of appropriateness and success (Gioia & Thomas, 1996; Rutherford, Fleming, & Mathias, 1985).

Legitimacy. While an innovation must embody an organization's ideals, in complex professional organizations it must also embody the professional values and knowledge of the adopters (Van Driel et al., 1997). Professional knowledge exerts a major influence on the ways in which professionals respond to innovations. It appears they are rarely open to all possible innovations and will only consider those for which their basic disciplinary assumptions hold (Van Driel et al., 1997; Cannon & Lonsdale, 1987). An innovation becomes relevant to a potential adopter when the innovation achieves both cognitive legitimacy ("I think it's okay to change") and social-political legitimacy ("Others think it's okay to change") (Hargrave & Van de Ven, 2006). Since colleges and universities are embedded in highly institutionalized fields (Meyer et al., 2008)—with the influence of regional and specialized accrediting agencies, professional associations, and state and federal governments to spread coercive, mimetic, and normative change (DiMaggio & Powell, 1983)—the need to establish the legitimacy of the innovation is particularly relevant. As a result, innovations that are identified to solve real organizational problems may not be viewed as legitimate, while legitimate innovations that are adopted at the organizational level are not necessarily designed to solve specific organizational problems (Meyer & Rowan, 1991). Argyris and Schön (1996) argued that change at the individual level must precede changes at other levels, including organizational. Since the decision to adopt an innovation is a personal one, each new adopter goes through a similar filtering process of alignment with values and previous experience (Kozma, 1985) prior to the adoption choice.

Training. An employee's knowledge and capacity are important components of adoption and successful implementation (Rogers, 2003). The concept of training includes tools and adequate resources to address motivation and competence of personnel through training and professional development (Eraut, 1975; Greenhalgh et al., 2004; Kezar, 2003, 2006).

Usefulness. Research on the adoption of technology and information systems points to the importance of usefulness in an individual's decision to adopt and continue to use an innovation (Davis, 1989; Wixom & Todd, 2005). The concept of usefulness indicates that users find that an innovation improves their ability to complete organizational responsibilities and increase their effectiveness better than previous programs or tools (Wixom & Todd, 2005).

ORGANIZATIONAL AND INDIVIDUAL USE OF DATA ANALYTICS

According to academic leaders who participated in this study, data analytics is a topic that is receiving increasing attention and

Table 8.2. Which statement best describes the status of data analytics at your institution?

Response	Percent
A major priority institution-wide	23.6%
A major priority for some units but not the entire institution	41.9
An interest for some units	26.9
Not a priority or interest	5.4
Don't know	2.4

Source: Table by Lisa Helmin Foss.

Table 8.3. Individual usage of data analytics during the last year

	Great extent	Somewhat	Very little	Not at all
Used data analytics to guide your own decision making in the last year	37.4%	46.2%	14.5%	1.9%
Used data analytics in discussions at college or department meetings in the last year	35.9%	46.9%	13.4%	3.8%
Used data analytics during informal conversations with colleagues in the last year	23.7%	51.9%	21.0%	3.4%

Source: Table by Lisa Helmin Foss.

Table 8.4. How do you anticipate your usage of data analytics will change in the next year?

Response	Percentage
Increase substantially	37.4%
Increase slightly	42.4
Stay about the same	19.1
Decrease slightly	0.4
Decrease substantially	0.8

Source: Table by Lisa Helmin Foss.

prioritization on college campuses across the United States. More than 65% of respondents said data analytics was a priority either for their entire institution or for some units on their campus, and only 5.4% responded that it was not a priority or interest (table 8.2). These perceptions of prioritization of data analytics were not significantly different across academic discipline, geographic region, size, institutional control, or Carnegie Classification. That is, all institution types were experiencing an increasing pressure to engage in data analytics.

Consistent with an organizational focus on analytics, academic leaders are increasing their personal use of data analytics (table 8.3). One-third of respondents said that they used data analytics to a great extent in the last year in their own practice—to guide decision making, during formal unit meetings, and during informal conversations with colleagues. More importantly, fewer than 4% of respondents indicated that they are not using data analytics at all. While the largest percentage of respondents said that they use data to some extent in their daily practice, a large majority (79.8%) anticipated increasing their use in the next year (table 8.4). These findings indicate that data analytics is a topic of increasing importance for academic leaders, and quality implementation of data analytics programs will become an increasingly relevant topic on U.S. college campuses in the coming years.

A MODEL OF INDIVIDUAL ADOPTION OF DATA ANALYTICS

Through the survey, deans and department chairs were asked a series of questions to gauge their attitudes toward and usage patterns of data analytics. The questions were designed to capture the dimensions of each of the factors that may influence their adoption of data analytics. The questions were converted to factor scales, and their influence was tested using data from the survey. Based on the findings from regression analysis, a model for the individual adoption of data analytics at higher education institutions was developed (figure 8.2).

Adoption of data analytics by academic leaders appears to be the result of the interaction between: (1) the organizational context in which the data analytics program is being implemented; (2) the

Figure 8.2. Model of the individual adoption of data analytics at higher education institutions

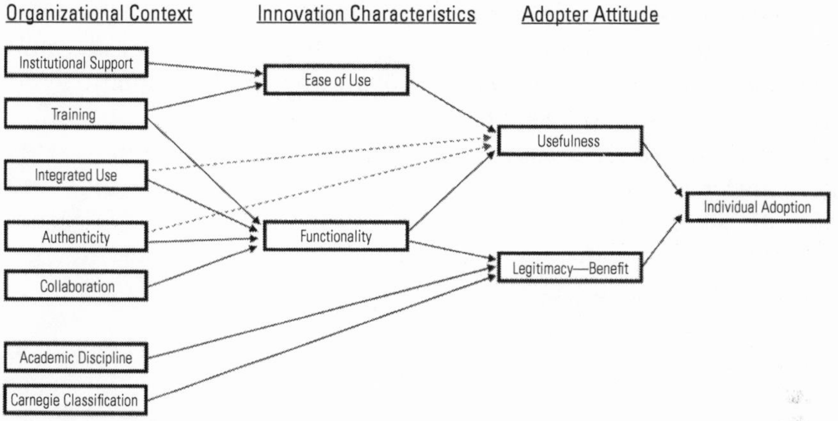

Source: Table by Lisa Helmin Foss.

innovative characteristics of the data analytics program; and (3) the attitude of the individual toward data analytics.

The extent of individual adoption is most directly influenced by the adopter's attitude toward the data analytics tool set available to them and their perception of the legitimacy of data analytics as an appropriate innovation for higher education. From the perspective of academic leaders, data analytics must be both useful, meaning that use enhances their ability to do their job, and it must be legitimate, meaning academic leaders must believe that use of data analytics is the right tool to improve or address different challenges facing their organization. The factors of usefulness (p<.01) and legitimacy-benefit (p<.05) made significant contributions to a regression model that explained nearly 50% of the variability in the level of individual adoption (R^2=0.486; p<.001). The extent of individual adoption was positively influenced by the respondent's perception of the usefulness of data analytics and by his or her attitude that data analytics would provide a benefit to higher education or his or her organization.

Usefulness and legitimacy are not inherent characteristics of data analytics but are acquired through actions of the organization and individual adopters as an innovation is implemented and supported.

The perception of usefulness is influenced by both the characteristics of the data analytics program and by the organizational context in which the program is implemented. When academic leaders experience their institution as having a data-driven culture, they are more likely to perceive data analytics as useful to them personally. In addition, when available data are of good quality, easy to use, and integrated with other systems and data within the organization, the academic leader's perception that data analytics is useful is enhanced. Ease of use (p<.01), functionality (p<.001), authenticity (p<.05), and integrated use (p<.01) contribute significantly to a model that explains more than 70% of the variability in the academic leader's perception that data analytics is useful (R^2=0.722; p<.001).

The drivers of the perception of legitimacy are more difficult to interpret. An academic leader's perception that data analytics could provide substantial benefit to higher education is influenced by the functionality of the data analytics program at her institution, by academic discipline, and by the type of organization in which she works. Functionality (p<.001), academic discipline (p<.05), and Carnegie Classification (p<.05) made significant contributions to a model that explained 33% of the variability in the respondent's perception that data analytics was legitimately beneficial to higher education (R^2=0.329; p<.01). Academic leaders from more applied disciplines perceived data analytics to have greater potential for providing benefit than those from more traditional disciplines, and those from baccalaureate institutions perceived data analytics to have less benefit.

The innovation characteristics of ease of use and functionality are, in turn, influenced most directly by the organizational context in which a data analytics program is implemented. When an institution provides appropriate funding, tools, and staff to support and maintain data analytics and provides training and professional development for the end user to successfully use data analytics, academic leaders perceive the data analytics program at their institution as easy to use. The factors of institutional support (p<.05) and training (p<.01) contributed significantly to a model that explains more than 50% of the variability in the academic leaders' perception that data analytics were easy to use (R^2=0.534; p<.001).

When an institution has a data-driven culture, involves academic leaders in the collaborative development of the program, uses data analytics for multiple purposes, successfully integrates data analytics with other information within the institution, and provides appropriate training, academic leaders perceive data analytics as more functional. The factors of training (p<.01), integrated use (p<.01), authenticity (p<.05), and collaboration (p<.01) contribute significantly to a model that explains more than 60% of the variability in academic leaders' perception that the data analytics program is functional (R^2=0.609; p<.001).

CONCLUSIONS

The results of the study provide empirical support to the premise that the successful implementation of data analytics in higher education organizations is more complex than simply acquiring the best technology or information system. It appears successful adoption and implementation results from the active management of the relationship between the organizational context, the data analytics system, and the academic leaders who are expected to adopt the practice and technology. Based on findings from this study, it appears that the extent of individual adoption of data analytics is driven by the two critical elements. From the perspective of the academic leader, data analytics must be useful, meaning that use enhances his or her ability to do the job, and it must be legitimate, meaning the academic leader must believe that use of data analytics is the right tool to improve or address different challenges facing the organization or industry. Usefulness and legitimacy are not inherent characteristics of data analytics. The usefulness of data analytics is acquired through actions of the organization and individual adopters as it is implemented and supported within a specific organization. The characteristic of legitimacy is influenced not necessarily by the direct actions of the organization to implement data analytics but through the disciplinary experiences of academic leaders and the organizational context in which they work. The use of data analytics to inform decision making is not seen as equally legitimate by all disciplines or types of institutions, creating a significant challenge for those responsible for implementation across the entire organization.

As senior administrators think about developing or expanding data analytics at their institutions, they must give careful consideration to the technical aspects of data analytics—such as software, data, and training—and resource aspects—such as staffing and funding. These elements are foundational to any data analytics effort and directly influence academic leaders' perception of data analytics at their institution. Senior administrators must also consider the softer side of implementation, however. Factors such as the level of collaborative development that engages deans and departments chairs in the design, testing, ongoing improvement of data analytics, and the visibility of senior leaders' use of and support for data analytics are equally, if not more, important for successful implementation and use. It is the quality of the experience with the implementation process and the consistency with the culture of the organization that influence academic leaders' attitudes about the functionality and usability of data analytics at their institution.

Also important is the translation of the pressures for adoption from the external environment. External pressure is universal and is felt at similar levels across different institution types and disciplines, but external calls for the acceptance of more data-driven practices are not sufficient to drive the adoption of data analytics by academic leaders. If not appropriately translated, external pressure may actually result in increased levels of concern among academic leaders about adoption, which may negatively influence their adoption choice. Senior leaders play a critical role in the translation of external pressure into institution-specific actions that compel academic leaders to integrate more data-driven practices into their daily routines.

Finally, data analytics, like any innovation deployed in higher education organizations, should be implemented in a way that gives consideration to the specific institution in which it is being developed. The higher education sector is not homogeneous. Institutional cultures and professional norms vary substantially across institutions based on mission, constituencies served, and mix of academic programs. Similarly, individual institutions are not homogeneous. Deans, department chairs, and faculty members within a particular institution come from various disciplines and work and educational experiences that influence their perception of what is legitimate and appropriate for their programs and students. Any strategy to implement data analytics must be technically excellent, but equally critical is the strategy to engage a diverse set of academic leaders fully in the process of moving to a campus culture of data-driven decision making, of which the adoption of data analytics is only a part. It is only when campuses can reach a consensus on the purpose and need for deploying data analytics and create a shared responsibility for its development and use that campuses will begin to experience the improved effectiveness, efficiencies, and student success that are promised.

NOTES

1. See http://www.educause.edu/ero/article/top-ten-it-issues-2013-welcome-connected-age for details.
2. Survey questions were designed to capture different dimensions of nine factors that were proposed to influence individual adoption of data analytics. Academic leaders from 255 U.S. institutions of higher education that had previously participated in the EDUCAUSE 2012 analytics study (Bichsel, 2012) were invited to participate in the survey. The institutional response rate was 70.2%, with 313 surveys completed from 179 different higher education institutions.

REFERENCES

Argyris, C., & Schön, D. A. (1996). *Organizational learning II: Theory, method, and practice.* Reading, MA: Addison-Wesley.

Baldridge, J. V. (1980). Managerial innovation: Rules for successful implementation. *Journal of Higher Education 51*(2), 117–134.

Bichsel, J. (2012). *Analytics in higher education: Benefits, barriers, progress, and recommendations.* Retrieved from EDUCAUSE Center for Applied Research website: http://www.educause.edu/library/resources/2012-ecar-study-analytics-higher-education

Cameron, K. S. (1984). Organizational adaptation and higher education. *Journal of Higher Education 55*(2), 122–144.

Cannon, R. A., & Lonsdale, A. J. (1987). A "muddled array of models": Theoretical and organisational perspectives on change and development in higher education. *Higher Education 16*(1), 21–32.

Cohen, M. D., March, J. G., & Olsen, J. P. (1972). A garbage can model of organizational choice. *Administrative Science Quarterly 17*(1), 1–25.

Davenport, T. H., & Harris, G. H. (2007). *Competing on analytics: The new science of winning*. Boston, MA: Harvard Business School.

Davis, F. D. (1989). Perceived usefulness, perceived ease of use, and user acceptance of information technology. *MIS Quarterly 13*(3), 319–340.

Davis, R. H., Strand, R., Alexander, L. T., & Hussain, M. N. (1982). The impact of organizational and innovator variables on instructional innovation in higher education. *Journal of Higher Education 53*(5), 568–586.

DiMaggio, P. J., & Powell, W. W. (1983). The iron cage revisited: Institutional isomorphism and collective rationality in organizational fields. *American Sociological Review 48*(2), 147–160.

Dill, D. D., & Friedman, C. P. (1979). An analysis of frameworks for research on innovation and change in higher education. *Review of Educational Research 49*(3), 411–435. doi:10.3102/00346543049003411

Easterby-Smith, M. (1987). Change and innovation in higher education: A role for corporate strategy? *Higher Education 16*(1), 37–52.

EDUCAUSE. (2012). *Findings of the Expert Panel on Analytics*. Retrieved from http://www.educause.edu/library/resources/findings-expert-panel-analytics

Eraut, M. (1975). Promoting innovation in teaching and learning: Problems, processes and institutional mechanisms. *Higher Education 4*(1), 13–26. doi:10.1007/BF01569099

Fonseca, J. (2002). *Complexity and innovations in organizations*. New York, NY: Routledge.

Gioia, D. A., & Thomas, J. B. (1996). Identity, image, and issue interpretation: Sensemaking during strategic change in academia. *Administrative Science Quarterly 41*(3), 370–403.

Goldstein, P. J., & Katz, R. N. (2005). *Academic analytics: The uses of management information and technology in higher education*. Retrieved from EDUCAUSE website: http://www.educause.edu/library/resources/academic-analytics-uses-management-information-and-technology-higher-education

Grajek, S. (2011). Research and data services for higher education information technology: Past, present, and future. *EDUCAUSE*

Review 46(6). Retrieved from http://www.educause.edu/ero/article/research-and-data-services-higher-education-information-technology-past-present-and-future

Green, K. C. (2012, January 25). (Not) using data for decisions. *Inside Higher Ed*. Retrieved from www.insidehighered.com/blogs/not-using-data-decisions

Green, R. (2003). Markets, management and "reengineering" higher education. *Annals of the American Academy of Political and Social Science 585*, 196–210. doi:10.1177/0002716202238575

Greenhalgh, T., Robert, G., MacFarlane, F., Bate, P., & Kyriakidou, O. (2004). Diffusion innovations in service organizations: Systemic review and recommendations. *Milbank Quarterly 82*(4), 581–629. doi:10.1111/j.0887-378X.2004.00325.x

Hargrave, T. J., & Van de Ven, A. H. (2006). A collective action model of institutional innovation. *Academy of Management Review 31*(4): 864–888.

Heckscher, C., & Adler, P. (2006). *The firm as a collaborative community: The reconstruction of trust in the knowledge economy*. New York, NY: Oxford University Press.

Hrabowski, F. A., III, Suess, J. & Fritz, J. (2011). Assessment and analytics in institutional transformation. *EDUCAUSE Review 46*(5). Retrieved from http://www.educause.edu/ero/article/assessment-and-analytics-institutional-transformation

Johnson, L., Adams, S., & Cummins, M. (2012). *The NMC horizon report: 2012 higher education edition*. Retrieved from New Media Consortium website: http://www.nmc.org/publications/horizon-report-2012-higher-ed-edition

Kezar, A. (2003). Enhancing innovative partnerships: Creating a change model for academic and student affairs collaboration. *Innovative Higher Education 28*(2), 137–156. doi:10.1023/B:IHIE.0000006289.31227.25

Kezar, A. (2006). Redesigning for collaboration in learning initiatives: An examination of four highly collaborative campuses. *Journal of Higher Education 77*(5), 804–838. doi:10.1353/jhe.2006.0043

Klein, J. T. (2010). *Creating interdisciplinary campus cultures: A model of strength and sustainability*. San Francisco, CA: John Wiley & Sons.

Kozma, R. B. (1985). A grounded theory of instructional innovation in higher education. *The Journal of Higher Education 56*(3), 300–319.

Liberatore, M., & Luo, W. (2011). INFORMS and the analytics movement: The view of the membership. *Interfaces 41*(6), 578–589. doi:10.1287/inte.1110.0599

Manyika, J., Chui, M., Brown, B., Bughin, J., Dobbs, R., Roxburgh, C., & Byers, A. H. (2011). *Big Data: The next frontier for innovation, competition, and productivity*. Retrieved from McKinsey & Company website: http://www.mckinsey.com/insights/mgi/research/technology_and_innovation/big_data_the_next_frontier_for_innovation

Meyer, J. W., Ramirez, F. O., Frank, D. J., & Schofer, E. (2008). Higher education as an institution. In P. J. Gumport (Ed.), *Sociology of higher education: Contributions and their contexts* (pp. 187–221). Baltimore, MD: Johns Hopkins University Press.

Meyer, J. W., & Rowan, B. (1991). Institutionalized organizations: Formal structure as myth and ceremony. In W. W. Powell & P. J. DiMaggio (Eds.), *The new institutionalism in organizational analysis* (pp. 41–62). Chicago, IL: University of Chicago Press.

Norris, D. M., & Baer, L. L. (2013). Building organizational capacity for analytics. Retrieved from EDUCAUSE website: http://www.educause.edu/library/resources/building-organizational-capacity-analytics

Oblinger, D. G. (2012). Let's talk . . . analytics. *EDUCAUSE Review 47*(4). Retrieved from http://www.educause.edu/ero/article/lets-talk-analytics

Petersen, R. J. (2012). Policy dimensions of analytics in higher education. *EDUCAUSE Review 47*(4). Retrieved from http://www.educause.edu/ero/article/policy-dimensions-analytics-higher-education

Rogers, E. M. (2003). *Diffusion of innovations* (5th ed). New York, NY: Free Press.

Rutherford, D., Fleming, W., & Mathias, H. (1985). Strategies for change in higher education: Three political models. *Higher Education 14*(4), 433–445.

Savenjie, B., & Van Rosmalen, K. (1988). Innovation in a professional organization. *Higher Education 17*(6), 683–698.

Schein, E. H. (2004). *Organizational culture and leadership* (3rd ed.). San Francisco, CA: Jossey-Bass.

Stiles, R. J. (2012). *Understanding and managing the risks of analytics in higher education: A guide*. Retrieved from EDUCAUSE website: http://net.educause.edu/ir/library/pdf/EPUB1201.pdf

Van de Ven, A. H. (1986). Central problems in the management of innovation. *Management Science 32*(5), 590–607. doi:10.1287/mnsc.32.5.590

Van de Ven, A. H., Polley, D. E., Garud, R., & Venkataraman, S. (2008). *The innovation journey*. New York, NY: Oxford University Press.

Van de Ven, A. H., & Poole, M. S. (1985). Explaining development and change in organizations. *Academy of Management Review 20*(3), 510–540.

Van Driel, J. H., Verloop, N., Van Werven, H. I., & Dekkers, H. (1997). Teachers' craft knowledge and curriculum innovation in higher engineering education. *Higher Education 34*(1), 105–122. doi:10.1023/A:1003063317210

Weick, K. E. (1976). Educational organizations as loosely coupled systems. *Administrative Science Quarterly 21*(1), 1–19.

White, S. C., & Glickman, T. S. (2007). Innovation in higher education: Implications for the future. *New Directions for Higher Education 2007*(137), 97–105. doi:10.1002/he.248

Wixom, B. H., & Todd, P. A. (2005). A theoretical integration of user satisfaction and technology acceptance. *Information Systems Research 16*(1), 85–102. doi:10.1287/isre.1050.0042

9

The Opportunities, Challenges, and Strategies Associated with the Use of Operations-Oriented (Big) Data to Support Decision Making within Universities

JOHN CHESLOCK, RODNEY P. HUGHES, AND MARK UMBRICHT

ABSTRACT

To support operations, universities collect vast amounts of information regarding students, faculty, courses, finances, and other matters, and often store that information within large data warehouses. These data can be employed within research that informs the decision making of university leaders, but such work is challenging because these data are often structured, measured, and segmented in ways that advance operations but complicate research. On the other hand, an operations orientation can promote reporting accuracy in a manner that research-oriented data collection never can. After describing the forces shaping operations-oriented data, we present recommendations for how analysts can best extract the valuable information

The authors wish to thank Mike Dooris, Betty Harper, Heather Kelly, Nick Warcholak, and Alex Yin for helpful conversations and suggestions. All errors and opinions are those of the authors.

contained within institutional databases. Throughout the chapter, we illustrate our points using examples pertaining to data elements describing courses and instructors.

INTRODUCTION

The emergence of gigantic data sets that contain information such as the exact time a student logs in to an online course system, the specific keystrokes that the student performs while in the course system, and the moment the student logs out of the course system is an important development that receives much of the attention during discussions of the promises associated with Big Data. The focus of this chapter lies with another important data-related development: advancements in the collection and storage of data regarding key operations within higher education institutions. These data, often organized within data warehouses, are not as new, gigantic, or attention-grabbing as data describing online interactions, but they are still substantial in size and potential value. To function effectively, a college or university must record key bits of information each time a student enrolls in a class, completes a course, graduates, or is awarded financial aid; an instructor is assigned to teach a course; an employee is compensated; a research grant is completed; and a variety of other activities occur. The adjective *big* can be used to describe such data, especially when information is pooled across activities and years.

The presence of these data has little consequence if valuable information cannot be extracted from them. Multiple challenges make extraction difficult. As Varian (2009) famously noted, although Big Data is now ubiquitous in many settings, personnel who can process these data, extract value, and communicate that value effectively are scarce. Thus, most organizations will only enjoy a fraction of the potential benefits made available by Big Data.

The need for highly skilled personnel grows rapidly if data quantity is not accompanied by data quality. Institutional databases often contain data elements that are measured inaccurately or in confusing ways, are structured so that important information is obscured, and are included in multiple data systems that can only be made interoperable through considerable effort. The addition of flawed data elements allows the data to grow "bigger" but can complicate or detract from research seeking to advance decision making within colleges and universities. Institutional researchers must now sift through the data warehouse seeking to identify those data elements that can be used effectively in their current format, to determine which elements could potentially be made useful with proper cleaning, and to identify effective cleaning procedures. If data analysts exert such effort, they may waste time examining data elements whose flaws can only be identified or eliminated through efforts requiring more time than is available. If researchers instead commence analysis with little consideration for data quality, the results of the research will mislead decision makers when the biases created by the flaws in the data overwhelm the true information that researchers are seeking to extract.

This chapter seeks to advance our understanding of these challenges and the potential strategies for addressing them. A central theme is that much of the data in warehouses are collected with operational goals, not institutional research, in mind. Operational goals are central to the well-being of higher education institutions because students want to easily and effectively enroll in courses, learn about the time and location of their courses, and demonstrate their performance to future employers; employees of the institution wish to receive compensation and benefits in a convenient fashion; and administrators need to track the employment status of their personnel accurately. For these goals to be attained, voluminous data systems that contain detailed information about students, personnel, classes, finances, and other items must be developed and maintained. In other words, operational pressures cause universities to collect large amounts of data.

The operations orientation of data systems has mixed implications for data quality. As we describe in our next section, the data structures, measures, and segmentation required to advance operations often complicate institutional research because the data elements and structures that best advance operations are often quite different from those that would best advance research. On the other hand, an operations orientation can promote reporting accuracy in a manner that research-oriented data collection never can, a topic discussed in our third section. The strengths and weaknesses of operations-oriented data mean that data analysts must proceed thoughtfully, and in our fourth section, we describe how researchers might identify data elements containing high-quality information, data elements containing major limitations, and potential strategies that can be employed to overcome these limitations.

Since discussions about data are most effective when accompanied by examples, we illustrate our points using data elements pertaining to courses and instructors. These examples are easy to understand because instructor data are simple conceptually and course data are drawn from the course scheduling system, which most readers have likely used as a student to learn about course availability or as a faculty member or administrator to monitor enrollment levels and course offerings. Simplicity and familiarity are not the only virtues associated with our examples, as our chosen data elements also demonstrate well the importance and challenges of analyzing operations-oriented data effectively.

Analyses of course- and instructor-related data elements can inform important questions regarding instructional productivity and costs, which are growing in prominence due to the financial challenges faced by colleges and universities. Most schools are seeing little growth or declines in governmental funding, are unable to further increase their net tuition revenue substantially as they reach their tuition ceilings, and have limited opportunities to increase revenues from other sources (Cheslock & Gianneschi, 2008). At the same time, expense pressures continue to increase due to a variety of forces including the cost disease affecting personnel-services industries, such as higher education, that rely heavily on highly educated skilled labor and cannot easily reduce costs through technological progress (Archibald & Feldman, 2011).[1] These problematic trends in revenues and expenditures are a major reason why a recent survey revealed that only 27% of chief business officers of higher education institutions strongly agree that they are confident about the sustainability of their institution's financial model over the next five years, and only 13% strongly agree when the considered time span increases to 10 years (Jaschik & Lederman, 2013). Operational data contain information pertaining to a number of cost drivers within education, and analyses of these data that allow university leaders to better understand the cost structure of their institution and how it could change in the future will only grow in value as financial challenges mount.

Course- and instructor-related data demonstrate well the challenges of using operations-oriented data because these data are often structured, measured, and segmented in ways that impede institutional research. In a recent study of issues pertaining to non-tenure-track faculty at 10 leading research universities, Cross and Goldenberg (2009) found numerous instances of such impediments. Since certain conclusions and quotes from their study are quite compelling, we often reference their findings in this chapter to further demonstrate the systematic challenges we discuss.

OPERATIONAL GOALS, RESEARCH GOALS, AND INSTITUTIONAL DATA

After interviewing institutional leaders and researchers at 10 well-resourced institutions, Cross and Goldenberg (2009) came to several striking conclusions:

> [U]niversity information systems are inadequate for administrative decision-making. Presidents lack information about fundamental aspects of their institution and lack the means to track instructional changes or evaluate education policies. (pp. 2–3)

> No university in our study was able to provide student-oriented teaching data by faculty type—that is, how many students are taught in classes led by tenure-track faculty, non-tenure-track-faculty, and graduate students. (pp. 22–23)

The interviews revealed a number of specific data challenges created by the operations-oriented nature of institutional data, and we classify these challenges into three categories: structure, measurement, and segmentation.

Structure. The following observation from a participant in Cross and Goldenberg's (2009) study highlights a key structure-related challenge relating to course data: "I've never been really confident about the accuracy of the student system with respect to who's teaching what. In some departments, the faculty instructor will be listed for all the labs or sections, and in others, the TAs themselves will be listed" (p. 23). This quote relates to courses that contain multiple student experiences: a common session attended by a large number of

Table 9.1. Alternative Reporting Structures for Courses

Course	Section	Students	Listed Credits	Student Credits	Appt Type: Fac. #1	Appt Type: Fac. #2	Date/Time	Bldg.
A. Case #1: Optimal research-based structure								
PHYS 211R	1	30	1	30	Grd. St. #1		F 2-3pm	James 302
PHYS 211R	2	30	1	30	Grd. St. #2		F 1-2pm	James 302
PHYS 211R	3	30	1	30	Grd. St. #3		R 2-3pm	James 304
PHYS 211R	4	30	1	30	Grd. St. #4		R 1-2pm	James 304
PHYS 211L	1	120	2	240	Full Prof		MW 1-2pm	Smith 100
B. Case #2: Optimal operations structure (listing common lecturer)								
PHYS 211	1	30	3	90	Full Prof		MW 1-2/F 2-3pm	Smith 100/James 302
PHYS 211	2	30	3	90	Full Prof		MW 1-2/F 1-2pm	Smith 100/James 302
PHYS 211	3	30	3	90	Full Prof		MW 1-2/R 2-3pm	Smith 100/James 304
PHYS 211	4	30	3	90	Full Prof		MW 1-2/R 1-2pm	Smith 100/James 304
C. Case #3: Optimal operations structure (listing break-out instructor)								
PHYS 211	1	30	3	90	Grd. St. #1		MW 1-2/F 2-3pm	Smith 100/James 302
PHYS 211	2	30	3	90	Grd. St. #2		MW 1-2/F 1-2pm	Smith 100/James 302
PHYS 211	3	30	3	90	Grd. St. #3		MW 1-2/R 2-3pm	Smith 100/James 304
PHYS 211	4	30	3	90	Grd. St. #4		MW 1-2/R 1-2pm	Smith 100/James 304

Table 9.1. Alternative Reporting Structures for Courses (continued)

D. Case #4: Optimal operations structure (listing both faculty)

Course	Section	Students	Listed Credits	Student Credits	Appt Type: Fac. #1	Appt Type: Fac. #2	Date/Time	Bldg.
PHYS 211	1	30	3	90	Full Prof	Grd. St. #1	MW 1-2/F 2-3pm	Smith 100/James 302
PHYS 211	2	30	3	90	Full Prof	Grd. St. #2	MW 1-2/F 1-2pm	Smith 100/James 302
PHYS 211	3	30	3	90	Full Prof	Grd. St. #3	MW 1-2/R 2-3pm	Smith 100/James 304
PHYS 211	4	30	3	90	Full Prof	Grd. St. #4	MW 1-2/R 1-2pm	Smith 100/James 304

E. Differences Across Cases in Key Statistics

Case	Average Class Size		% Credits Taught By	
	Course[a]	Student[b]	Full-Prof	Grd. St.
#1: Optimal research-based structure	48	90	67%	33%
#2: Operations (listing common lecturer)	30	30	100%	0%
#3: Operations (listing break-out instructor)	30	30	0%	100%
#4: Operations (listing both faculty)	30	30	50%c	50%c

a. The average class size for listed courses.
b. The average class size experienced by students for every course hour taken.
c. We weight each listed instructor equally when determining credit generation for co-taught courses. A sophisticated data system would include a measure of faculty effort which could be used to more accurately assign credits.

students and break-out discussion or lab sessions containing smaller numbers of students. For the purposes of research, we would want to list these two student experiences separately. Any analysis of class sizes and the student composition of particular classes would be confounded by the combination of two vastly different student experiences into one observation. Furthermore, the separate listing of experiences would make it easy to identify which instructor taught the large common session and which instructor taught the small individual sessions. Section A of table 9.1 demonstrates a reporting structure that would align well with institutional research.

Such a structure, however, would not work well in terms of operations because the data elements are used within a course scheduling system used by students to enroll in classes. Students may be confused by the separate listing of the common session and the break-out session and may sign up for the common session but not the smaller break-out sessions (or vice versa). Scheduling complexities become even more daunting if multiple common sessions are offered in the same semester, and the instructors do not want students from different common sessions in the same break-out sessions. If the common session and break-out session are not associated with separate grades, then instructors will be required to enter grades twice or IT professionals will be required to develop a system in which the grade from one course is automatically entered into another course. Although these and other challenges could be overcome with careful planning, that work would require precious time and attention from personnel.

The importance of operational goals means that the course data will likely be structured in the manner described by sections B–D in table 9.1. In these cases, multiple student experiences (a common session and a break-out session) are combined into the same course. The common session instructor is the listed instructor in section B, the break-out session instructor is listed in section C, and both instructors are listed in section D. The decentralized nature of most higher education institutions means that academic programs would likely vary in which instructor they report for these types of classes so that no consistent standard is present within an institution.

As section E of table 9.1 outlines, the average class size and the credits generated by each type of instructor vary drastically across all four cases. The figures for the first case would provide an accurate picture of what is transpiring at the institution and would best advance decision making. The latter three cases, however, are what will typically occur in practice as data are created to support operations rather than research.

A course structure that combines a common lecture and a break-out session is not the only structure that inhibits institutional researchers. Additional complexities are created by courses that contain multiple sections that are cross-listed across academic programs, courses that combine a non-honors section and an honors section, and a variety of other possibilities. These complexities are less daunting than those introduced by courses that combine common and break-out sessions but can still be difficult to resolve. The degree to which data complexities are solved is typically determined by the initiative of individual data analysts rather than broad institutional initiatives (Cross & Goldenberg, 2009; Hess & Fullerton, 2010).

Some institutions may not possess many courses that have common and break-out sessions or other complexities, so this particular structure-related issue may not create substantial challenges. The goal of this discussion, however, is to make a larger point about data structure rather than a specific point about data elements relating to courses and instructors. Structural challenges can be found in other parts of the data warehouse and need to be identified and considered by researchers seeking to extract value from the Big Data that is collected to support operations.

Measurement. If all data were collected solely for research that supports decision making, some measurement decisions would be daunting while others would be relatively straightforward. For example, no widespread agreement exists regarding the proper way to measure the degree to which students learn during their period of enrollment, but consensus would be easy to achieve for measurement decisions regarding the appointment type of personnel who teach courses. In the real world—where data-related decisions are heavily driven by considerations unrelated to research—even easy-to-measure items may not be calculated in a manner well suited for research. For example, the title of the instructor teaching a class could be an informative data element for those seeking to describe instructional personnel within a college or university. The assignment of titles, however, may vary across academic programs. Some programs may want to distinguish between tenure-track and non-tenure-track faculty members by describing the former as professors and the latter as instructors or lecturers, while other programs may want to reduce status differentiations across faculty types and provide them with similar titles. Title assignment can vary within programs as well. If a prominent former official or professional is more likely to accept a position if the title of professor is attached, an academic program may gladly deviate from the norms it traditionally uses to assign titles. This discussion implies that operational considerations, such as employee preferences and the norms of academic programs, will often drive data decisions more than research considerations, which can complicate research efforts, as this quote from an institutional data expert demonstrates: "When departments hire NTT [non-tenure-track] people, they can throw any title at them they want. . . . I can't find any consistent way to figure out who they are, so I don't include them in my tables [which he prepares for the president]" (Cross & Goldenberg, 2009, p. 21).

Data segmentation. Data for a higher education institution are often collected within very different systems. The student information system can operate separately from the human resources system, the budget system, or other systems. Data systems were created and enhanced over time to digitize key functions and tasks (e.g., enroll students, pay employees) as technological advances made it more practical and less costly to conduct these activities using large databases. The timelines associated with each system varied because the operational pressures and technological options associated with each area emerged at different speeds. When a system was developed or updated, considerable thought was not expended toward ensuring that the system aligned with the other systems in ways that aided future research seeking to support decision making. Developers faced considerable challenges simply meeting the operational goals that were driving the creation or updating of each system, and the performance of the system would be primarily judged by its ability to meet these operational goals, so the lack of attention to research goals is quite understandable. The resulting systems complicate efforts by analysts who seek to conduct research using data elements that span systems, as Cross and Goldenberg (2009) concluded after interviewing a number of these analysts: "The software databases themselves are frequently incompatible, so that even if universities were inclined to merge all of this information into one whole, the technical barriers would be nearly insurmountable" (p. 23). The severity of these technical barriers likely differs across institutions. For example, the data systems at some schools may have appropriately placed identification codes for individual students, employees, academic programs, or other items that allow analysts to merge data from separate databases without considerable effort. Although the severity of challenges may vary, the segmentation of information into separate data systems complicates research efforts at all institutions.

THE ACCURACY OF OPERATIONS-ORIENTED DATA

The previous section explained how the presence of operations-oriented data could complicate efforts to conduct research to support decision making within higher education institutions, but the operational nature of institutional data also promises good news for researchers. An operational orientation can promote data accuracy in a manner that research-orientated data collection never can because inaccurate data within certain types of operations can create large problems within an organization. Students get upset when their transcripts are wrong or class schedules list the wrong room or time. Employees become angry when they are incorrectly denied access to benefits or receive a salary well below what was promised. These consequences create pressure on data entrants to enter information accurately and lead to corrections being made once errors are identified. When data are collected primarily for research efforts, such accuracy-promoting forces are not present.

Skilled research analysts must determine which variables are highly accurate and center their research strategies on those variables while avoiding the use of variables possessing considerable error. The following three questions, which examine how operational pressures affect data reporting, are helpful for analysts who are seeking to determine the quality of any specific data element.[2]

1. Are there consequences to the data entrant if data are entered incorrectly so that the entrant will spend considerable effort ensuring data accuracy?
2. If data are entered incorrectly, would the errors rise to anyone's attention in a manner that would lead to the correction of the database?

3. Would these factors be similar across the institution, so that the data reporting would be consistent across units?

We turn now to a discussion of operational forces—relating to ritual classifications, resources, and logistics—that promote data accuracy. Our goal is not to provide an exhaustive classification of potential forces but instead to provide examples that further explain the basic logic underlying our argument.

Ritual classifications. In a book chapter written while they were shaping new institutionalism, a prominent tradition within organizational theory, Meyer and Rowan (1978) highlighted the key role that ritual classifications play within the educational system:

> The tight control educational organizations maintain over the ritual or formal classification systems is central to our understanding of education as an institution. To a considerable extent, educational organizations function to maintain the *societally agreed-on rites defined in societal myths (or institutional rules) of education.* Education rests on and obtains enormous resources from central institutional rules about what valid education is. These rules define the ritual categories of teacher, student, curricular topic, and type of school. When these categories are properly assembled, education is understood to occur. (pp. 84–85)

Meyer and Rowan implied that colleges and universities must consider societal expectations when determining how to measure key items relating to students, instructors, and the education that occurs. If a school does not employ the reigning ritual classifications when measuring key items, its legitimacy and effectiveness within society is diminished. Furthermore, higher education institutions must measure variables relating to ritual classifications very accurately because these data are used within society in very important ways.

A specific example illuminates these points. Society currently expects colleges and universities to classify the education that students receive using credentials based on the level of their education (e.g., associate's, bachelor's, master's) and the primary subject area of their education (e.g., English, sociology, accounting). Society also currently expects colleges and universities to classify the specific portions of a student's education by describing each portion as a class and describing each class in terms of topic, amount, and performance level. The topic needs to be described using a subject area, a number, and a course title; the amount needs to be described using the Carnegie credit hour; and the performance level needs to be described using a letter grade.[3]

Colleges and universities that conform to these rules allow their students to list their credential at the top of their resume; to list specific items regarding their education using a transcript; and to communicate information, in both instances, in a manner that key audiences (e.g., employers, admissions committees) find *easily understandable* and *trustworthy*. Such information will only be easily understandable if the information is organized using the prevailing ritual classifications, which are familiar to employers and admissions committees. The information will only be deemed trustworthy if the university is viewed as a legitimate provider of education, and society expects legitimate providers to communicate information about their activities using the prevailing ritual classifications. Trustworthiness also requires accuracy, which implies that schools are under tremendous pressure to measure items pertaining to ritual classifications in a *highly accurate* manner.

Consequently, the items within a data warehouse pertaining to key ritual classifications, such as information relating to student transcripts, will be precisely measured. If such data contained major errors, the institution would be viewed negatively by alumni, potential students, and employers, which would have major consequences. Therefore, great care is taken when entering these data, and mistakes—with the exception of course grades that accidently exceed the assigned grade—are quickly corrected in response to student complaints.

Resources. Fiduciary responsibilities cause financial data elements to receive special attention as the dollar figures associated with specific financial transactions and groups of transactions must be recorded accurately. Similar pressures occur for data elements—such as those that determine whether employees qualify for benefits—that determine the expenditure of resources. If benefit eligibility is not recorded accurately, data entrants will receive feedback after complaints are received from angry employees or from administrators concerned about the high costs of benefits. Other aspects of the employee arrangement, such as whether the contract relates to a standing appointment or a fixed-term appointment, will also be precisely measured at most institutions.

Logistics. Certain activities can only be performed effectively if key pieces of information are accurately communicated to participants through central data systems. Imagine the chaos that would ensue during the first week of classes at a school whose course scheduling system contained major errors so that multiple classes are listed with the same time and location information. Data entrants would certainly endure harsh reprimands, and data errors would be quickly rectified. Mundane logistical challenges can cause certain data elements, such as room and location information, to be some of the most precisely measured items in the data warehouse.

When pressures for data accuracy are absent. Data warehouses also contain a number of items measured with considerable error, and those inaccuracies can appear in a variety of contexts: (1) data elements collected to support operations but not used within operations in a manner that promotes accuracy, (2) data elements collected to augment research designed to support decision making, (3) data elements collected to satisfy data requests by external entities, and (4) data elements whose accuracy cannot be determined by anyone other than the data entrant. Errors have the potential to arise in these scenarios because data entrants will not feel pressure to report accurately and errors will not be identified and corrected. Specific examples from each scenario best demonstrate this point.

To run a higher education institution effectively, administrators need to know which faculty members are tenured and which are not, but this requirement does not imply the information in the data warehouse regarding the tenure status of faculty members is accurate. In practice, central databases may measure tenure with considerable error at some institutions because institutional leaders may not take regular actions for which they need data analysts to generate an exhaustive and extremely accurate list of tenured faculty members. Actions may occur primarily at more local levels (e.g., colleges within a university), and lists may be easy to maintain within informal local databases because the number of tenured individuals is relatively small, and the importance of tenure means that these lists are easy to generate because the status of each faculty member is well known locally. Therefore, although an institution may have included the tenure variable within central databases because planners thought such information would be helpful to operations in the future, in reality, the information may not be used within operations in important ways that create pressure on data entrants to report accurate information. As a result, the central data systems may not be properly updated when faculty members are awarded tenure, and because the information is not being used for important tasks, the errors may not be identified and corrected.

Our earlier discussion regarding table 9.1 described how researchers may have difficulty identifying common lectures because data within the course scheduling system lists each break-out session as a separate course. Our analysis highlighted how this data structure can make research into class sizes, credit generation by instructor types, or others topics difficult, and those challenges may lead database planners to add a data field that indicates whether a listed course shares a common session with other courses. The information reported for each academic program, however, may contain substantial errors, as staff members supporting the programs may have difficulty understanding what is meant by a common session and how to determine whether the courses in their program possess a common session. Since these data will be used primarily for research rather than operations, the incentives for data entrants to spend time learning how to enter this information correctly will be weak. When errors occur, staff members will likely not be alerted, which ensures that past errors are not corrected and strengthens the belief among data entrants that this data field is of low importance.

A number of state governments, seeking to ensure productivity among faculty members, have required their public higher education institutions to report a variety of figures relating to their faculty, and in certain states, the mandated figures include the average number of hours faculty spend per week on specific tasks (e.g., undergraduate teaching, research). Such a requirement is fascinating for the purposes of this chapter because so many forces work against the collection of accurate data on faculty time allocation. Accurate reporting requires great effort by data entrants (i.e., individual faculty members), because the human mind has great difficulty recalling the average amount of time spent per week on specific activities over an extended period of time (Porter, 2011). Faculty members, however, would be unlikely to expend such effort because time is scarce, inaccuracies carry no penalty as no one other than the data entrant knows the true values, and efforts to monitor performance often create resistance. Inaccuracies are also difficult to detect at the institution level through benchmarking because similarities across schools could be due to similar reporting errors, and observed differences could be due to difficult-to-detect differences in mission or fields of study. Thus, pressures for data accuracy are absent at both the level of the individual data entrant and the institution.

PRINCIPLES AND STRATEGIES FOR EXAMINING OPERATIONS-ORIENTED DATA

Researchers should consider these general principles when seeking to use operations-oriented data skillfully to support decision making: (1) think theoretically, (2) learn how data elements are used within operations in practice, (3) perform internal consistency checks, (4) employ time and coding expertise, (5) find simplicity on the other side of complexity, and (6) plan data systems with research (partially) in mind. The first three principles represent three different ways to investigate data quality. Using a mix of logic and theory similar to that employed earlier in this chapter, the analyst should predict which data elements are crucial to operations and likely to be accurately reported and which data elements are not. The analyst can then query members of the organization who understand how specific data elements are actually used within operations and how they are reported by data entrants. The third step is to examine whether the patterns contained within key data elements suggest accuracy or error. For example, the data elements pertaining to tenure can be investigated by checking whether tenure status changes when a professor with a standing appointment moves from assistant professor to associate professor and whether observed irregularities represent idiosyncrasies or errors.

Once data analysts understand the nature of the data, they can employ time and coding expertise to investigate how the data could be restructured, cleaned, and merged, so that effective research can be conducted. Such work can be time-intensive and complex, which requires analysts to regularly contemplate whether the benefits of additional data improvements exceed the costs of their time. Analysts must identify simple descriptions that effectively explain the complexities contained within data flaws and the corrections employed to address those flaws because the findings emanating from big operations-oriented data will not be used to improve decision making if administrators do not trust and understand the underlying analysis.

In addition to spending time correcting flaws in the existing institutional databases, data analysts should seek to prevent future flaws by participating in discussions supporting the creation or alteration of institutional data systems. Analysts can recommend changes that will allow for future research to be conducted more easily and more effectively. Such recommendations may need to be discarded if they would weaken the ability of data systems to support operations, but they may often enhance research at no cost to operations.

In addition to general principles, the data analyst must also consider specific challenges associated with operations-oriented data. We turn now to a discussion of strategies, informed by the aforementioned six principles, that could be employed in response to specific challenges associated with data structure, measurement, and segmentation, the three categories of data challenges discussed earlier.

Structure. As discussed earlier, accurate research into key instruction-related topics requires data structured in the manner described in section A of table 9.1 while operating pressures cause data to be structured in the manner described in sections B–D. How might colleges and universities still provide an accurate description of instruction? The university could adjust data collection procedures so the resulting data are well suited for research, but such an approach could create greater problems within operations than it would solve through improved research. As noted earlier, a course scheduling system based on data framed primarily for research could lead students to sign up for courses incorrectly, faculty to spend additional time entering grades, or other operational problems. In other contexts, the conflict between operations and research may be slight or nonexistent, and the inadequacy of existing data for research simply reflects a lack of thought and/or effective communication. Although problems of this type seem easy to reconcile, thought and effective communication require personnel time, which will likely become increasingly scarce given the financial challenges facing higher education institutions.

Suitable data could be alternatively produced by requiring each academic program to report both operations-oriented data (sections B–D of table 9.1) and research-oriented data (section A) regarding its courses. Such an approach, however, would increase workload and be unlikely to yield good data because as described in the previous sections, academic programs are unlikely to report accurate data to a database designed solely for research. The research-oriented database will only be accurate when individuals throughout the organization possess an unusual commitment to ensuring data quality for the sake of future research.

A third option for producing suitable data relies upon the restructuring of operations-oriented data (a mixture of the data described in sections B–D of table 9.1) so that they resemble research-oriented data (described in section A). Such restructuring requires data analysts to identify those courses that contain separate experiences and adjust the data so that each experience is associated with the proper course size, students, and instructors. Such identification could occur through the use of data elements that identify cross-listed courses, common lectures, and other course structures, but as noted earlier, these data elements may be entered with considerable error. As the location and time of each student experience should be accurately recorded, researchers could instead use this information to identify separate experiences within the same course and shared experiences across courses. The primary challenge associated with restructuring existing data is that it requires substantial expertise and time to implement successfully.

Measurement. Employing our general strategies, a data analyst can identify those data elements from the warehouse that are accurately measured and those elements containing considerable error. Our earlier discussion indicated that the title of a faculty member may be a poor measure of instructor type given the way titles are used within operations, while other aspects of the employment arrangement, especially those relating to access to benefits, may be measured with considerable accuracy. Often, the data analyst may wish to create new variables that aggregate information from a variety of data elements. For example, instructor type may be best measured by combining the information contained in appointment title with multiple pieces of data concerning employment status: (a) full-time versus part-time, (b) standing appointment versus fixed-term appointment, (c) faculty appointment versus administrative appointment, (d) tenure-track versus non-tenure-track appointment, and (e) graduate student status.

Data segmentation. As universities developed and updated a range of data systems, considerable thought was not expended toward ensuring that these data systems were aligned in ways that aided future research seeking to support decision making. As a result, analysts seeking to use data simultaneously from the course system, the human resources system, and other data systems to study instructional costs and productivity often face considerable technical challenges. Such challenges can be lessened in the long run through careful planning whenever data systems are updated so that adjustments to these systems are made with research partially in mind. In the short run, skilled analysts must employ their time and expertise to develop methods that allow data from a range of data systems to be employed effectively.

PAST RESEARCH INTO INSTRUCTIONAL
PRODUCTIVITY AND COSTS

Earlier in this chapter, we illustrated our points using data pertaining to courses and instructors because these data have not been examined widely in past research, and financial pressures are causing many higher education institutions to examine issues pertaining to instructional productivity and costs more closely. We describe here several prominent examples of research in this area to illuminate this topic and the associated data challenges.

Delta Cost Project. The Delta Cost Project examines productivity and costs using institution-level data reported to the federal government through the Integrated Postsecondary Education Data System (IPEDS). Among other items, this project measures costs per student and per degree by employing data on the total education and related costs associated with instruction, student services, and a portion of spending related to academic and institutional support and maintenance of buildings. Comparisons of figures over time and between different states and sectors allow for a national portrait of costs within higher education (Desrochers & Kirshstein, 2012). Although this chapter focuses on analysis of detailed data housed within specific colleges and universities rather than the aggregated data reported to IPEDS, the work done by the Delta Cost Project paints an important national portrait that serves as the backdrop for more detailed institutional studies.

Institutional consortiums. Two consortiums of institutions collect data on institutional costs and productivity: the National Study of Instructional Costs and Productivity and the National Community College Costs and Productivity Project, commonly referred to respectively as the Delaware Study and the Kansas Study. Each study examines factors such as faculty workload, instructional costs per credit hour or student, and the proportion of credit hours taught by each faculty type. The data, collected at the academic discipline level, allow for discipline-specific comparisons across institutions. Although they allow for more detailed comparisons than IPEDS data do, consortium data are not publicly available to researchers and do not provide a nationally representative portrait of the higher education system. For the institutions in the consortium, however, these data allow for helpful comparisons with peer institutions. Participation also forces institutional researchers at these schools to produce student-oriented teaching data by faculty type, information that the researchers at the universities studied by Cross and Goldenberg (2009) were unable to produce. A key question, for the purposes of this chapter, is whether participation in such consortiums leads researchers to address fully the wide range of data flaws that are present in the operations-oriented data available for research. Institutional participation in such consortiums will be of greatest value when accurate figures are produced, but that incentive may not lead institutions to devote the substantial amount of time required to address a number of the severe data challenges noted in this chapter and elsewhere (e.g., Middaugh, 2001).

Comparative case study. In *Buying the Best: Cost Escalation in Elite Higher Education*, Clotfelter (1996) examined a range of cost drivers at four elite, private institutions. He argued that the price increases caused by exogenous forces, such as the cost for faculty or library books, could only explain a portion of the increase in tuition, which implies that other areas, such as instructional productivity, must be responsible for the remaining rise in expenditures. When examining instructional costs and productivity using detailed data from these four institutions, Clotfelter identified and sought to correct for many of the data flaws highlighted in this chapter. For example, the class sizes for courses containing both common and break-out sessions were weighted by the amount of class time spent in each venue, and the faculty effort associated with such courses was adjusted to account for break-out sessions conducted by teaching assistants. While describing his approach to data preparation, Clotfelter provided several general statements quite relevant to this chapter:

> Although this approach may appear relatively straightforward, the customs and peculiarities of college and university teaching make it necessary to make use of several simplifying and, ultimately, arbitrary assumptions. As with the exclusion of all hours of teaching effort that do not occur in the classroom—an exclusion necessitated by the absence of data—these assumptions can be justified only by arguing that rough quantification of what can be observed will be a useful addition to our knowledge of resource allocation in these institutions. (p. 189)

Clotfelter only examined three academic departments because "[t]he volume of information required to make calculations (for course loads) for an entire institution made it impractical to examine more than a few departments" (p. 16). For big operations-oriented data to advance decision making within higher education institutions, practical data preparation procedures must be developed so that analysts can examine the full range of departments within an institution and provide a complete portrait of activities to university leadership.

Institution-specific studies. In recent years, several detailed and highly controversial studies about faculty productivity emerged from Texas (Mangan, 2010; Musick, 2011; O'Donnell, 2011; Vedder, Matgouranis, & Robe, 2011). Very different findings were drawn from the same set of original data, which highlights the importance of decisions pertaining to variable selection, measurement, sample construction, and other areas. The promise of Big Data would be much easier to realize if such decisions only needed to address the technical challenges that could be solved in an objective fashion that enjoyed widespread support. But data preparation decisions often require assumptions about fundamental items, such as the mission of higher education institutions, which are a source of deep disagreement.

The initial study in Texas, conducted using data from Texas A&M University, illustrated tension over the activities that should be conducted by faculty (Mangan, 2010). This study sought to estimate the benefits and costs of each individual faculty member by comparing the revenue associated with teaching activity with the costs of salary and benefits. Proponents of the study emphasized that educating large numbers of students in formal classes is the primary activity of the university, while critics noted that a range of other important activities, such as conducting and publishing high-quality research, advising students, serving on committees, and educating students in specialized topics, were not properly recognized in the analyses (Fairbanks, 2011; Mangan, 2010; Middaugh, 2011).

Similar data from the University of Texas at Austin were later released and generated a flurry of reports. O'Donnell (2011) and Musick (2011) both examined credit-hour production and research grant procurement using the same data but found very different levels of variability across faculty members. The varying findings reflected very different decisions by the researchers. O'Donnell (2011) only adjusted for the employment intensity of faculty members (full-time or part-time) and full-time administrative appointments, while Musick (2011) analyzed faculty members by appointment and rank, separating tenured and tenure-track professors, fixed-term faculty, and graduate student instructors. Furthermore, Musick (2011) excluded research scientists, adjunct instructors, retired faculty, and graduate students who appeared in the public employee data and might have taught courses occasionally but were not employed primarily to be full-time instructors. The results were also sensitive to measurement decisions, such as the decision of whether and how to weight student credit hours by the level of instruction.

Few studies will be conducted in as politicized an environment as these Texas studies were, but a discussion of this extreme case is worthwhile because most research initiatives will face decisions regarding data preparation and analysis that require assumptions that will be deeply disputed. Skilled analysts will seek to identify robust findings that hold true across the range of reasonable assumptions that could be held. At the same time, institutional researchers must contend with the less contentious but still daunting technical challenges described in this chapter. Unless addressed properly, those technical challenges can lead to gross inaccuracies within the data, which makes it unsurprising that the Texas A&M University System decided to remove its faculty productivity data from its website after initial release because many aspects of the data were found to be inaccurate (Fairbanks, 2011).

DISCUSSION AND CONCLUSION

Technological advances have allowed colleges and universities to increase drastically the collection and storage of data pertaining to a wide array of operational activities. Such data can allow universities to become "smarter" in many areas, the most prominent being teaching and learning, the area that receives the greatest attention in discussions of Big Data. This chapter has focused more on financial considerations, which often lead to analysis of personnel and their activities, given the personnel-intensive nature of higher education. The financial challenges present in higher education cause institutional leaders to face numerous decisions that could be made easier if accurate and insightful information about the organization could be extracted from the large amounts of data being collected.

How do we extract this information? Or, to use the framework recently popularized by Silver (2012), how do we separate the signal from the noise? This chapter advanced our thinking on these questions through big-picture conceptual discussions of the nature of the data collection process employed within higher education institutions. The operations orientation of that process often creates considerable noise by measuring, structuring, and segmenting the data in a manner poorly aligned with research goals, but that orientation also can substantially reduce noise by promoting highly accurate reporting. We provide a number of strategies that can identify the volume and nature of the noise within the data and help guide data collection or restructuring procedures that better allow detection of the signal.

The applications of these strategies, especially in regard to the restructuring of data, will often require tedious and time-intensive examination and cleaning of institutional data, as described in this quote from a date scientist: "I'm a data janitor. That's the sexiest job of the 21st century? It's very flattering, but it's also a little baffling" (Leber, 2013). The underlying tension within this humorous quote is a serious one. Although many stakeholders are excited about the promise of Big Data, few are qualified and willing to do the work required to realize that promise.

Who will conduct that work for colleges and universities? Institutional researchers will play an important role as they possess the greatest understanding of the databases, context, and leaders of their institutions, but these researchers often face a large array of short-term deadlines and are tasked with advancing their institution rather than higher education as a whole. As the challenges associated with big operations-oriented data require long-term, sustained attention with delayed rewards and are similar across institutions, institutional researchers will be aided by partnerships with researchers and organizations that have the time and resources to engage in long-term projects with delayed rewards and have an incentive to develop industry-wide strategies (Hess & Fullerton, 2010). These partners can supply the basic institutional research that can support applied efforts at individual institutions.

For-profit firms will be most effective as partners when they have a financial incentive to invest heavily in the required research and development and can use that R&D to advance products and services in both higher education and other industries, which would lead them to charge relatively low prices for universities if a competitive marketplace were to exist. The arena of learning analytics may prove to be such a context as companies learn general strategies for turning key strokes of learners—in K–12, higher education, employee training, and other settings—into clear signals regarding what instructional materials to provide next to individual learners.

Academic research centers will be most effective as partners in those arenas where interesting conceptual challenges exist alongside technical challenges. The operations orientation of institutional data, which causes the basic structure of the data to be misaligned with research goals, can create challenges that institutional researchers can more easily navigate when aided by basic conceptual ideas, such as the differences between course-level and student-experience-level data structures outlined in this chapter. Much greater conceptual challenges are caused by the complicated nature of key aspects of higher education such as costs that are nonlinear and difficult to separate across activities (e.g., undergraduate education, graduate education, research, service).

The quotes from Cross and Goldenberg (2009) presented earlier highlight the challenges that researchers face when seeking to enhance decision making through the analysis of institutional data. Such challenges are regularly overcome in a variety of academic fields, and thoughtful and sustained partnerships can produce similar results in this domain. The primary challenge will likely be the successful formation and implementation of such partnerships, but the promise of Big Data suggests the rewards for success will be considerable.

NOTES

1. Expenditures increase in industries afflicted by the cost disease because the number of personnel required to provide the service does not decrease over time but the salaries associated with these personnel increase. The excitement associated with Big Data partially lies in its potential to break the cost disease by allowing higher education institutions to replace instructional personnel with computerized learning (Bowen, 2013). These potential changes are mostly beyond the scope of this chapter, but they are partially related in that operational data are needed to determine the effect of new forms of instruction on expenses. This effect is not straightforward: Although instructional personnel can be replaced with technology, the personnel and infrastructure required to support the technology are substantial in cost.

2. Pressures relating to operations are not the only forces shaping data quality. The training and experience of data entrants, the clarity of reporting screens, the complexity of the information being reported, and other considerations will also play an important role.

3. Proponents of competency-based education are seeking to alter these expectations by encouraging key actors within governments and the higher education system to allow for alternative descriptions of educational attainment. The power of ritual classifications explains why reformers are targeting the credit hour and

student evaluation methods and why reform is difficult, although not impossible, to achieve.

REFERENCES

Archibald, R. B., & Feldman, D. H. (2011). *Why does college cost so much?* Oxford, UK: Oxford University Press.

Bowen, W. G. (2013). *Higher education in the digital age.* Princeton, NJ: Princeton University Press.

Cheslock, J. J., & Gianneschi, M. (2008). Replacing state appropriations with alternative revenue sources: The case of voluntary support. *Journal of Higher Education 79*(2), 208–229. doi:10.1353/jhe.2008.0012

Clotfelter, C. T. (1996). *Buying the best: Cost escalation in elite higher education.* Princeton, NJ: Princeton University Press.

Cross, J. G., & Goldenberg, E. N. (2009). *Off-track profs: Nontenured teachers in higher education.* Cambridge, MA: MIT Press.

Desrochers, D. M., & Kirshstein, R. J. (2012). *College spending in a turbulent decade: Findings from the Delta Cost Project.* Retrieved from the Delta Cost Project website: http://www.delta-costproject.org/pdfs/Delta-Cost-College-Spending-In-A-Turbulent-Decade.pdf

Fairbanks, A. (2011, April 7). College professor rankings in Texas spark national debate. *The Huffington Post.* Retrieved from http://www.huffingtonpost.com/2011/04/07/college-professor-salary-texas_n_845667.html

Hess, F. M., & Fullerton, J. (2010). The numbers we need: How the right metrics could improve K–12 education. *Education Outlook 2.* Washington, DC: American Enterprise Institute for Public Policy Research. Retrieved from American Enterprise Institute website: http://www.aei.org/article/education/k-12/the-numbers-we-need-how-the-right-metrics-could-improve-k-12-education/

Jaschik, S., & Lederman, D. (2013). *The 2013 Inside Higher Ed survey of college and university business officers.* Washington, DC: Inside Higher Ed.

Leber, J. (2013, May 22). In a data deluge, companies seek to fill new role. *MIT Technology Review.* Retrieved from http://

www.technologyreview.com/news/513866/in-a-data-deluge-companies-seek-to-fill-a-new-role/

Mangan, K. (2010, September 15). Texas A&M's bottom-line ratings of professors find that most are cost-effective. *The Chronicle of Higher Education*. Retrieved from http://chronicle.com/article/Texas-A-Ms-Bottom-Line/124451/

Meyer, J., & Rowan, B. (1978). The structure of educational organizations. In M. W. Meyer (Ed.), *Environments and organizations* (pp. 78–109). San Francisco, CA: Jossey-Bass.

Middaugh, M. F. (2001). *Understanding faculty productivity: Standards and benchmarks for colleges and universities*. San Francisco, CA: Jossey-Bass.

Middaugh, M. F. (2011, August 28). Measuring faculty productivity: Let's get it right. *The Chronicle of Higher Education*. Retrieved from http://chronicle.com/article/Measuring-Faculty/128802/

Musick, M. A. (2011). *An analysis of faculty instructional and grant-based productivity at the University of Texas at Austin*. Retrieved from the University of Texas at Austin website: http://www.utexas.edu/news/attach/2011/campus/32385_faculty_productivity.pdf

O'Donnell, R. F. (2011). *Higher education's faculty productivity gap: The cost to students, parents & taxpayers*. Retrieved from the *Texas Tribune* website: http://static.texastribune.org/media/documents/Higher_Eds_Faculty_Productivity_Gap.pdf

Porter, S. (2011). Do college student surveys have any validity? *Review of Higher Education 35*(1), 45–75. doi:10.1353/rhe.2011.0034

Silver, N. (2012). *The signal and the noise: Why so many predictions fail—but some don't*. New York, NY: Penguin Press.

Varian, H. (2009). *Hal Varian on how the web challenges managers*. Retrieved from McKinsey Quarterly website: http://www.mckinseyquarterly.com/Hal_Varian_on_how_the_Web_challenges_managers_2286

Vedder, R., Matgouranis, C., & Robe, J. (2011). *Faculty productivity and costs at the University of Texas at Austin: A preliminary analysis*. Retrieved from Center for College Affordability and Productivity website: http://www.centerforcollegeaffordability.org/uploads/Faculty_Productivity_UT-Austin_report.pdf

10

Measuring the Internationalization of Higher Education

Data, Big Data, and Analytics

JASON E. LANE AND RAJIKA BHANDARI

ABSTRACT

Once almost entirely domestically focused, many colleges and universities are increasingly competing in a global marketplace for students, scholars, prestige, and resources. However, few institutions have historically gathered data about their internationality or developed analytics to support strategic decision making about their global engagements. The gap between wanting to be more strategic and not having the appropriate data has led many academic leaders to begin to develop internal and external capacities to support their international work. This chapter examines the importance of measuring an institution's internationality; what resources are available to understand global higher education trends; and how institutions can harness data, Big Data, and analytics to become more strategic in their global engagements.

Higher education data systems have traditionally been domestically focused, largely because higher education has been domestically focused. However, the environment in which colleges and universities now operate is increasingly international in scope, and academic leaders are considering, more and more, how to internationalize their home campuses and pursue global engagements for their institutions. The most recent *Mapping Internationalization* survey by the American Council on Education (ACE) found that in 2011, 93 percent of doctoral institutions, 84 percent of master's institutions, 78 percent of baccalaureate institutions, and approximately 50 percent of associate institutions and special focus institutions perceived that internationalization has accelerated on their campuses in the previous three years (American Council on Education, 2012). Indeed, a growing proportion of student enrollments comes from outside of the national boundaries of where a campus is located, and many domestic students spend some part of their college years in another country (Farrugia & Bhandari, 2013). Faculty members partner with colleagues in other countries on activities ranging from coauthoring journal articles to codirecting research teams. Institutions engage in a range of institution-to-institution partnerships, including student exchanges, joint and dual degree programs, and formal research collaboration. Some colleges and universities are even developing their own global footprints, operating physical locations in more than one country. Many of these activities are done outside of traditional data reporting contexts, which makes it difficult for academic leaders to engage in data-informed decision making when creating a global strategy and pursuing internationalization activities.

We acknowledge that for many academic administrators international activities are often not viewed as part of the core mission of their institution, and there has thus been very little interest in collecting and analyzing data about these activities. In fact, historically, there have been conscious efforts among some public institutions, particularly in the United States, to not raise awareness of such activities out of fear that it might provoke the ire of elected officials or the general public for taking resources away from activities within the state or nation. But these general sentiments about higher education's international engagements and collecting corresponding data seem to be changing.

More than collecting data, institutions need to develop analytical models and incorporate international data into existing models as a means for informing their global strategy development. As discussed throughout this volume, the emergence of Big Data is transforming many aspects of how higher education operates—from how we recruit students, to the interventions that we provide to keep them on track to graduation, to measuring their post-collegiate success in the workforce (a measure that does not fully capture the value of a college education but is a reality of the current times).[1] To date, however, these transformations are occurring mostly in the domestic context.

An important predecessor to developing analytical models is understanding what data exist to be fed into the models. Unlike many of the other areas discussed in this volume, data collection around international engagements is still relatively limited. That being said, there are a growing number of national and international organizations that are seeking to collect data related to student mobility. The context of this volume provides an opportunity to reconsider all aspects of data related to the international activities of colleges and universities. Some of this chapter directly addresses both the advantages and disadvantages of Big Data in relation to international higher education, but we also focus on traditional (yet under-utilized) forms of data in this context. We begin with a discussion of some of the reasons why institutions and governments are increasingly interested in creating and harnessing data in this arena. We then provide information about some of the existing data sources upon which an institution might draw. Finally, we discuss cautionary considerations about using data in the international context and look to the future of data in the higher education internationalization arena.

WHY MEASURE INTERNATIONALIZATION?

It may seem curious to some that international activities have not been captured by the traditional data systems. One reason is that many of the international activities in which faculty members engage occur in a grassroots fashion, not from top-down directives. So, faculty members may collaborate with colleagues in foreign countries on a range of research and academic issues, without the senior administration ever being made aware. Even if administrators are informed of such activities, many campuses do not have the sophisticated database systems or computer applications to allow for tracking of such initiatives in a systematic way. For some institutions, students who are temporarily enrolled in programs outside their home country or

state are often not permitted to be included in some standard enrollment reporting processes, particularly those affecting resource allo-
cations from the government. In some cases, the mandated reporting mechanisms have not been designed to capture all international
student data. For example, the Integrated Postsecondary Education
Data System (IPEDS), the U.S. Department of Education's system of
surveys of postsecondary institutions, only provides reporting categories for foreign students legally attending class in the United States.
All nonresident alien students and students who are studying with
the institution in a foreign location are required to be reported as
"unknown."

This is not to say that data about international activities are not
available. Within the United States, the Institute for International Education (IIE) has been tracking the mobility of students into and out
of the United States since 1948 through their annual Open Doors®
survey. The National Science Foundation tracks the involvement of
international students and scholars in STEM fields at U.S. colleges
and universities. In addition, the U.S. Department of Homeland Security requires that institutions that provide visa sponsorship for international students and scholars regularly report their activities via
the Student and Exchange Visitor Program.

These collections of data have been motivated by various reasons
ranging from a desire to raise awareness of the flow of international
students to a post-9/11 concern about national security threats potentially posed by international students. For this chapter, though, we
are primarily concerned with what, how, and why institutions would
want to gather data related to international higher education.

Improve recruitment of students. One of the major advances being attributed to the new data available via the digital revolution
is the ability to improve the effectiveness of an institution's recruitment efforts (see chapter 4). While the admissions and recruitment
profession has been increasingly data-driven since at least the 1970s,
Big Data allows for more individualized analysis of student behavior
when it comes to the college selection process. Within the United
States, there has been a push to use the personal information of prospective students to target those with certain traits (e.g., ethnicity,
academic achievement, family income) as well as predict who is most
likely to enroll and stay in college (Rivard, 2013). These analyses are
often then used to target resources to recruit these students and tailor

the message they receive, rather than spread the resources across very broad efforts with generic messages. This approach is a version of what political campaigns refer to as *microtargeting*—techniques used to tailor messaging to prospective voters based on where they live, how they have voted, and what websites they visit (Vega, 2012). While data on individual prospective students from foreign countries remain largely inaccessible, at least in the short term, more and more data on existing students are available, particularly via their digital activities. Collecting and analyzing these data could be used to develop patterns of activity, such as certain geographic hotspots of interest (possibly targeted to the village/province/district level), how interests in programs might vary by country of origin, and which students are most likely to complete a full course of study. A new firm based in Silicon Valley, Anyadir Education, is developing software for institutions to improve international student recruitment by using Facebook data to target students in India and Vietnam who may have an interest in the institution based on their online activities as well as whether any of their Facebook friends attended the institution. This type of data could allow institutions to target their limited resources both in terms of location and messaging. Such data would also allow institutions to know which regions may need additional resources or different marketing strategies if they want to increase enrollments from those locations.

Provide resources for student success. Another way in which Big Data is being used to improve the college experience of students is by using learning analytics to identify at-risk students and provide real-time interventions to ensure that they stay on track to complete their courses and eventually graduate (rather than waiting for their grades to come in at the end of the semester; additional information on some of these techniques is available in chapter 6). While not widely discussed elsewhere, these emerging analytic platforms can be very helpful for international students in two different ways.

First, many international students, particularly those from non-English-speaking nations, have a difficult time adjusting to study in the United States (see, e.g., Constantine, Okazaki, & Utsey, 2010; Gareis, 2012; Lin & Yi, 1997). Unfortunately, they often do not know where to seek assistance, and it can be difficult for campus officials to identify these students before they begin to founder academically. The analytical tools now being developed to intervene with domestic at-risk students can be tweaked to develop models specifically for international students. They will help international office staff members to develop appropriate interventions to ensure the success of these students.

Second, student culture and behavior can vary across campuses, particularly when those campuses are in different countries. However, institutions often develop models of student success based on the behavior of students at the home campus and then apply those models to students at other locations. This approach can be problematic as the model often does not meet the needs of the students studying in a different location. The growing availability of data can allow institutions to develop separate models for different campuses and provide individualized interventions based on the needs of the student.

Inform institutional strategy (internal and external). A growing number of colleges and universities are incorporating international components into their institutional strategies, though they still are not usually mainstream components. In a review of system-level strategic plans, Lane (2013b) found that the plans of only 12 of 38 higher education systems included a reference to internationalization activities, and according to the ACE internationalization survey only 26 percent of U.S. institutions had an internationalization plan, although about 44 percent did have in place some sort of campus-wide committee or taskforce dedicated to advancing internationalization (ACE, 2012). In the absence of hard data about how many institutions are pursuing a global strategy, anecdotal evidence suggests that it is modest but increasing. New York University is now a geographically disbursed institution with 13 academic centers around the world. Texas A&M University is creating a second branch campus in the Middle East.

Even if not part of an official strategy, international students already comprise a not insignificant proportion of enrollments. In 2012, international students in the United States comprised just under 4% of all higher education enrollments nationally and 15% of graduate enrollments (Farrugia & Bhandari, 2013; Gonzales, Allum, & Sowell, 2013). And, current indicators suggest these numbers will continue to grow. For example, many campuses are trying to take advantage of Brazil's commitment to send 100,000 students overseas for study (Balan, 2013). Moreover, 35% of postdoctoral students in the United States are foreign students on temporary visas, and post-docs and other nonfaculty researchers supported the development of 54% of patents issues by universities in 2011 (Kang, 2012; Partnership for a New American Economy, 2012). In sum, whether by drift or design, higher education in the United States is international, but academic leaders need additional data to be more strategic about global engagement.

Enhance student and staff security. Given the increasing political instability in some parts of the world, as well as the increasing likelihood of extreme weather events, institutional leaders are becoming more aware of their responsibility for the safety and security of their students and staff in foreign locations. Already, most institutions have developed risk management policies related to their international engagements, and many have insurance policies that cover evacuation of individuals from crisis situations. How can this new data environment help with these situations? No amount of planning can ever fully prepare an institution (or those traveling abroad) for an extreme event, and no amount of data (at least currently) can completely predict when in the future such events will occur. It is possible, though, for institutions to develop mechanisms to track the mobility of individuals operating overseas as well as monitor potentially dangerous situations. Devices with GPS can track the mobility of students in real time. A more passive monitoring can occur via social networking and students' engagement with an institution's website. We know that these strategies sound a bit like "Big Brother," and we are not proponents of regularized tracking of individual activity. However, we also know there are times when security concerns become preeminent, and institutions need to be aware of what data may now be available to them that were not previously.

Leveraging existing international networks. As we noted at the beginning of this chapter, most colleges and universities already have extensive international engagements, but these activities are largely unknown to senior administrators. Consequently, if the senior leaders of an institution are looking to create an engagement in Mexico, for example, they often have to start from scratch and identify experts to assist. The irony is that members of their faculty may already have relationships and expertise that could be leveraged to advance new initiatives. If institutions knew what existing research collaborations, geographic and language expertise, and academic engagements were already in place, they could avoid duplication of effort and instead focus on expanding relationships rather than continually building them from scratch. While some initiatives such as UCosmic[2] (UC Online System for Managing International Collaboration) and ACE's *Mapping Internationalization* tool have attempted to devise a way of centralizing information about an institution's internationalization activities, very little attention has been paid to how Big Data could be leveraged in this context. Most of these data would be collected through traditional venues, such as a standard database to start, and could be augmented by additional data through tracking how often and from where users visit the websites of specific international projects and by using social network data to track international engagements of students and staff (we encourage getting their consent before engaging in these activities).

Evidence the value of international education to external stakeholders. Over the last decade, there has been increasing interest in international higher education among external stakeholders, particularly national governments, due to a desire to enhance public diplomacy, economic competitiveness, and national security (Lane, 2013a). This interest has been much greater outside of the United States than within, although even in the United States state governments are beginning to recognize the benefits associated with international engagements among institutions of higher education (Lane, Owens, & Ziegler, 2014). As data become more available, this information allows for academic leaders and others to better evidence the value of internationalization, whether it be from enhancing intercultural understanding of the local region, strengthening connections with other countries, helping to attract international trade and foreign direct investment, or advancing the nation's innovation agenda. More than simply being informative, such data can reinforce arguments for needed resources and public policies that support, rather than hinder, the international activities of colleges and universities.

MEASURING INTERNATIONAL ASPECTS OF HIGHER EDUCATION: SOURCES AND METHODS

Among the great challenges and opportunities associated with measuring higher education internationalization is understanding the various flows of students, scholars, partnerships, and knowledge around the world. Understanding these flows can be a significant advantage for academic leaders and policy makers, but there is no one repository of data related to higher education internationalization, so it can be a challenge for those looking to analyze global trends. Thus, for those looking to obtain data about these flows, the landscape can appear to be a tangled web.

In this section we explore the various types of mobility data that currently exist, both at the national and international levels. Even though the unit of analysis in these data-gathering efforts tends to be the student, the data can and are being leveraged to drive decision making at the institutional and policy levels. Although it is important to note that such data may already exist at the institution level, we do not explicitly discuss here institutionally collected data, as such data will likely vary markedly among institutions.

Statistics and indicators of student mobility (national level). Many countries (and the institutions within them) track data related to the mobility of their international students (as well as their domestic students who study abroad). In the United States, for example, the Institute of International Education (IIE) has been collecting these data since the 1920s and publishing the material since 1954 as the *Open Doors Report on International Educational Exchange*, with support from the U.S. Department of State since 1972.[3] An annual census of U.S. international educational exchange, *Open Doors* presents mobility statistics based on data collected from all regionally accredited U.S. higher education institutions. Similar data for Australia are gathered by Australian Education International (AEI), for the United Kingdom by the Higher Education Statistics Agency, and for Germany by the German Academic Exchange Service (DAAD). Countries such as China and Mexico have more recently developed mechanisms to collect these data. One key difference in approach is that in some countries (such as the United States and Germany) the data are gathered directly from institutions; in other countries (such as Australia) the data collection is part of the government agency or branch that gathers visa and other immigration statistics. There are tradeoffs with either approach: The former, which by definition is a voluntary survey approach, might suffer from lower response rates if institutions choose not to respond. However, one of the advantages of the institutional data collection approach is that it allows for easier and timelier modifications to the data collection process as definitions and measures of mobility change over time. Mandated reporting, on the other hand, ensures comprehensive data and complete coverage since response rates are typically not an issue—all institutions or education providers are required to report the data.

Additional, albeit smaller, efforts to gather mobility data on specific subsets of international exchange include organizations that focus on specific aspects of higher education. For example, the three-part annual international graduate students survey carried out by the Council of Graduate Schools (CGS) tracks the number of international students applying to graduate school in the United States, the numbers that subsequently receive offers of admission, and the final number that actually enrolls in U.S. institutions. Similarly, the National Science Foundation (NSF) collects data about the citizenship, among other indicators, of those who earn doctoral degrees from U.S. institutions. Although both surveys are small in scope and cover in-bound students from a handful of countries and world regions, they are useful resources for understanding graduate-level mobility trends for the United States.

Statistics and indicators of student mobility (international level). Since most current sources of information and knowledge about international students are derived from national data collection organizations such as those mentioned earlier in the chapter (and listed in table 10.1), the resulting data vary widely from country to country in terms of their timeliness, data definitions, and scope. Country-specific data are limited in that they tell us little about the implications of each country's mobility statistics within a global context. Variations in national degree and qualification structures across countries also make comparative analysis difficult.

What is needed is a global and consistent source of baseline data, as well as a forum within which national efforts may be compared and benchmarked. Global data collection efforts by nongovernmental organizations such as the Organisation for Economic Co-operation (OECD) and the United Nations Educational, Scientific and Cultural Organization (UNESCO) attempt to track the flow of students into and out of their member countries, as well as a few other nations that tend to be major senders of students.[4] These efforts are intended to provide a comprehensive picture of student flows around the world, but they suffer from some obvious limitations. First, there is typically a significant time lag between data collection and data release. Second, because the data are primarily collected through ministries of education, they do not always capture enrollments at private institutions. The result is an underestimate of international students, since private institutions represent the fastest growing education sector in many countries. Third, only students enrolled for a year or more are counted in the data. Since internationally mobile students from the United States, Japan, and the European Union (EU) often study abroad for less than a full academic year, it can be safely assumed that the actual number of students who are globally mobile significantly exceeds the 4.3 million currently reported by the OECD (2013). A final consideration is that these types of multinational collection efforts may leave out certain types of mobility, such as that which occurs between two nations in the global South.

One effort to build upon the work of UNESCO and OECD and address some of its limitations is Project Atlas, an initiative that brings together a community of researchers from around the world to share more harmonized and current data on student mobility (see table 10.1). Initiated in 2001 with support from the Ford Foundation and subsequently supported by the U.S. Department of State and participating partners in other countries, Project Atlas and its associated web portal, the *Atlas of Student Mobility*, provide a comprehensive global picture of international student mobility for 28 leading destination countries and enrollments by students from 76 places of origin. The initiative provides a shared framework within which to collect, synthesize, and disseminate data on the migration trends of the millions of students who pursue education outside of their home countries each year. The aim was to address the need for global migration data that measures student flows not just to the United States but also to several other leading and emerging destinations for transnational higher education. These data are gathered through data-sharing agreements with researchers based at national academic mobility agencies around the world. *Project Atlas* also helps IIE and the other member organizations to consider how international education patterns relate to other national developments such as home country investment in human capital, population growth, and the level of technological capacity, as well as how these patterns are affected by international and transnational economic, diplomatic, and political factors. An improved understanding of these dynamics might also

Table 10.1. Sources of international student mobility data for Project Atlas

Country	Agency/Organization	Website
Australia	Australian Education International (AEI)	https://aei.gov.au/Pages/default.aspx
Brazil	Coordenação de Aperfeiçoamento de Pessoal de Nível Superior (CAPES)	http://www.capes.gov.br/
Canada	Canadian Bureau for International Education (CBIE)	http://www.cbie.ca/
Chile	Ministry of Education, Higher Education Division	http://www.mineduc.cl/
China	China Scholarship Council	http://en.csc.edu.cn/
Denmark	Danish Agency for Universities and Internationalisation	http://fivu.dk/en/
Finland	Centre for International Mobility (CIMO)	http://www.cimo.fi/english
France	Campus France	http://www.campusfrance.org/en
Germany	The German Academic Exchange Service (DAAD)	https://www.daad.org/
India	Association of Indian Universities (AIU)	http://www.aiuweb.org/index.asp
Ireland	Education in Ireland	http://www.educationinireland.com/en/
Japan	Japan Student Services Organization (JASSO)	http://www.jasso.go.jp/index_e.html
Malaysia	Ministry of Higher Education Malaysia	http://mohe.gov.my/
Mexico	National Association of Universities and Higher Education Institutions (ANUIES)	http://www.anuies.mx/
Netherlands	Netherlands Organization for International Cooperation in Higher Education (NUFFIC)	http://www.nuffic.nl/
Norway	Norwegian Centre for International Cooperation in Education (SIU)	http://www.siu.no/eng
New Zealand	New Zealand Ministry of Education	http://www.minedu.govt.nz/
South Africa	International Education Association of South Africa (IEASA)	http://www.ieasa.studysa.org/
Spain	Fundación Universidad.es	http://www.universidad.es/en
Sweden	Swedish Institute	http://www.swedishinstitute.edu/
United Arab Emirates	Center for Higher Education Data and Statistics, Ministry of Higher Education and Scientific Research (MOHESR)	http://www.mohesr.gov.ae/En/Pages/default.aspx
United Kingdom	British Council	http://www.britishcouncil.org/

help potential international students make better-informed choices regarding their study destinations.

Student perception and attitudinal data. Another source of student-level data that can be used for institutional decision making and enrollment management is student perception data such as those gathered through opinion surveys and similar instruments. In contrast to the student-level data discussed in the preceding section, this type of data tends to be largely qualitative and entirely perception based. Such surveys mostly focus on either prospective international students or current international students and are geared toward better understanding the student decision-making process and the myriad factors that affect a student's choice of study destination. Examples of these types of efforts include the global I-Graduate surveys (the International Student Barometer and StudentPulse) and IIE's surveys of prospective international students in 20 countries. While the data gathered through these surveys play a key role in understanding the international student market and the story behind the mobility numbers, by their very nature, these data tend to be significantly biased. For example, current international students in a country are likely to report high levels of satisfaction with their chosen destination since they have already invested a considerable amount of time, effort, and resources in gaining entry to an institution in their selected country.

Comparative national data. In addition to data about student mobility, institutional leaders may also desire information about the education systems of nations where they are looking to expand their global engagement. Such data might include, for example, the structure of the educational system; enrollment patterns at the primary, secondary, and tertiary levels; and government support for education. There is no one place to obtain this information for all countries, though there are several sources that individuals may reference. We list some organizations in this chapter that provide relevant data that readers may want to explore, although we note that this list is not exhaustive. Many of the sources described provide information on all levels of education and, in general, there tends to be more comparative data on the primary and secondary levels than on the tertiary level. (Primary and secondary education data are important, of course, for understanding a country's educational pipeline.)

ASIAN DEVELOPMENT BANK (ADB). Demand for postsecondary education has been rapidly increasing across Asia, and countries have been responding in a variety of ways. While educational information about some Asian countries is included in international data sets, ADB has been collecting a range of data about developments in all levels of education across the region. ADB, with the purpose of improving people's lives in Asia and the Pacific, collects a host of demographic and societal measures beyond education as well.

EUROPEAN COMMISSION. Through its Eurydice network, the European Commission provides information related to Europe-level analysis and information related to education systems and policies in Europe. This information includes description of how educational systems are structured; comparative analysis on a host of different issues; and comparative data on student fees, education budgets, academic calendars, and salaries (at the secondary level).

INSTITUTE FOR EDUCATIONAL STATISTICS (IES). IES, a division of the National Center for Education Statistics (NCES) in the United States, tracks comparative information related to U.S. adults, students, teachers, principals, and schools. Using data from a set of international surveys,[5] the International Activities Program of IES provides comparative data on education participation rates, education outcomes, school contexts, students' experiences and attitudes about education, and characteristics of education systems.

ORGANISATION FOR ECONOMIC CO-OPERATION AND DEVELOPMENT (OECD). In addition to the tracking of student mobility (mentioned earlier), the OECD tracks data in their online education database as well as their annual report, *Education at a Glance*. These sources provide compilations of statistical data related to education, including information on a range of topics related to (a) the output of educational institutions and the impact on learning; (b) financial and human resources invested in education; (c) access to education, participation, and professions; and (d) the learning environment and organization of schools.

UNITED NATIONS EDUCATIONAL, SCIENTIFIC AND CULTURAL ORGANIZATION (UNESCO). UNESCO's Institute for Statistics (UIS) collects information on all types of education, from preprimary through tertiary, from more than 200 countries. Each year, the *Global Education Digest* presents statistical data from education sectors around the globe. UIS also uses the data it collects to produce a range of indicators that tracks tertiary education trends at the global, regional, and national levels, including enrollment patterns, completion rates by area of study, and the international mobility of students (discussed earlier).

WORLD BANK. EdStats is the World Bank's database for education statics. This resource compiles data on more than 200 countries collected by national and international organizations. The site also provides information on education projections on attainment, enrollments, primary completion, and gender parity (mostly for the primary and secondary levels). An EdStats app even provides users with mobile access to more than 2,000 education-related indicators tracked by the World Bank.

Research, science, and innovation. Another important component to understanding data related to higher education internationalization is that it is packaged in a variety of ways, depending on the interests of the groups collecting the information. Many of those who work in the profession of international education focus primarily, though not exclusively, on student and scholar mobility. However, those in the research and science policy areas are also increasingly interested in the internationalization of science, particularly in terms of the development of research partnerships and the flow of resources (see, e.g., The Royal Society, 2011). Many colleges and universities are just beginning to track these engagements, although governmental agencies such as the NSF and Germany's Wissenschaft weltoffen have been tracking a wide variety of data related to the internationalization of science.[6]

Efforts are also underway to track the funding of research and development in the international context. This information is often collected and reported separately from educational indicators. One of the best sources of these data is the OECD, which collects this information as part of its Research and Development Statistics. Unlike some of the OECD's education data, which are collected in a wide range of countries, these indicators are only tracked among the 34 member nations of the OECD. These nations are among the most well-developed economies and have the highest investments in R&D. The World Bank also collects data on science and technology, including research and development expenditures, scholarly publications, high-tech exports, and patent production. The UNESCO Institute for Statistics also tracks similar data on more than 150 nations, including indicators that reflect the situation in developing economies (as opposed to the developed economies tracked by the OECD). In addition, the Network for Science and Technology Indicators—Ibero-American and Inter-American collects data from 28 nations across North America and South America, as well Portugal and Spain. Battelle, a nonprofit research organization in the United States, produces an annual funding forecast for research and development around the globe. The report does not focus exclusively on higher education, but a significant amount of this funding does flow to colleges and universities.

Academic program partnerships. International mobility is not limited to students or science. More and more colleges and universities are developing joint- and dual-degree partnerships with institutions in other countries, in addition to other academic linkages. In recent years, new forms of international collaborative partnerships— such as joint- and dual-degree programs, consortial arrangements, twinning, and other forms of close curricular integration—have been rapidly gaining attention at colleges and universities around the world as a way to offer particularly deep and meaningful international experiences to college and university students. Although the United States has relatively few international joint- and dual-degree programs—especially when compared to European countries, where such degrees have long been a vital part of internationalization strategies in higher education—U.S. interest in such degrees has increased substantially. A survey of U.S. and European institutions conducted in 2008 by IIE and the Freie Universität Berlin found that universities on both sides of the Atlantic are working to establish more international joint- and dual-degree programs, with 87% of respondents saying that they wanted to develop more of these degree programs, especially with countries such as China and India (Kuder, Lemmens & Obst, 2014).

Moreover, a small but growing number of institutions are developing physical outposts in other countries. Some of these outposts provide an opportunity to teach a few courses or provide research experiences. Other are full-fledged branch campuses where students can attend an entire course of study and receive a degree from the home campus, such as Texas A&M University's campuses in Qatar and Israel (in development). Still others have begun to acquire existing institutions in foreign countries, such as when Manipal University in India purchased the American University of Antigua (AUA). AUA continues to operate with the same faculty and curriculum, but it became part of the Manipal family of educational institutions around the globe. All of these efforts might be viewed as a form of "internationalization abroad" that takes education to the students, as compared with the more traditional form of "internationalization at home" (Klyburg, 2012; Mestenhauser, 2003; Wachter, 2003). University-based and independent research centers such as the Cross-Border Education Research Team (C-BERT) at the State University of New York at Albany and the Observatory on Borderless Higher Education (OBHE) work to track the global development of different forms of international engagements, in this case the growth of branch campuses and other foreign higher education outposts.

When considering the many ways in which institutions are taking education to the student, the explosion of virtual learning—namely, online courses and MOOCs—must be addressed, especially given the complete lack of data on the extent to which institutions are offering such courses and the frequency with which students are participating in these courses. There is a fundamental question, however, of whether these types if courses should even be regarded as a form of internationalization for an institution. This type of internet-based learning may undercut the need for students to cross physical borders to obtain an international credential. Among the many challenges of internet-based education are monitoring of quality and equity of access. Universities around the globe are developing creative ways of delivering education remotely and reaching students and professionals who may never have considered studying abroad. The internet can also be an invaluable tool for alumni of study abroad programs to stay in touch with their host campuses after they return home and to benefit from the continuing educational opportunities available online.

CAUTIONARY CONSIDERATIONS

The rapid proliferation of data that are publicly and privately available has raised awareness of issues related to data governance and security. Many of these issues are addressed elsewhere in the book (see chapters 1 and 3). There are specific concerns, however, about which those using data in the international context should be aware.

Privacy is a constant concern related to data. Institutions now collect a wide array of information about students, including traditionally privileged information such as Social Security Numbers, passport numbers, birthdays, financial information, and so on. These data also increasingly include information about student behaviors, both in and out of the classroom. This information is collected from different sources, including ID card usage, engagement with course management software, and activity on social networks (e.g., Facebook, Twitter, etc.). While some of these data are in the public domain, aggregating this information into a dataset that links with specific students makes it easier to track student activities as well as potentially compromise their privacy.

While the aggregation of these data may be useful for identifying at-risk students and developing individualized interventions, disclosure of these data may be problematic, if not dangerous, for students from countries with restrictive cultural norms and/or government regulations. This concern is particularly relevant if the data reveal the student to be engaged in activity or behaviors that might not be in line with the expectations of the home country. For example, during the Arab Spring, the media uncovered evidence that representatives of the Bahraini government were watching the Facebook pages of at least some Bahraini students studying abroad (Wheeler, 2011). When a student studying in the United Kingdom posted the location of an Arab Spring protest in Manchester, Bahraini security officials back home allegedly visited the student's family and questioned her relatives about the post and their child's involvement, including pictures of the student's Facebook page.

A final concern about using data is a more fundamental one. It is critical in this age of data overload to have a clear understanding of the underlying definitions of the data, especially when the information is being used for strategic planning purposes. One of the main reasons why there is little consistency in measuring mobility and other forms of internationalization is that there is widespread disagreement and debate on what constitutes mobility and internationalization, how these phenomena should be defined, and how they should be measured. For example, some countries distinguish between master's degrees that are primarily coursework versus those that include a research component. Some countries count overseas enrollment at their branch campuses as a key component of internationalization, while others do not. Being cognizant of the underlying differences among the many data sources available to international educators is critical to using the data in an appropriate and responsible way.

WHAT DOES THE FUTURE HOLD?

The effects of this data revolution are just beginning to be realized and are likely to have significant impacts on those who work in international higher education. Already, the data needed to make decisions about the international efforts of higher education institutions are vastly better than they were even a decade ago. Data on student mobility are more complete than ever. The sources of comparative national data are growing. Information about research, science, and technology is expanding. And new tools to track the global engagements of colleges and universities are being developed and implemented right now. All these initiatives mean that there is growing awareness of the world around us. As these new data are combined with new technologies and new forms of analysis, they have the potential to reshape how we recruit, educate, and engage. "The possession of knowledge, which once meant an understanding of the past, is coming to mean an ability to predict the future" (Mayer-Schonberger & Cukier, 2013, p. 180).

Part of this new future rests in the increasing availability of individual-produced data. This idea was highlighted in a report from a High-Level Panel of Eminent Persons on the Post-2015 Development Agenda (2013) convened by the secretary general of the United Nations. This panel called "for a data revolution for sustainable development, with a new international initiative to improve the quality of statistics and information available to citizens. We should actively take advantage of new technology, crowd sourcing, and improved connectivity to empower people with information on the progress towards the targets" (p. 7). Much of the information that will be collected in the future will come not only from governments but directly from individuals. Social networks are a current example of how individual data in the digital world are being collected, but there will surely be new advances that have not yet been considered, let alone developed.

What these developments mean for international educators and institutional leaders looking to make strategic decisions about the global engagements of their college or university is that data will become increasingly available from a variety of different contexts. We can harness and use more information than ever before. Increasingly, we will be able to target our international recruitment efforts at the regional and individual levels to maximize return on investment. Data may be able to help us to identify the most beneficial places to locate study abroad sites, research centers, or branch campuses. Data may even eventually be able to help predict the success of joint academic and research partnerships—not to mention how this data revolution is transforming the entire research enterprise. The problem with data will no longer be scarcity. Rather, the challenge will be (over)abundance. International educators will have to learn to parse out what is relevant and use it to inform their activities.

The current data revolution will help international educators improve what they do already. It will also provide for new opportunities yet to be considered. What is important to remember is that data alone will not change the world or how we operate within it. Data cannot ensure that all international students are successful when they study at our campus, but they can provide opportunities to intervene when those students may be at risk. Data will not go out and recruit students, but they can help target precious resources toward areas where the returns on investment are most likely. These and similar changes will take a reorientation among those who work in international education, within our institutions' faculties and administrations alike.

NOTES

1. Chapter 1 provides a description of Big Data and its broader impact on higher education.
2. See www.uscosmic.org for more information.
3. See www.iie.org/opendoors for more information.
4. Student mobility information can be found in the annual OECD *Education at a Glance* report (http://www.oecd-ilibrary.org/education/education-at-a-glance_19991487) as well as via the UNESCO Institute for Statistics, which also tracks global mobility and

has developed interesting visualization packages for this information (http://www.uis.unesco.org/education/Pages/international-
student-flow-viz.aspx).
5. These surveys include the Programme for the International Assessment of Adult Competencies (PIAAC), Progress in International
Reading Literacy Survey (PIRLS), Programme for International
Student Assessment (PISA), Teaching and Learning International
Survey (TALIS), and Trends in International Mathematics and
Science Study (TIMSS).
6. NSF data can be accessed through the National Center for Science and Engineering Statistics (http://www.nsf.gov/statistics/
index.cfm), and data about the internationalization of German higher education are available on the Wissenschaft weltoffen website (http://www.wissenschaftweltoffen.de/daten/
index_html?lang=en).

REFERENCES

American Council on Education. (2012). *Mapping internationalization on U.S. campuses.* Retrieved from http://www.acenet.edu/
news-room/Documents/MappingInternationalizationonUSCam-
puses2012-full.pdf
Balan, J. (2013). *Latin America's new knowledge economy: Higher
education, government, and international collaboration.* New
York, NY: Institute for International Education.
Constantine, M. D., Okazaki, S., & Utsey, S. O. (2010). Self-con-
cealment, social self-efficacy, acculturative stress, and depres-
sion in African, Asian, and Latin American international college
students. *American Journal of Orthopsychiatry 74*(3), 230–241.
doi:10.1037/0002-9432.74.3.230
Farrugia, C., & Bhandari, R. (2013). *Open doors report on international education exchange.* New York, NY: Institute of International Education.
Gareis, E. (2012). Intercultural Friendship: Effects of Home and Host
Region. *Journal of International and Intercultural Communication 5*(4), 309–328. doi:10.1080/17513057.2012.691525
Gonzales, L. M., Allum, J. R., & Sowell, R. S. (2013). *Graduate enrollment and degrees: 2002 to 2012.* Washington, DC: Council
of Graduate Schools.

High-level Panel of Eminent Persons on the Post-2015 Development Agenda. (2013). A new global partnership: Eradicate poverty and transform economies through sustainable development. Retrieved from http://www.post2015hlp.org/wp-content/uploads/2013/05/UN-Report.pdf.

Kang, K. (2012). *Graduate enrollment in science and engineering grew substantially in the past decade but slowed in 2010.* Retrieved from National Center for Science and Engineering Statistics website: http://www.nsf.gov/statistics/infbrief/nsf12317/

Klyberg, S. G. F. (2012). *The faculty experience in internationalization: Motivations for, practices of, and means for engagement.* Doctoral dissertation. Center for the Study of Higher Education, Department of Educational Policy Studies, Pennsylvania State University, University Park, PA.

Kuder, M., Lemmens, N., & Obst, D. (2014). *Global perspectives on international joint and double degree programs.* New York, NY: Institute of International Education.

Lane, J. E. (2013a). Why governments should care about the internationalization of higher education. In M. Larinova & O. Perfilieva (Eds.), *Rationales for internationalization* (pp. 139–160). Moscow: Logos Publishing House. (Published in Russian.)

Lane, J. E. (2013b). The systemness of internationalization strategies: How higher education systems are aiding institutions with globalization. In J. E. Lane & D. B. Johnstone (Eds.), *Higher education systems 3.0: Harnessing systemness, delivering performance* (pp. 261–282). Albany, NY: State University of New York Press.

Lane, J. E., Owens, T. L., & Ziegler, P. (2014). *The international higher education public agenda: How states are promoting economics, efficiencies and quality.* Albany, NY: Rockefeller Institute of Government.

Lin, J. G., & Yi, J. K. (1997). Asian international students' adjustment: Issues and program suggestions. *College Student Journal* 31(4), 473–479.

Mayer-Schonberger, V., & Cukier, K. (2013). *Big Data: A revolution that will transform how we live, work, and think.* Boston, MA: Houghton Mifflin Harcourt.

Mestenhauser, J. A. (2003). Building bridges. *International Educator* 12(3), 6–11.

Organisation for Economic Co-operation and Development (2013). *Education at a glance 2013: OECD indicators.* Retrieved from http://www.oecd.org/edu/eag.htm

Partnership for a New American Economy. (2012). *Patent pending: How immigrants are reinventing the American economy.* Retrieved from http://www.renewoureconomy.org/wp-content/uploads/2013/07/patent-pending.pdf

Rivard, R. (2013, October 24). Micro-targeting students. *Inside HigherEd.* Retrieved from http://www.insidehighered.com/news/2013/10/24/political-campaign-style-targeting-comes-student-search

Vega, T. (2012, February 20). Online data helping campaigns customize ads. *New York Times.* Retrieved from http://www.nytimes.com/2012/02/21/us/politics/campaigns-use-microtargeting-to-attract-supporters.html

Wachter, B. (2003). An introduction: Internationalisation at home in context. *Journal of Studies in International Education 7*(1), 5–11. doi: 10.1177/1028315302250176

Wheeler, D. (2011, November 29). In the Arab Spring's wake, Twitter trolls and Facebook spies. *The Chronicle of Higher Education.* Retrieved from http://chronicle.com/blogs/planet/2011/11/29/in-the-arab-springs-wake-twitter-trolls-and-facebook-spies/.

11

BIG DATA AND HUMAN CAPITAL DEVELOPMENT AND MOBILITY

BRIAN T. PRESCOTT

ABSTRACT

Since the advent of the global knowledge economy, more has been asked of colleges and universities, as well as the policy structures that support them, in terms of preparing graduates for the workforce. Aligning educational outputs with state workforce needs has, however, always been an elusive goal. States, with a substantial infusion of investment from the federal government, have been hard at work building data systems to equip policy makers and practitioners with information about how to promote greater student success. Even as these innovations evolve, policy makers are demanding additional information on students' subsequent employment outcomes. Many in the higher education community remain skeptical of Big Data efforts focused on the intersection between education and employment, sometimes for good reason. This chapter reviews developments in

The author would like to thank the following people for their contributions to or feedback on this chapter: Karen Paulson and Peter Ewell of the National Center for Higher Education Management Systems (NCHEMS); Hans L'Orange of the State Higher Education Executive Officers Association (SHEEO); David Longanecker of the Western Interstate Commission for Higher Education (WICHE); and Denise Deutschlander, currently a PhD student at the University of Virginia.

this area—with a particular focus on one project that has taken a regional, rather than a single-state, perspective on human capital development and mobility—and outlines the potential for the use of such information for institutions as well as policy makers and researchers.

Fed by rapidly rising tuition prices and a globalized economic environment that rewards societies with high levels of educational attainment, the current policy climate facing postsecondary education in the United States is increasingly dominated by a focus on return on investment. Research has documented that individual opportunities are enjoyed predominantly by those with an education beyond high school (Baum, Ma, & Payea, 2013), and with citizens quick to recognize this relationship (Immerwahr & Johnson, 2007), colleges and universities have seen record enrollment levels in recent years (National Center for Education Statistics, 2012). Perhaps no better evidence exists than the extent to which those individuals with postsecondary educations were able to weather the economic recession more effectively than those whose education ended with high school or less (Carnevale, Smith, & Strohl, 2013). Despite this fact, and reinforced by the difficulties that recent college graduates have faced in finding employment, many prominent voices—including a one-time presidential candidate—and media outlets have raised questions about whether the high costs of college are worth the expense (Vedder, 2012).

Although some observers are challenging the value of higher education, policy makers at both the state and federal levels are increasingly conscious of how state and national economic prosperity is linked to educational attainment. They are starting to demand better information about postsecondary success and employment outcomes in an effort to calculate return on investment. In part spurred by President Obama's goal to ensure that the United States regains its place as the most well-educated nation, policy makers have focused attention on improving degree-completion rates, perhaps most notably by designing and implementing new models of performance-based funding that allocate all or a portion of state appropriations to public institutions based on the extent to which their students are able to make progress toward and complete degrees.[1] Just as these reforms are being implemented in many states, policy makers are also looking beyond college for evidence of how well graduates are prepared for the workforce.[2] The employment outcomes in question have multiple uses: Policy makers want to know to what extent recent graduates are able to find productive employment in order to meet their own debt obligations, to help build the economy, and to contribute to the tax base. They also want to use information about postgraduate employment to help potential college students make informed choices about major and institution.

Twin pressures arise out of these conditions: demand for better information about educational productivity and about employment outcomes. Both require access to more comprehensive data about human capital development. This chapter reviews developments in this area and how policy makers and members of the postsecondary education community can constructively employ linked longitudinal data to spur human capital development and examine economic and workforce development. After a brief discussion of the limitations of traditional data sources for contemporary needs, the chapter describes a pilot project spanning education and workforce sectors across multiple states and presents lessons learned to date.

In the end, the most effective solution will balance linked longitudinal data capacity to meet demands for accountability with its potential to aid strategic planning and formative evaluation needs. In other words, the optimal solution will not simply provide evidence on which to reward institutions or, conversely, to hold them to account. It will also equip them with the data they need to examine and refine their institutional priorities, curricular offerings, and the performance of their academic and student support units. These expectations require that the solution preserve high standards for data security and privacy protection in ways that ensure that the utility of data to inform and improve policies and practices will not be handicapped. For these reasons and because higher education policy falls principally within the purview of the states, this chapter argues that the most appropriate solution for housing linked longitudinal data spanning education and labor (the "Big Data" to be harnessed for understanding human capital development and mobility) in service to policy and practice improvements is with the states collectively, operating in partnership with and through support from the federal government.

DEMAND FOR LINKED LONGITUDINAL DATA

Currently, the kinds of information that policy makers and institutional planners need for calibrating postsecondary education services with state workforce needs is not widely available. The traditional sources of data either rely on institutions as the unit of analysis (as the nation's principal data source for postsecondary education, the Integrated Postsecondary Education Data System, or IPEDS, does) or on sample surveys. IPEDS is an essential resource for understanding the higher education landscape, but it comes up short in providing information about student success. Specifically, by measuring graduation rates for full-time, first-time students only, IPEDS relies on inadequate or imprecise proxies and fails to capture the experiences of a large and growing share of the postsecondary student population (Committee on Measures of Student Success, 2011).[3] IPEDS and other common data sources typically focus more on processes rather than outcomes. For instance, they might provide an estimate of how much money is spent per graduate but lack information about the likelihood of student completion, and they provide even less information about what happens to students after their educational experiences are concluded (whether or not they graduate).

The federal longitudinal sample surveys can provide more comprehensive information about students' academic progress and outcomes, but because they generally lack the ability to provide information that is representative at the state level, where policies affecting statewide educational attainment are crafted and implemented, their utility in informing state policy makers with actionable evidence is limited.[4] For example, the National Postsecondary Student Aid Study (NPSAS, which is not itself a longitudinal database, although it does form the basis for the Beginning Postsecondary Students data set, which is longitudinal) provides nationally representative information about the average net price that students pay after accounting for grant aid. Net prices in public higher education are, however, largely a function of state appropriations, tuition levels, and financial aid policies, which vary considerably among states. NPSAS, therefore, generally cannot provide accurate state-level net price estimates, let alone variations within net price or actionable information about how state and institutional financial aid is distributed. Also, the federal longitudinal sample surveys are incapable of serving as the underlying data for accountability concerns because institutions cannot be identified in the samples.

Recognizing that a much larger resource containing individual student-level data would be required to capture all of this variation, the federal government examined the feasibility of creating a "unit-record" data system that would track individuals throughout college (Cunningham, Milam, & Statham, 2005). Those efforts ran into stiff opposition from a coalition of postsecondary institutions, especially from the independent sector, as well as citizens concerned about privacy protections. The end result was that the U.S. Congress included in the Higher Education Opportunity Act of 2008 a prohibition against further federal efforts to build a unit-record system.[5]

As an alternative to a federally managed unit-record data system, the U.S. Department of Education has partnered with 47 states and the District of Columbia, Puerto Rico, and the U.S. Virgin Islands to invest $613 million in statewide longitudinal data systems (SLDSs) to address data gaps (U.S. Department of Education, 2013). With states at the helm of these projects, there has been a variety of approaches and priorities in terms of integrating individual-level data across the education and workforce spectrums (Garcia & L'Orange, 2012). More recent rounds of SLDS grant making have required states to combine K–12 and postsecondary education data with data captured by state labor agencies on employment outcomes through their unemployment insurance (UI) wage record files. A number of states have already connected these data sources and are using the resulting information in various ways, including conducting academic program reviews and providing consumer information (Aspen Institute, 2013; Whitfield & Crouch, forthcoming).[6]

BORDERS CAN HINDER DATA FLOW

One promising way in which states can use these combined data is by developing a more informed and nuanced understanding of how human capital—expanded through knowledge, talent, and skills development—and individual mobility combine to fulfill state workforce needs (Prescott & Ewell, 2009). The capacity to create such a comprehensive approach is beyond the ability of states acting individually because they only have access to their own workforce information.

To administer unemployment insurance (UI), states must obtain wage records for all employees at private firms, nonprofit organizations, and state and local government entities operating in the state on a quarterly basis. The resulting database is a rich resource for examining employment and compensation patterns on a statewide basis, but since each state administers its own UI, each state generally does not have information on its own residents who work for employers in other states, let alone individuals educated by the state who then move away. Moreover, they cannot identify individuals participating in their workforce but who were educated in other states. In most states, the only identifying data element in the UI wage record files is the Social Security Number (SSN), which makes linking UI data with any other data source at the individual level dependent on collecting SSNs. Also, UI files do not capture employment of individuals who are self-employed or work for the federal government, including the military (employment information for these categories is captured at the federal level in two other data systems, and many states are working to gain access to those data as well).

These characteristics leave many gaps in the information that a state can obtain from its own UI data. Nevertheless, UI data are still the principal source of information available to states investigating the relationship between postsecondary education and employment. The information gap created by the tendency of individuals to cross state borders is, however, particularly significant given that college students are extremely mobile throughout their educational pathway (Adelman, 2006; Hossler et al., 2012a; Hossler et al., 2012b; Shapiro et al., 2012). More to the point, individuals' tendency to migrate rises as they achieve higher levels of education (Malamud & Wozniak, 2010; Molloy, Smith, & Wozniak, 2011; Schachter, 2004) in order to take advantage of economic opportunities available to them due to their educational achievements (Bound & Holzer, 2000; Wozniak, 2010). Additionally, states with better labor market conditions disproportionately attract more highly educated talent (Wozniak, 2010). Consequently, analyses restricted to data available within a single state fall short of a complete picture of where students come from and go to, both for college and for work, and how a state's workforce is being filled. This shortcoming is only likely to grow as public institutions increasingly covet out-of-state students for their nonresident tuition revenue (Jaschik & Lederman, 2012).

Some options for gaining access to state-border-spanning data are available. The National Student Clearinghouse warehouses data on student enrollments and awards at nearly all postsecondary institutions (and a large number of K–12 schools as well). For employment information spanning state lines, the Wage Record Interchange System (WRIS) captures UI wage record data over the most recent eight fiscal quarters for all 50 states, but access to and use of these data are extremely restricted to applications directly related to states' operational management of their UI programs. About two-thirds of the states (and Puerto Rico) also have signed on to a mirrored version of WRIS (known as WRIS2) that allows aggregate data to be prepared for examining the employment outcomes of education programs. A serious drawback is that educational institutions or agencies are unable to perform their own analyses on any data supplied through WRIS2 because the underlying data-sharing agreement limits them from receiving anything other than aggregated results. What remains elusive is a single way in which policy makers and practitioners can obtain information spanning K–12 and postsecondary education and employment that can also account for mobility from state to state.

THE WICHE MULTISTATE DATA EXCHANGE PILOT

To fill this hole, the Western Interstate Commission for Higher Education (WICHE) has been leading a pilot effort to construct a multistate data exchange as part of a grant supported by the Bill and Melinda Gates Foundation. WICHE has brought together four states that are mostly contiguous—Washington, Oregon, Idaho, and Hawaii—to determine whether individual-level data can be shared among states and across sectors, including K–12 education, postsecondary education, and workforce information, and to offer insights on the extent to which the combined data might inform public policy makers and practitioners. The first goal of the project is to construct such a data exchange as a resource, owned and directed collectively by the participating states, that would supply more accurate answers to pressing public policy questions related to human capital creation, mobility, and economic development. The second goal is to document the extent to which the exchange of data among states can reduce or eliminate the uncertainty in outcomes that each state, relying solely on its own data, faces.

Working with the four states, WICHE developed the pilot Data Exchange based largely on a framework outlined by Prescott and Ewell (2009). Most importantly, the Data Exchange was guided from the very start by two principal policy questions: (1) How are former high school students performing in postsecondary education? (2) How are former high school and postsecondary students performing in the workforce? Each of these questions was broad enough to capture a range of more specific questions, such as, What are the employment outcomes of graduates of different academic programs? Naturally, the specific questions focused on the issue of mobility, especially across state lines—from high school to college, during college, and into the workforce. The two principal questions were written into the memoranda of agreement (MOAs) that made possible an initial exchange of data.[7]

Given the nature of the pilot, however, a third research question became important and was also included in the MOAs. It aimed more narrowly at establishing how much additional insight would be provided through the Data Exchange. The question was: By more fully accounting for individual mobility across state lines, to what extent does sharing data among states supplement existing state data resources available for conducting evaluations leading to policy and program improvements?

The mechanics of the Data Exchange. To answer these questions, the project defined two cohorts of students that it would track: (1) graduates from public high schools in any of the four states during the 2004–2005 academic year, and (2) first-time postsecondary students in public institutions in any of the four states in 2005–2006. Obviously, there would be overlap between the two cohorts consisting of those students who went directly to college after completing high school. With the first cohort the project also captures information about the paths of students who did not immediately go to college. With the second cohort, the project is able to examine the paths of students who began their college education as nontraditionally aged adults.

There are two main ways in which the Data Exchange closes gaps in the availability of employment outcomes data for a participating state. First, the exchange simply supplements states' employment records. Recall the sources of missing data in the UI wage records described earlier. Figure 11.1 shows what would happen if Washington

Figure 11.1. Unpacking the sources of missing data in UI wage record files in Washington State.

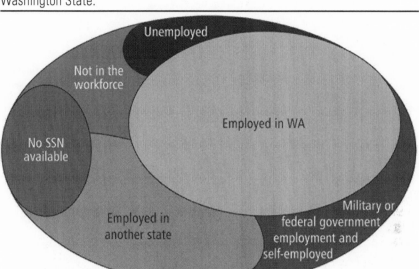

Source: WICHE's Multistate Longitudinal Data Exchange Pilot.

State were to investigate the labor market outcomes of a hypothetical group of graduates. The state would be blind to all the information in the larger circle that is outside the "Employed in Washington" subcircle, but by combining its data with those of other states participating in the Data Exchange, Washington is able to fill in the portion of the missing information represented by the "Employed in another state" piece (for the pilot, this piece applies just to the other three participating states).

The second way in which the Data Exchange supplies information not otherwise available is by capturing additional data elements, including SSNs, for students who at one time or another were enrolled in a state's public education system—individuals about whose subsequent enrollments or employment experiences the state would have a legitimate interest in knowing. What becomes evident is that the amount of information a state can access about educational and employment outcomes, in order to understand human capital development and mobility, depends in part on the choices a student makes about where he or she attends college and subsequently works. Using

Figure 11.2. The availability of individual-level data depends on students' post-secondary educational pathways.

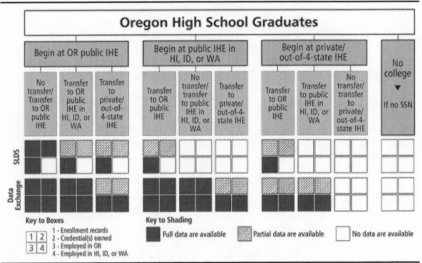

Notes: SLDS representations do not include data made available through its own use of National Student Clearinghouse data or through bilateral data- sharing agreements with other states. The lack of employment data for those who don't attend college is tied to the absence of SSNs common in K-12 data systems, though some states are seeking ways to obtain one from other sources. Employment data for states not included in the data exchange are unavailable for all student pathways.

a cohort of public high school graduates from Oregon as an example, figure 11.2 illustrates how students' pathways into and through college determine the extent to which Oregon's longitudinal data system contains the information it needs to fully recognize patterns in student completion and employment. Note that much of the information concerning students' subsequent postsecondary enrollment and awards and their employment experiences, which remains invisible to Oregon's longitudinal data system, is revealed by exchanging data. Without beginning to fill in the gaps in these data, states conducting similar analyses risk having to rely on an assumption that is unlikely to bear out: that individuals who move out of state, who move into the state from elsewhere, or who are more chaotic in their postsecondary enrollment behaviors are not much different than those individuals who stay put or who proceed in a linear, lockstep manner through college and into the workforce in the same state.

The pilot Data Exchange might be viewed principally as an extension of the four individual states' own SLDS efforts, which—like most similar projects across the nation—capture data about students in public institutions. However, by partnering with the National Student Clearinghouse, the pilot Data Exchange also includes enrollment and awards records for students in either of the original two cohorts who enrolled in or graduated from private institutions nationwide as well as public institutions outside of the four states in the pilot. Since the NSC is prohibited from sharing any student SSNs that it may have collected, however, as a general rule the Data Exchange can only obtain employment information for those students attending or graduating from private institutions or public schools in other states if they at some point "touched" one of the public postsecondary institutions in one of the four states participating in the pilot Data Exchange and in the process provided their SSN to that institution. Consequently, the pilot Data Exchange has fairly complete coverage of students' postsecondary progress and outcomes no matter where they attended college, but information about employment outcomes is much more limited based on where students enrolled in college and subsequently worked.

Reducing gaps in available data. The analysis shows that the pilot Data Exchange supplied information about the employment outcomes for a substantial additional portion of students who completed an associate's degree or higher and had a valid SSN. The proportion of additional information ranged from 9% to 22% (table 11.1). These estimates are likely to be low because they do not account for students who elected to continue their postsecondary careers in pursuit of additional credentials such as a baccalaureate or graduate degree. It is also likely that a similar analysis involving states in parts of the country where heavily populated areas are more commonly found along state borders (e.g., New England) would demonstrate substantially more mobility among students and graduates. The implication here is that a data resource that does not take mobility into account is less than satisfying not only because relying on a single state's data alone is incomplete and may lead to misleading or inaccurate results but also because, as the Data Exchange has shown, it is possible legally and technically to create a resource that captures that mobility.

While policy makers' attention has concentrated on states' natural interest in how well students educated in their publicly supported

Table 11.1. Employment outcomes and mobility of recent college graduates

State Where Associate's or Higher Was Conferred	Hawaii	Idaho	Oregon	Washington
Number of Completers with a Valid SSN	2,617	3,158	11,380	22,278
Number of Completers without an Employment Record in State	1,386	1,405	4,683	10,470
Number of Completers with an Employment Record in 1 of the Other 3 States	233	303	653	989
Percent with an Employment Record in at Least 1 of the Other 3 States, among Completers without an Employment Record within State Where Degree Was Conferred	16.8%	21.6%	13.9%	9.4%

Notes: Data apply to all students who graduated from a public high school in 2004–2005 or entered a public postsecondary institution in 2005–2006 in any of the four states and who obtained at least an associate's degree from any institution in one of the four states, public or private, by December 2010. Employment is measured for the quarter that is closest to one year after the date of completion of the highest award.

institutions fare in the workforce, they should also be interested in how states address their workforce needs by attracting graduates from elsewhere. Indeed, states actively cultivate strategies to recruit talent from outside their borders to meet their workforce needs, but by looking only at their own data resources, states have little capacity to evaluate those recruitment efforts in relation to their ability to develop and retain in-state talent. The pilot's initial analysis shows that recently educated incoming talent had a substantial impact on each state's workforce. As table 11.2 indicates, of the employment records that could be linked to recent graduates, between 9% and 24% of employed workers received their degrees from somewhere other than the state in which they were employed.

As policy makers and practitioners are naturally interested in how well graduates succeed in the workforce, the focus on employment outcomes has been largely restricted to what happens to college graduates in the workforce. With the costs of a higher education rising rapidly, however, student debt levels are increasing, and attention

Table 11.2. Retention and recruitment of recent college graduates for employment

State of Employment	Hawaii	Idaho	Oregon	Washington
Number of Completers Retained in State	1,231	1,753	6,697	11,808
Number of Completers Recruited to State	205	550	1,227	1,198
Percent of Completers Recruited among All Found to Be Employed in State	14.3%	23.9%	15.5%	9.2%

Notes: Data apply to all students who graduated from a public high school in 2004–2005 or entered a public postsecondary institution in 2005–2006 in any of the four states and who obtained at least an associate's degree from any institution anywhere in the nation, public or private, by December 2010. Employment is measured for the quarter that is closest to one year after the date of completion of the highest award.

should also be paid to those who fail to complete postsecondary programs of study. The employment outcomes of these former students are likely to be less positive than for graduates, but thus far efforts to link employment outcomes with education records has ignored those students who were diverted along the path to a postsecondary degree. The project's preliminary work is guilty of this oversight as well, but the data exchanged among the four states will allow an examination of those students' outcomes. Lastly, if policy makers are really interested in understanding employment outcomes related to education, they also should be knowledgeable about what happens to students who opt not to attend college, just as they are demanding that information for the students who do. Such information is a crucial aspect of the context when stakeholders examine the relationship between postsecondary education and job placement rates. Unfortunately, the ability to collect this information is limited by prohibitions at the K–12 level on collecting specific data elements vital to matching workforce records, namely, the SSN.

CONSIDERATIONS IN MAKING APPROPRIATE AND EFFECTIVE USE OF LINKED LONGITUDINAL DATA

In addition to providing new information about how much mobility matters to states' workforces, work on the Data Exchange pilot has also led to lessons about how policy makers and institutional leaders can make the best and most appropriate use of longitudinal data spanning education and labor. These lessons address issues around balancing accountability pressures with the capacity to make evidenced-based decisions for strategic planning and program improvement. In addition, they identify how to equip the education and policy communities most effectively with the information that they need to make informed decisions, without undermining data security and individual privacy protections.

Accountability cautions. There is a natural tendency among policy makers to seek objective measures of institutional and individual performance for accountability purposes. The rise of longitudinal data systems is rapidly expanding the building blocks available for the development of such measures. This contribution is, in fact, one of the more promising goals of these projects: As measures become more precise, policy makers can use them to shape the changes that they want to see in institutional operations—through the allocation of public funds or through regulation, and in student and family decision making regarding the higher education marketplace—through more complete and less ambiguous consumer information. Outcomes-based performance funding is perhaps the most obvious example of this effect. To the extent that such financing reforms will provide incentives to institutions to devote greater attention to student success, especially among those who come from traditionally underserved populations, they will help ensure that postsecondary institutions continue to be drivers of economic development and economic mobility.

Despite the potential usefulness of these data, the data systems in which the individual-level data needed for accountability and funding allocation decisions reside were not designed for research and evaluation—and certainly not for the purpose of making politically sensitive high-stakes decisions. Instead, they are administrative databases built for operational purposes. Even if these data could be used to help states be better informed about institutional performance, and in some cases aid in the allocation of funding, not all conceivable metrics are suitable for inclusion in accountability schemes. Even some that may be conceptually sound indicators of performance cannot yet be measured with enough precision or sufficiently without bias for use in allocating resources to institutions or in the implementation of regulations. For example, developing a measure for "placement rates" with these data might be appealing from an accountability mindset, but many questions remain about whether these data are ready to calculate such a metric with reasonable accuracy and how it might be constructed.

These data do, however, offer both policy makers and institutions clues about how they might be able to better serve the needs of students or the state. Therefore, they are becoming essential tools for visionary strategic planning. In their quest for accountability, policy makers should try to avoid creating a system that advances the accountability agenda but fails to equip states and institutions with the comprehensive information that they need to examine critically their own programs and to make decisions about their own investments.

This caution is especially appropriate for data systems that link education and employment records. The way in which these data are brought together will matter a great deal on two counts: the extent to which the findings are an accurate reflection of students' employment outcomes and how useful they are to state policy makers and institutional leaders. Through the Internal Revenue Service and the Social Security Administration, the federal government has the means to provide information about individual income, occupation, location of employment, and a range of other information that, if linked to educational records, may be able to establish how education and employment are related. Notwithstanding highly technical arguments about how calculations are made, analyses drawn from this data would be powerful in that they would come closest to being able to cover the population of U.S. residents. Indeed, the federal government's recent attempt to develop gainful employment regulations sought to achieve exactly this goal, in order to restrict student financial aid dollars from going to institutions with poor employment and repayment outcomes.

For many reasons, policy makers will need to be cautious before adopting linked education-employment analyses for institutional accountability purposes, beginning with the reality that any measures constructed will be subject to the prevailing conditions of an unpredictable business cycle. This effect is likely to be exacerbated by local conditions that also vary, potentially yielding biased results for institutions that serve more predominately place-bound students. Bias creeps in as well through unequal treatment of graduates from some institutions relative to others who have achieved the same credentials, based on perceptions of institutional prestige. Additionally, it is not immediately clear how an accountability mindset would encourage institutions to behave in response to employment outcomes data. Too much direction in terms of compelling or incentivizing institutions to produce certain types of graduates starts to take on the characteristics of a planned economy or at least may invite policy makers to believe they can rather effectively direct supply and demand for talent. In addition, it fails to account for student choices, both in terms of college majors and in the workforce. After all, a postsecondary education is not narrow training for one specific job to be sought immediately upon completion of a program but rather education for a longer career (Kelly, 2011).

Instead, these linked data are far better positioned for formative evaluation and for use in strategic planning and direction setting by both states and institutional leaders. These data are useful in describing the extent to which brain drain (or gain) is depleting (or enhancing) the level of talent available in the state workforce. They can inform states and institutional leaders about how well aligned supply and demand for particular kinds of workers are. They can also be used to provide additional consumer information to students and families to make informed decisions about the relative payoffs of academic or vocational programs, as well as whether continued education beyond an initial program will be needed (Kelly, 2011).

Optimizing productive use. Beyond the tension between accountability and strategic planning, some deeper thinking is needed about how linked longitudinal data spanning education and employment can most effectively be deployed for the greatest impact on student success. A particular concern for that role is how to distribute access to information, especially when it comes to personally identifiable information. There is understandable concern about how to balance the growing expectations that data can constructively inform public policy and institutional practice and the concern that individuals' information be kept private and confidential. Consistent with the principles of data security and privacy protections, not everyone needs access to personally identifiable data or to all the data elements captured within a data system. In fact, a great many of the analyses needed to inform public policy and to stimulate improvements in practice can be accomplished with de-identified data sets consisting of only a handful of data elements (Ewell & L'Orange, 2009). Even if de-identified data were able to meet these requirements, however, we still would be better off with a means through which to eliminate holes in the data fields that are necessary to answer pressing analytical questions before a data set gets de-identified. Not doing so risks falling into the trap of making policy and practice based on incomplete and potentially biased data.

In that regard, it may be useful to think about at least two distinct data uses: administrative/operational and policy/planning. The former type of use is characterized by identifiable data captured at a highly granular level that exists to support the operation of an institution. These data are updated routinely, often in real time, and help practitioners and institutional leaders understand how students are interacting with the curriculum and with institutional operations. In the era of Big Data, these data are increasingly being mined for predictive analytics that are intended to engage students and promote their success by identifying patterns that tend to be more or less correlated with academic progress and degree completion. It is necessarily identifiable; in fact, it is there in part so that faculty and support staff can intervene with individual students for whom early warning indicators show to be in danger of going off course. Purdue University's Signals project, the Open Learning Initiative at Carnegie Mellon University, the Predictive Analytics and Reporting Framework managed by the WICHE Cooperative for Educational Technologies (WCET), and other efforts exemplify this type of data use.[8] In general, these data do not require information about students to be shared outside of the institutional context.[9] Other operational necessities may require sharing identifiable data for a very narrow purpose. For instance, a campus financial aid office needs to know if a student is eligible for a federal Stafford loan before originating one, which may require exchanging information about that student's debt and repayment information from prior college enrollment.

The ways in which data can be most productively used for policy/planning purposes may be less straightforward, however, particularly with regard to the level of specificity and identifiability needed. As Ewell and L'Orange (2009) noted, de-identified data sets with a rather limited set of data elements are sufficient for many policy-relevant questions. Along with Prescott and Ewell (2009), though, they also indicated a need for state data systems to be able to match individuals across state lines both for analyzing postsecondary performance and for understanding how well connected the state's educational programs are to the labor market. Accordingly, given what we know about the propensity of individuals to move, it is clear that some facility to match individuals across data systems in multiple states would meet a pressing need. That matchmaking process necessarily involves individually identifiable pieces of information. It is true regardless of whether the federal government, the states, or some other entity is responsible for putting the data together. Once the matchmaking process has occurred, the data can be de-identified or aggregated at the appropriate level before it is shared, which is how the federal government manages its longitudinal sample surveys, the results from its gainful employment analysis, census data products, and other databases. And with the Student Right to Know Before You Go Act (S. 915, 2013) under consideration in the U.S. Congress, there remains the possibility that the federal government might reconsider its role in managing an educational unit-record system in spite of the prohibition against it in the Higher Education Opportunity Act (2008). Certainly, the federal government could assume this responsibility, but the pilot Data Exchange effort has identified several reasons why the effort may most productively be taken on primarily by the states, with support from the federal government.

Our experience with the pilot Data Exchange suggests that a de-identified data set of a handful of elements, although clearly able to improve the quality of information available for policy making and accountability, falls short of optimizing the potential utility of these data in helping states, sectors, and institutions to plan. Two examples from the project illustrate this point. A participating state agency insisted from the first day that unless the Data Exchange actually operated as an exchange, namely, by providing individually identifiable data back to the source after records were enhanced with other states' data, the project would not be worth the trouble. That assertion reflected a reality that became clearer as time passed: The value proposition in being involved in the project differed for each state agency. For this particular agency, the Data Exchange created solely as a de-identified source of information seemed potentially more like an intrusion than an aid to accomplishing the goals of improving institutional performance and student success. In contrast, the project would be a significant boon to its work if it were developed in a way that allowed data (on its own students only) to flow back and forth seamlessly because doing so would enhance its ability to understand more accurately how well its own students performed in subsequent (or prior) institutions and in the workforce.

This point was reinforced in a subsequent discussion during which representatives from each state talked about what data elements should actually be exchanged. Many elements were obvious, and the release of the Common Education Data Standard[10] eased the need to translate data element definitions—until someone argued that remediation had become a pressing policy matter in her state, and to better understand the outcomes of students who needed remedial courses, the Data Exchange should include one or more variables to address that issue. Quickly it became apparent that the pilot participants were not going to be able to come to agreement over a common definition for such a variable, and we elected not to develop one for the pilot, although there remains interest in doing so in the future. Without it, though, the de-identified data set is incapable of addressing the downstream effects of remediation on regional educational attainment levels and the regional labor market. The question remains important to public policy makers and institutional planners, and participating states potentially could analyze their own data to determine answers for themselves about students who received remedial education. If they like, they can do it by de-identifying their data set before conducting the analysis. But the data needed to be personally identifiable in the first place for the cross-state database to be built.

It may well be that a study of remediation's effects on eventual success in college or the workforce may be adequate even if it only extracts data from a single statewide database. If there is not a mechanism to match data on individuals through some centralized and appropriately secure process, however, the analytical ability of state policy makers and institutional leaders is limited. SLDSs, sector-based data systems, and institutional databases are rich in data elements well beyond that which could conceivably be exchanged and de-identified before sharing. So long as states (or institutions) are seeking information on their own current or former students to perform evaluation of publicly supported education programs, they would be operating under well-recognized authority to exchange education records (EducationCounsel, 2011).

Perceptions of unequal value. Another lesson from the pilot effort relates to how different the value proposition for the Data Exchange is for different states and state agencies. The most obvious beneficiaries of the pilot effort have been the agencies with responsibility for assembling the SLDSs and those that coordinate or govern postsecondary institutions. K–12 agencies have shown relatively greater interest in how a multistate data exchange could provide more operational data, such as assessment information for students who relocate or prior educational and work experience for teachers who do the same. Due to the prohibition on collecting SSNs that applies to many states' K–12 agencies' data systems, the Data Exchange is largely unable to provide employment information about students who have never passed through a public postsecondary institution in a participating state, so what can be learned about students who go directly into the workforce is limited. Additionally, under the pilot's design, the workforce agencies are simply providing the UI wage data. Restricted by the MOAs (and possibly the Family Education Rights and Privacy Act of 1974 [FERPA]) from researching questions that are most salient for the issues they focus on, the workforce agencies have been good partners to date by assisting the project in gaining access to and interpreting the UI wage record data. It is necessary, however, to overcome the tendency to think about pathways through education and into work as linear and to restrict our perspective on how human capital development happens based on that false assumption. While it is not possible under the pilot's MOAs, a Data Exchange could conceivably allow a workforce agency to examine the educational experiences of a cohort of incumbent workers—for instance, those displaced by economic cycles or employer relocations—and how they relate to future employment (Prescott & Ewell, 2009).

The value proposition may differ by the size of states as well. What the Data Exchange can tell a smaller state such as Idaho is more significant compared to Washington, even when the two states are looking at the exact same individuals moving between them, because these relatively few individuals will be a larger proportion of Idaho's smaller population.

What is needed is a resource that makes it possible to fill in gaps in existing data systems so that decision makers are not doing their work relying on evidence that may be skewed. But to the extent that a federal data collection would create a de-identified data set, whatever possibilities exist for helping states or institutions fill in missing data needed for their own analyses may be limited or nonexistent. A federal data collection may also take longer to implement due to the necessity of setting up a system in consultation with representatives from all states and sectors, including the various interest groups and membership associations in higher education. The Common Education Data Standard (CEDS) would be an obvious starting point for selecting the variables to collect, but since CEDS is based on voluntary adoption, the discussions about which variables to collect could be time consuming and ultimately limit the scope of what is captured.

Readiness for use. If a federal database were established, it is unclear how long it may take to assemble all the data needed to explore postsecondary and employment outcomes. Unless a cohort of students is defined retroactively and tracked effectively, the data collection process would require at least six years before it could replace existing data sources. For purposes of comparison, the complete data set for the federal Beginning Postsecondary Students data set, which tracked first-time postsecondary students from 2003–2004 longitudinally, was not released until the spring of 2011, and it remains the most recent federal source of individual-level data on students' educational outcomes.

A matchmaking resource such as the Data Exchange, on the other hand, would not require all states and sectors to participate at the initial stage. As a "coalition of the willing," states and sectors that come to the governance table would be motivated to make sure that the resource operated most effectively for their own use. This approach could reduce the amount of time needed to create the resource and improve its functionality. As states are able to show evidence available only by sharing data across states and sectors, pressure would mount on states that are reluctant to participate because their policy makers would begin to demand similar information. This strategy has the additional virtue of complementing the substantial investments that the federal government and individual states have made in building statewide longitudinal data systems by linking them rather than by building a federal one from scratch. The federal government could support this effort with funding backed up with statutory or regulatory requirements or incentives for states or institutions to participate. The federal government's role in this regard would be particularly helpful in encouraging or requiring private institutions to participate.

CONCLUSION

As this chapter points out, what is missing from state longitudinal data systems is often along the periphery, especially information about students whose enrollment patterns are chaotic, who enter and leave postsecondary education, who attend part-time, and who move among institutions. Information about employment outcomes also may disappear most regularly for those who have the most talent and who, by virtue of their talent, have more opportunities to be mobile. Our historic reliance on the kind of institutional proxies for performance that IPEDS provides has resulted in a blurry view of institutional and student performance. The federal longitudinal sample surveys fill in many of the gaps, but the actionable information they provide to policy makers, institutions, and consumers is limited. Meanwhile, the data collection strategies for these data sets rely on costly surveys of individual students for many of the most valuable elements, and when information in them goes missing the research community routinely has found it necessary or expedient to exclude data of which it cannot make sense.

As states build their own longitudinal data systems, they equip themselves with information needed to do their own accountability reporting. However, without linking individual records across data systems, including with other states, states will go on making decisions without particularly good peripheral vision. As a result, leaders will continue to make important decisions about policy and practice, and increasingly invite consumers to do so as well, on the basis of incomplete and potentially biased information. Such a situation is calling for a resource that more comprehensively captures the information, and a multistate data exchange built off administrative data systems linked across state lines offers a workable solution that broadens our field of vision.

NOTES

1. See Jones (2013) for a recent summary of state efforts to implement outcomes-based performance funding policies.
2. Many will note with dismay the dominant focus on the instrumental role of postsecondary education in preparing the future

workforce, largely at the expense of other broad educational purposes (Labaree, 1997). Without trying to suggest that those other purposes are somehow less worthy, it is nevertheless apparent that policy makers are responding to public sentiment about college being necessary for better employment prospects (Immerwahr & Johnson, 2007), and that many of the other benefits of a higher education—such as civic engagement, volunteerism, good health, and aesthetic appreciation—accrue to those with a steady income. It is also the case that employment outcomes are the most systematically measurable through existing federal and state data collection activities.

3. Changes being made to extend IPEDS data collection (see the National Center for Education Statistics [2013] for details) to cover the experiences of more students are welcome, and they will extend our understanding of student outcomes and institutional performance, but they still will require broad analytical treatments that cannot fully capture the complexity of student enrollment paths both within and across institutions.

4. The National Center for Education Statistics runs a number of longitudinal sample surveys on a periodic cycle. These are principle sources of information about student behaviors, progress through educational institutions, and outcomes. Examples include Beginning Postsecondary Students, Baccalaureate and Beyond, and the Educational Longitudinal Study, among others.

5. Notably, that prohibition has not kept the federal government from developing "gainful employment" calculations based on individual-level data (some of which is provided by institutions themselves and some of which is linked from non-education federal databases) to regulate institutions' eligibility for federal financial aid based on their graduates' ability to repay their student loan debts.

6. See College Measures for an example of a website that is trying to consolidate these data and make them widely available (www.collegemeasures.org).

7. Assembling the data exchange required a memorandum of agreement with each state agency that served as a direct source of information to the project. WICHE's intent was to obtain data from the entity with responsibility for developing each state's statewide longitudinal data system (SLDS) wherever possible, relying on

the data-sharing agreements it had developed internally. But ultimately, the project required seven such MOAs: one each in Hawaii, Idaho, and Washington—the three states where all the data was provided through the agency managing the SLDS—and four in Oregon, where no single entity could supply the data needed from data systems individually operated by the Department of Education, the Department of Community Colleges and Workforce Development, the Oregon University System, and the Employment Department.

8. Information about these projects can be found at the following web addresses: Purdue's Signals project: http://www.itap.purdue.edu/learning/tools/signals/index.html; Carnegie Mellon's OLI: http://oli.cmu.edu/; and WCET's PAR project: http://wcet.wiche.edu/par.

9. WCET's PAR project is one exception. Its goal is to combine similar data from multiple institutions to gather additional insights. As the project is not trying to match individual students across participating institutions, there is no need for it to capture identifiable data on the students.

10. http:\\ceds.ed.gov

REFERENCES

Adelman, C. (2006). *The toolbox revisited: Paths to degree completion from high school through college*. Retrieved from Office of Vocational and Adult Education, U.S. Department of Education website: http://www2.ed.gov/rschstat/research/pubs/toolboxrevisit/toolbox.pdf

Aspen Institute. (2013). *A guide for using labor market data to improve student success*. Retrieved from http://www.aspeninstitute.org/sites/default/files/content/upload/AspenGuideforUsingLaborMarketData.pdf

Baum, S., Ma, J., & Payea, K. (2013). *Education pays: The benefits of higher education for individuals and society*. Retrieved from the College Board website: http://trends.collegeboard.org/sites/default/files/education-pays-2013-full-report.pdf

Bound, J., & Holzer, H. (2000). Demand shifts, population adjustments, and labor market outcomes during the 1980s. *Journal of Labor Economics 18*(1), 20–54.

Carnevale, A. P., Smith, N., & Strohl, J. (2013). *Recovery: Job growth and education requirements through 2020.* Retrieved from Georgetown University Center on Education and the Workforce website: http://www9.georgetown.edu/grad/gppi/hpi/cew/pdfs/Recovery2020.FR.Web.pdf

Committee on Measures of Student Success. (2011). *A report to Secretary of Education Arne Duncan.* Retrieved from U.S. Department of Education website: http://www2.ed.gov/about/bdscomm/list/cmss-committee-report-final.pdf

Cunningham, A. F., Milam, J., & Statham, C. (2005). *Feasibility of a student unit record system within the Integrated Postsecondary Education Data System.* Retrieved from National Center for Education Statistics website: http://nces.ed.gov/pubs2005/2005160.pdf

EducationCounsel. (2011). *U.S. Department of Education final FERPA regulations: Advisory and overview.* Retrieved from Data Quality Campaign website: http://www.dataqualitycampaign.org/files/1475_2011%20Final%20FERPA%20Regulations_Advisory%20and%20Overview%20FINAL.pdf

Ewell, P., & L'Orange, H. (2009). *The ideal state postsecondary data system: 15 essential characteristics and required functionality.* Retrieved from State Higher Education Executive Officers Association website: http://www.sheeo.org/sites/default/files/publications/ideal_data_system.pdf

Family Education Rights and Privacy Act of 1974, Pub. L. 113-31, Stat., codified as amended at 20 U.S.C. § 1232g.

Garcia, T. I., & L'Orange, H. P. (2012). *Strong foundations: The state of state postsecondary data systems.* Retrieved from State Higher Education Executive Officers Association website: http://www.sheeo.org/sites/default/files/publications/StrongFoundations_Full.pdf

Hossler, D., Shapiro, D., Dundar, A., Ziskin, M., Chen, J., Zerquera, D., & Torres, V. (2012a). *Transfer & mobility: A national view of pre-degree student movement in postsecondary institutions.* Retrieved from National Student Clearinghouse Research Center website: http://www.studentclearinghouse.info/signature/2/NSC_Signature_Report_2.pdf

Hossler, D., Shapiro, D., Dundar, A., Chen, J., Zerquera, D., Ziskin, M., & Torres, V. (2012b). *Reverse transfer: A national view of student mobility from four-year to two-year institutions.* Retrieved from National Student Clearinghouse Research Center website: http://www.studentclearinghouse.info/signature/3/NSC_Signature_Report_3.pdf

Higher Education Opportunity Act of 2008, Pub. L. 110-315, 122 Stat. 3078.

Immerwahr, J., & Johnson, J. (2007). *Squeeze play: How parents and the public look at higher education today.* Retrieved from National Center for Public Policy and Higher Education website: http://www.highereducation.org/reports/squeeze_play/squeeze_play.pdf

Jaschik, S., & Lederman, D. (2012). *The 2012 Inside Higher Ed survey of college and university admissions directors.* Retrieved from http://www.insidehighered.com/news/survey/debt-jobs-diversity-and-who-gets-survey-admissions-directors

Jones, D. P. (2013). *Outcomes-based funding: The wave of implementation.* Retrieved from Complete College America website: http://www.completecollege.org/pdfs/Outcomes-Based-Funding-Report-Final.pdf

Kelly, P. (2012). *The fast-approaching frontier: Employment outcomes of college graduates. How do we make sense of it all?* Retrieved from Education Commission of the States Boosting College Completion website: http://www.boostingcollegecompletion.org/wp-content/uploads/2012/07/BCC-Legislative-Workshop-Patrick-Kelly-Presentation.pdf

Labaree, D. F. (1997). Public goods, private goods: The American struggle over educational goals. *American Educational Research Journal 34*(1), 39–81.

Malamud, O., & Wozniak, A. K. (2010). *The impact of college education on geographic mobility: Identifying education using multiple components of Vietnam draft risk* (NBER Working Paper 16463). Retrieved from National Bureau of Economic Research website: http://www.nber.org/papers/w16463

Molloy, R., Smith, C. L., & Wozniak, A. (2011). Internal migration in the United States. *Journal of Economic Perspectives 25*(3), 173–196. doi:10.1257/jep.25.3.173

National Center for Education Statistics (2012). *Digest of education statistics.* Retrieved from U.S. Department of Education website: http://nces.ed.gov/programs/digest/

National Center for Education Statistics (2013). *Integrated Postsecondary Education Data System (IPEDS) 2013–2016*. Docket ID: ED-2013-ICCD-0128. Retrieved from regulations.gov website: http://www.regulations.gov/#!docketDetail;D=ED-2013-ICCD-0128

Prescott, B. T., & Ewell, P. (2009). *A framework for a multi-state human capital development data system*. Retrieved from Western Interstate Commission for Higher Education website: http://www.wiche.edu/info/publications/FrameworkForAMultistate-HumanCapitalDevelopmentDataSystem.pdf

Schachter, J. P. (2004). *Geographic mobility: 2002–03. Current Population Reports*. Washington, DC: U.S. Department of Commerce.

Shapiro, D., Dundar, A., Chen, J., Ziskin, M., Park, E., Torres, V., & Chiang, Y-C. (2012). *Completing college: A national view of student attainment rates*. Retrieved from National Student Clearinghouse Research Center website: http://www.studentclearinghouse.info/signature/4/NSC_Signature_Report_4.pdf

Student Right to Know Before You Go Act of 2013, S. 915, 113th Cong., 1st Sess. (2013).

U.S. Department of Education. (2013). *SLDS 101*. Retrieved from http:\\nces.ed.gov\programs\slds\ppt\SLDS_PPT.pptx

Vedder, R. (2012, April 9). Why college isn't for everyone. *BusinessWeek*. Retrieved from http://www.businessweek.com/articles/2012-04-09/why-college-isnt-for-everyone

Whitfield, C. & Crouch, A. (forthcoming). *State data profile: Kentucky Community and Technical College System*. Washington, DC: National Governors Association.

Wozniak, A. (2010). Are college graduates more responsive to distant labor market opportunities? *Journal of Human Resources* 45(4), 944–970.

CONTRIBUTORS

RAJIKA BHANDARI is deputy vice president of research and evaluation at the Institute of International Education, and provides strategic oversight of IIE's research and evaluation activities and leads the Open Doors and Project Atlas initiatives that measure international higher education mobility. She also directs IIE's Center for Academic Mobility Research. Dr. Bhandari serves on several international advisory groups, is a frequent speaker and widely published author on global student mobility, and has written four books on the subject. She also leads program evaluations of international scholarship and fellowship programs in higher education for IIE and for external clients. Prior to joining IIE in 2006, Dr. Bhandari was a senior researcher at MPR Associates, an educational research firm in California that provides research and evaluation services to the U.S. Department of Education. She also served as the assistant director for evaluation at the Mathematics and Science Education Network at the University of North Carolina at Chapel Hill. In addition to her work in international education research, Dr. Bhandari has a background in international development with a special focus on gender and education in developing countries. She holds a doctoral degree in psychology from North Carolina State University and a BA (Honors) in psychology from the University of Delhi, India.

ELIZABETH L. BRINGSJORD was appointed interim provost and vice chancellor by the SUNY Trustees as of August 2013. She is the chief academic officer for the SUNY system, leading system-wide academic initiatives and ensuring that all system administration activities align with and support SUNY's core academic mission. She supports the chancellor and Board of Trustees in carrying out their oversight responsibilities of SUNY's 64-campus system, serving as liaison to the board's Academic Affairs Committee. Dr. Bringsjord directs transformational work now underway in the areas of academic excellence: SUNY's commitment to access, completion, and success; institutional research and data analytics; educator preparation; strategic enrollment planning; student mobility and success; and diversity, equity, and inclusion. One of the hallmarks of her 15-year tenure at SUNY system administration has been a steadfast commitment to data-driven decision making, most recently marked by her spearheading the development of SUNY's policy on data reporting and transparency. She has written numerous academic policies and guidance documents for campuses on topics ranging from seamless transfer to remediation. Dr. Bringsjord led the preparation of SUNY's three most recent master plans as well as the New York State Commission on Higher Education's final report and recommendations. Dr. Bringsjord holds a PhD and MS in educational psychology and statistics from the University at Albany, an MS in nursing from the University of Pennsylvania, and a BS in nursing from Boston University.

SELMER BRINGSJORD specializes in the logico-mathematical and philosophical foundations of artificial intelligence (AI) and cognitive science, and in collaboratively building AI systems on the basis of computational logic. These systems are usually formal in nature and serve to model and simulate human cognition. Bringsjord has long been on the faculty at America's oldest technological university, Rensselaer Polytechnic Institute (RPI) in Troy, where he currently holds appointments in the Department of Cognitive Science (of which he is chair), the Department of Computer Science, and the Lally School of Management & Technology, where as a full professor he teaches AI, formal logic, human and machine reasoning, philosophy of AI, and other topics relating to formal computational logic. Before coming to RPI, Bringsjord received the PhD under Roderick Chisholm at Brown University. Funding for Bringsjord's R&D has come from the Luce Foundation, the National Science Foundation, the Templeton Foundation, AT&T, IBM, Apple, AFRL, ARDA/DTO/IARPA, ONR,

DARPA, AFOSR, and other sponsors. Bringsjord has consulted to and advised many companies in the general realm of intelligent systems and continues to do so. Many of Bringsjord's writings, including some unpublished ones, are available directly through hotlinks in his vitae, available (along with a lengthier bio) at http://www.rpi.edu/~brings.

JOHN CHESLOCK is director of the Center for the Study of Higher Education and associate professor in the Education Policies Studies department at the Pennsylvania State University. Dr. Cheslock obtained his PhD in labor economics from Cornell University, where he served as a research assistant at the Cornell Higher Education Research Institute (CHERI). After graduation, he was on the faculty of the University of Arizona for eight years. He currently serves as a consulting editor for *Research in Higher Education* and on the editorial boards of the *Review of Higher Education* and *Educational Evaluation and Policy Analysis*. Dr. Cheslock's research examines the financial sustainability challenges facing many colleges and universities through analysis of specific revenue sources, underlying cost structures, and the economics associated with specific activities. Most of his research into institutional revenues focuses on net tuition revenue through studies of institutional aid policies and enrollment growth initiatives, while expenditure-focused studies primarily examine faculty salaries and instructional productivity. When investigating specific activities within higher education, he primarily analyzes two areas: intercollegiate athletics and online education. His research employs quantitative methods and data drawn from either national surveys or databases maintained by higher education institutions.

B. ALEX FINSEL is a public high school economics and U.S. history teacher for North Colonie Central Schools in Latham, New York. He also serves as the district's summer school principal for grades 9–12. Previously, he served in the United States Marine Corps for ten years. Currently, Alex is a doctoral student in educational administration and policy studies at the University at Albany, State University of New York. His research interests include building school leadership, teacher evaluation, public education policy, and the economics of education. In 2011, Alex received an instructional technology grant from the New York State Association for Computers and Technologies in Education (NYSCATE) for real-T\time data collection, analysis, and decision making technology in social studies.

FRED FONSECA is currently the codirector of the Center for Online Innovation in Learning. From 2010–2012 he was the associate dean for education of the College of Information Sciences and Technology. During this time he led the online education operations of the college. His research is focused on the flow of information from its conceptualization in human minds to its implementation in computer applications. Currently he is studying the process surrounding the conceptualization, design, and instantiation of online courses. Dr. Fonseca received his PhD in spatial information science and engineering from the University of Maine in 2001. He joined Penn State in 2001 as an assistant professor. His work on three areas of research, geographic information science, information science, and information systems, led to several journal papers, research grants from NSF and other agencies, and to successful master's and doctoral students. He was promoted to associate professor in 2007. In his sabbatical leave (2008–2009) from Penn State he developed the project Global Forest Information Systems with Gilberto Camara at INPE and Clodoveu Davis at UFMG. His work on ontology-driven geographic information systems has been highly influential as demonstrated by the 2006 Researcher Award from the University Consortium of Geographic Information Science (UCGIS) for his foundational work on ontologies in GIS. His work on GIS is highly cited with more than 2,000 citations according to Google Scholar, including "Using Ontologies for Integrated Geographic Information Systems" with 400 citations and "Ontology-driven geographic information systems" with 220 citations.

JAY W. GOFF is vice president of enrollment and retention management at Saint Louis University. For more than 20 years, Mr. Goff has been a contributor to the higher education community in the areas of enrollment management, strategic planning, and institutional communication programs. His mission-centric approach has achieved record enrollments, retention, diversity, and graduation rates. Mr. Goff believes in a data-driven and team-oriented workplace that stresses service-focused student success plans. He has consulted with over 30 institutions and serves as a coordinator for AACRAO's Strategic Enrollment Management (SEM) conference. He has also provided advisory board service to ACT, the Educational Policy Institute, and the National Student Clearinghouse. Goff earned his master's in communication studies from the University of Kansas. His doctoral studies are focused on student development and effective change management in higher education.

LISA HELMIN FOSS is associate vice president and associate provost for strategy, planning, and effectiveness at St. Cloud State University in Minnesota. She holds a bachelor's degree in mass communication and a master in business administration from St. Cloud State University and is in the final stage of completing a doctoral degree in educational policy and administration–higher education from the University of Minnesota. Her dissertation topic is "Deploying Data Analytics: How Redefining, Clarifying and Integrating Factors Influence the Implementation of Organizational Innovations at US Colleges and Universities." She completed the Harvard Graduate School of Education's Management and Leadership in Higher Education Institute in 2010. She presents frequently at local, national, and international levels on change management and data analytics in higher education.

RODNEY P. HUGHES is a research manager for the Strategic Data Project (SDP) in the Center for Education Policy Research at Harvard University. With SDP, Rodney oversees analysis and data management for state- and district-level student, teacher, and school variables related to college-going and teacher policy. Prior to joining SDP, Rodney completed BS and MA degrees in economics and a PhD in higher education at Penn State University. While at Penn State, Rodney supported and conducted research around student outcomes associated with college match quality, state and institutional financial aid policy, demand-side influences on tuition pricing, faculty workload, and university costs. Rodney's work is informed by over three years of service as the student member of Penn State's Board of Trustees, for which he served on the Education Policy Committee, Campus Environment Committee, and Executive Committee, and gained exposure to a number of activities around planning and institutional assessment. Rodney also received a 2012–2013 dissertation grant from the Association for Institutional Research.

DANIEL J. KNOX is the director of student mobility with the State University of New York System office of academic affairs. In this role, Daniel is responsible for ensuring the flow of timely and accurate academic program information to promote student mobility and seamless transfer throughout the State University of New York. In addition to policy analysis on student mobility for the office of the provost, Daniel collaborates across functional areas to support the university's strategic priorities, including participation in NYS's P-20 integrated data effort and implementation of the Degree Planning and Audit initiative. Previously, Daniel taught eighth-grade English Language Arts in New York City as a member of Teach for America and earth science at a residential psychiatric treatment center in Chicago. Currently, he is a doctoral candidate in educational policy studies at the University at Albany. Through his doctoral research, he has published peer-reviewed articles and conference papers on accountability, cross-border regulation of branch campuses, and electronic monitoring in higher education.

JASON E. LANE is vice provost for academic affairs and senior associate vice chancellor at the State University of New York (SUNY) as well as deputy director for research at the Nelson A. Rockefeller Institute of Government, SUNY's public policy think tank. He is also an associate professor of educational policy, senior researcher at the Institute for Global Education Policy Studies, and codirector of the Cross-Border Education Research Team (C-BERT) at the University at Albany (SUNY). In addition to overseeing all academic program development across the system's 64 campuses, he is responsible for the graduate education, research, and economic development portfolios on behalf of the SUNY provost's office. Lane's research focuses on the organization and leadership of higher education institutions and their relationship to governments. Lane has written numerous articles, book chapters, and policy reports and authored or edited seven books, including *Higher Education Systems 3.0: Harnessing Systemness, Delivering Performance* (SUNY Press, 2013, with D. Bruce Johnstone), *Academic Leadership and Governance of Higher*

Education (Stylus Press, 2012, with Robert Hendrickson, James Harris, and Rick Dorman), and *Colleges and Universities as Economic Drivers* (SUNY Press, 2012, with D. Bruce Johnstone). He has served on the boards of the Comparative and International Education Society (CIES), Council for International Higher Education (CIHE), the Gulf Comparative Education Society (GCES), and SUNY Korea.

MICHAEL MARCINKOWSKI is a PhD candidate in the College of Information Sciences and Technology at Penn State University. Focusing on issues of design in socio-technical systems, his current research examines the use of student data in the design of online education. With specializations in qualitative and philosophically oriented research, Michael has presented his work at international conferences and has been awarded a University Graduate Fellowship from Penn State.

TAYA L. OWENS currently serves the State University of New York System office of academic affairs with system-wide program implementation and research. Taya's research addresses higher education system and organizational diversity, socioeconomic development, public education policy, and educational accountability at the state and international levels. Her approach to research is founded in academics, teaching, and learning, and emphasizes comparative state-level and international analysis.

BRIAN T. PRESCOTT is the director of policy research at the Western Interstate Commission for Higher Education (WICHE). In this role, he comanages WICHE's Policy Analysis and Research unit, with primary responsibility for obtaining and analyzing education and workforce data with public policy relevance. He is author of the two most recent editions of *Knocking at the College Door*, WICHE's widely used projections of high school graduates by state and race/ethnicity. Additionally, he manages grant- and contract-funded projects and authors occasional policy briefs, chapters, and research reports. Prescott has experience working directly with states on issues of access, success, affordability, accountability, workforce development, and data systems development. Currently, he is managing WICHE's Gates Foundation–funded project to develop a multistate longitudinal data exchange. Prescott earned a PhD in higher education from the University of Virginia and also holds degrees from the University of Iowa and the College of William and Mary.

CHRISTOPHER M. SHAFFER came to Shawnee State University from the Governor's Office of Appalachia working as a program manager and state alternate for the governor of the state of Ohio to the Appalachian Regional Commission, the regional economic development agency that represents a partnership of federal, state, and local government. The commission represents the thirteen Appalachian states. He was also the operations manager in the Governor's Office of Faith Based and Community Initiatives. He served as a field artillery platoon leader, fire direction officer, and battery executive officer. Chris also spent time on brigade staff as an assistant operations officer and rear detachment executive officer. He is a combat veteran of Operation Iraqi Freedom. He honorably left military services as a captain in the United States Army. Shaffer received his undergraduate degree at the United States Military Academy at West Point and received his MBA at Ohio Dominican University in Columbus, Ohio.

JEFFREY C. SUN is an associate professor of educational leadership and law at the University of North Dakota and a visiting scholar at the Ohio State University. He researches and writes in the area of higher education law. His publications have included venues such as the *BYU Education & Law Journal*, *Fordham Urban Law Journal*, *Journal of College and University Law*, *Review of Higher Education*, *Teachers College Record*, and the University of Pennsylvania's *Journal of Constitutional Law*. He serves on the Board of Directors for the Education Law Association (ELA), as editor of ELA and NASPA's *Legal Links*, as an editorial board member for the *Education Law & Policy Review*, as coeditor of the Law & Education Series for Information Age Publishing, and as an executive board member for the Law & Education SIG of AERA. Dr. Sun received an MBA from Loyola Marymount University, a law degree from the Moritz College of Law at the Ohio State University, and an MPhil and a PhD from Columbia University.

MARK R. UMBRICHT is a doctoral student in higher education at the Pennsylvania State University where he serves as a graduate research assistant for the Center for the Study of Higher Education. He previously worked for the Office of Community College Research and Leadership at the University of Illinois at Urbana–Champaign while completing his master's in educational organization and leadership. His thesis examined time-to-degree among first-generation students. His research interests include institutional research, student outcomes, and institutional finance and sustainability.

BEN WILDAVSKY is director of higher education studies at the State University of New York's Rockefeller Institute of Government and policy professor at SUNY–Albany. A former senior scholar at the Kauffman Foundation and guest scholar at the Brookings Institution, he is the author of the award-winning book *The Great Brain Race: How Global Universities Are Reshaping the World*. He is also the co-editor of *Reinventing Higher Education: The Promise of Innovation*. His articles have appeared in the *Washington Post*, the *Wall Street Journal*, *Foreign Policy*, *The New Republic*, *The Atlantic*, and many other publications. Wildavsky, a former education editor of *U.S. News & World Report*, has spoken on globalization and innovation to dozens of audiences in the United States and abroad, including at Google, Harvard, and the World Bank. He has convened gatherings of national education leaders, supervised the editorial operations of the bestselling *U.S. News* college guides, and managed a $2.5 million foundation grant portfolio. As a strategic and editorial consultant, he has provided advice to education leaders and has written influential policy reports, including the report of the secretary of education's Commission on the Future of Higher Education. He graduated from Yale University (Phi Beta Kappa, summa cum laude).

NANCY L. ZIMPHER became the 12th chancellor of the State University of New York, the nation's largest comprehensive system of higher education, in June 2009. A nationally recognized leader in education, Chancellor Zimpher spearheaded and launched a new strategic plan for SUNY in her first year as chancellor. The central goal of the plan, called *The Power of SUNY*, is to harness the university's potential to drive economic revitalization and create a better future for every community across New York. Chancellor Zimpher is active in numerous state and national education organizations and is a leader in the areas of teacher preparation, urban education, and university-community engagement. As cofounder of Strive, a community-based

cradle-to-career collaborative, Chancellor Zimpher has been instrumental in creating a national network of innovative systemic partnerships that holistically address challenges across the education pipeline. She has authored or coauthored numerous books, monographs,
and academic journal articles on teacher education, urban education,
academic leadership, and school-university partnerships. Chancellor
Zimpher currently serves as chair of the Board of Governors of the
New York Academy of Sciences and of CEOs for Cities. From 2005
to 2011, she chaired the national Coalition of Urban Serving Universities. She also recently cochaired NCATE's blue-ribbon panel on
transforming teacher preparation. She previously served as president
of the University of Cincinnati, chancellor of the University of Wis-
consin–Milwaukee, and executive dean of the Professional Colleges
and dean of the College of Education at the Ohio State University.
She holds a bachelor's degree in English education and speech, a master's degree in English literature, and a PhD in teacher education and
higher education administration, all from the Ohio State University.

Index

Made in the USA
Lexington, KY
20 January 2015